# Understanding Health Care Management: A Case Study Approach

Seth B. Goldsmith, ScD, JD

Professor Emeritus
University of Massachusetts
School of Public Health and Health Sciences
Amherst, Massachusetts

JONES & BARTLETT
L E A R N I N G

*World Headquarters*
Jones & Bartlett Learning
5 Wall Street
Burlington, MA 01803
978-443-5000
info@jblearning.com
www.jblearning.com

Jones & Bartlett Learning books and products are available through most bookstores and online booksellers. To contact Jones & Bartlett Learning directly, call 800-832-0034, fax 978-443-8000, or visit our website, www.jblearning.com.

*Understanding Health Care Management: A Case Study Approach* is an independent publication and has not been authorized, sponsored, or otherwise approved by the owners of the trademarks or service marks referenced in this product.

This publication is designed to provide accurate and authoritative information in regard to the Subject Matter covered. It is sold with the understanding that the publisher is not engaged in rendering legal, accounting, or other professional service. If legal advice or other expert assistance is required, the service of a competent professional person should be sought.

**Production Credits**
Publisher: Michael Brown
Managing Editor: Maro Gartside
Editorial Assistant: Kayla Dos Santos
Editorial Assistant: Chloe Falivene
Production Manager: Tracey McCrea
Production Assistant: Eileen Worthley
Senior Marketing Manager: Sophie Fleck Teague
Marketing Intern: Shayna Goodman
Manufacturing and Inventory Control Supervisor: Amy Bacus
Composition: Lapiz
Cover Design: Kristin E. Parker
Cover Images: © iStockphoto/Thinkstock
Printing and Binding: Edwards Brothers Malloy
Cover Printing: Edwards Brothers Malloy

**Library of Congress Cataloging-in-Publication Data**
Goldsmith, Seth B.
  Understanding health care management: a case study approach / Seth B. Goldsmith.
    p. ; cm.
  Includes bibliographical references and index.
  ISBN 978-1-4496-3210-6 (pbk.) -- ISBN 1-4496-3210-6 (pbk.)
  I. Title.
    [DNLM: 1. Health Services Administration--United States. 2. Organizational Case Studies--United States. W 84 AA1]
  362.1068--dc23

                2012015803

6048

Printed in the United States of America
16  15  14  13  12    10  9  8  7  6  5  4  3  2  1

# DEDICATION

*Dedicated to Olivia, Tessa, William, and Elise*

# CONTENTS

## Chapter 4  Organizational Management  77

## Chapter 10   Planning Through the OIG Advisory Opinion Process   273

## Index   313

# ABOUT THE AUTHOR

**Seth B. Goldsmith, ScD, JD,** is Professor Emeritus of Health Policy and Management at the University of Massachusetts at Amherst. Since 1995 he has been a director of Extendicare, a Toronto, Canada-based publicly owned company that is one of the leading providers of long-term care services in the United States and Canada. Dr. Goldsmith has also served on the faculties of Tulane University and Columbia University where he was director of the graduate program in health services administration. From 1996 through December 1998, Dr. Goldsmith served as Chief Executive Officer of the Miami Jewish Health System (formerly known as the Miami Jewish Home and Hospital for the Aged). For 15 years he was editor of the *Journal of Ambulatory Care Management* and for more than a decade he was Of Counsel to the Massachusetts law firm of Bowditch and Dewey. Dr. Goldsmith has served on numerous national and local boards, and he is the recipient of numerous awards. He is the author and editor of 16 books.

# ABOUT THE CASE CONTRIBUTORS

**Jonathan Bloomberg, MD,** is a clinical psychiatrist and director of the Bloomberg Institute in Northbrook, Illinois.

**Andrew R. Cagnetta Jr.** is president of Transworld Business Advisors, a national firm that values and sells a broad range of businesses including healthcare companies (healthcarebizsales. com). Andrew has served on numerous nonprofit and industry boards and is the former president of the International Business Brokers Association. He is a graduate of Lehigh University.

**James S. Davis, MD,** is a general surgery resident at Jackson Memorial Hospital, Miami, Florida. He is currently on a 2-year leave to pursue a research fellowship in trauma, burns, and surgical education.

**Jill Sanko** is a research and simulation education specialist at the University of Miami–Jackson Memorial Hospital Center for Patient Safety. In her position, she teaches teamwork communication skills, invasive bedside procedures, resuscitation using simulation, and manages multiple patient-safety research projects. Prior to moving back to her native Miami, Jill ran the simulation service at the National Institutes of Health. She has an undergraduate degree in anthropology and both bachelor and master's degrees in the field of nursing.

**Ilya Shekhter** is the medical simulation manager at the University of Miami–Jackson Memorial Hospital Center for Patient Safety. In his position, Ilya works with physicians and nurses from different clinical departments to create simulation courses based on the curricular needs of their learners and the safety needs of their patients. Before coming to Miami, he was the senior simulation engineer at the University of Rochester Medical Center in Rochester, New York. Ilya's educational background includes biomedical engineering and business administration.

**Alexander Szafran, MSPH,** is director of radiology at the Maine Medical Center in Portland, Maine. He has held similar positions with Baystate Medical Center in Springfield, Massachusetts, and the Lahey Clinic in Burlington, Massachusetts.

**Sheila H. Szafran, MS, OTR/L,** is a practitioner, consultant, and educator in Portland, Maine. She has practiced for more than 30 years in the field of rehabilitation medicine and has extensive experience in management, program development, and quality improvement.

# PREFACE

 ## INTRODUCTION

Learning via the case method is an established tradition in education. When Steve Jobs, the distinguished cofounder of Apple, passed away in 2011, a number of stories appeared in the press about "Apple University." The idea behind Apple University was to train the next generation of Apple leaders on the Jobs style and substance of management. This training was to be done via case studies of the critical decisions made in the company.

This book presents the opportunity for learners, whether they are experienced practitioners or novice students, to examine issues within the context of real organizations (almost all of which I have attempted to fictionalize). These cases are presented in a variety of settings including hospitals, nursing homes, medical centers, group practices, and public health agencies.

Every one of these cases is based on an actual situation that has required managerial decision making! It is my hope that the readers, in studying these cases, will, regardless of the problems presented and the organizational setting of the case, become more effective and efficient decision makers with a greater understanding of the implications of the decisions they are making.

Finally, allow me to note that despite the organization of the book around nine different themes, the fact is that there is an enormous overlap among these cases. Many of them could easily be placed in several categories, and it is well within the province of the reader or instructor to shift these cases for their own purposes.

## Organization of the Book

This book has been structured around nine themes that I believe are at the heart of effective healthcare management.

The first theme, found in Chapter One, is patients and their families. The cases in this section should serve to orient the reader to the reason we are in the healthcare business—that is, to serve the sick and needy. As a graduate student doing my administrative residency at Brookdale Medical Center in Brooklyn, New York, I was fortunate to have as one of my mentors a gentleman named Sydney Peimer who was an operating room nurse before he moved into hospital administration. On the first day of my residency, just as I was getting comfortably ensconced in the administrative offices, Peimer came in, told me to pack up, and sent me to nursing for an intensive course on being a nurse's aide. And so began a month of shift work on the patient floors. After that, I was transferred to a week in the operating room. Five weeks after first walking through the front door of Brookdale, I was finally back in the Executive Suite but with a new and profound appreciation for what patients and staff go through each day in receiving and delivering care. These cases are an introduction to the perspective of patients and their families.

The next group of cases, Chapter Two, focuses on corporate governance. Generally, we think of boards as governing the not-for-profit entities in the healthcare system, but clearly investor-owned facilities are also greatly influenced by their boards. The nine cases in this chapter will provide useful insights into boards and the board–management relationship.

Chapter Three focuses its numerous cases on human resource management. Years ago, the great management guru Peter Drucker noted in his book *Management* that the essential function of management was staffing. Indeed, the best and worst decisions managers typically make are related to HR issues. These cases address the myriad HR issues that managers deal with on both a day-to-day and a strategic basis.

In Chapter Four the cases examine a host of organizational issues that are oftentimes presented to managers. These cases offer the opportunity to consider real problems and how they might be effectively handled.

The theme of Chapter Five is managing change. Each of the cases in this section is about doing something different, new, or innovative. Change, as these cases illustrate, is difficult and demands considerable managerial expertise.

Chapter Six presents cases that revolve around the theme of planning—including one case about personal planning. A key aspect of effective management is planning for the future. These cases present an opportunity to consider management's role in the planning function.

Marketing is the focus of Chapter Seven. There was a time in the not-so-distant past when healthcare providers simply did not market themselves. Pick up any newspaper or magazine or examine any media source such as radio, TV, or the Internet, and it is absolutely clear that marketing in health care is a significant component of management.

No book on healthcare management would be complete without the themes of the final three chapters: financial and legal issues and planning for corporate compliance. Chapter Eight, "Financial Issues," presents cases on various aspects of financial management that challenge healthcare executives. The next chapter offers cases on various aspects of law and dabbles in corporate compliance. The last chapter focuses on avoiding problems through the mechanism of the Office of Inspector General's Advisory Process. The student will here be faced with figuring out the situation before it becomes a serious problem.

## Conclusion

In a federal legal case in which an issue might be a person's character, the Federal Rules of Evidence (Rule 405) allow for methods of proving character. The first method is reputational or opinion, and this happens when a lawyer wants to get in evidence a person's general character. For example, "In my opinion Jim Jones is a good guy." The standard of proof is essentially quite minimal because the judge or jury is just listening to one opinion. However, when an element of a person's character or a character trait such as honesty is an essential aspect of a charge or perhaps a defense, then the Federal Rules of Evidence allow the admission of "specific instances of conduct." The admission of specific instances of conduct are held to a higher standard than general opinion. Why?

In my judgment it is because the authors of the Federal Rules understood human nature and psychology. If a witness says to the jury, "Jim Jones is a good guy," that isn't as memorable or powerful as, "I saw Jim Jones race over to a burning car and pull an unconscious driver out of the car and give the driver CPR and save his life. Boy that Jim Jones is a good guy." So it is with case studies! I hope that as you read and work through these cases they prove to be useful as well as memorable.

# ACKNOWLEDGMENTS

The cases presented in this book have been generated over my many years of work as an academic, administrator, consultant, attorney, and researcher. In the course of preparing this manuscript, I have called on several colleagues and friends for advice, counsel, and material. I would specifically like to thank the following people for their contributions to this book: Alex Szafran; Michael Barrett; Jonathan Bloomberg, MD; James Davis, MD; Sheila Szafran, Ilya Shekhter, Jill Sanko, Andrew Cagnetta, and Drew Ben Aharon. I would also like to express my appreciation to Joel Dalva and Sol Goldner for their invaluable input to Chapter 8 of this text.

It has again been my privilege to work with Mike Brown and his staff at Jones & Bartlett Learning. It is indeed hard to believe that more than a quarter of a century has passed since we started working together. I would also like to thank Eileen Worthley, Production Assistant at Jones & Bartlett Learning.

Finally, I want to again thank my wife Wendy Benjamin Goldsmith for her support and encouragement!

CHAPTER 1

# PATIENTS AND THEIR FAMILIES

 **INTRODUCTION**

Patients and residents are at the core of the healthcare "business." As managers, the challenge is providing care that is accessible, of high quality, cost effective, and efficient. Ironically, this challenge is particularly difficult in this period where the patients' choices may be either limited by the health insurer or, in some cases, unlimited by the nature of their insurance.

Today's patients have the benefit of a vast amount of public information about their providers of care as well as their diseases. The manager's job is to be a provider of useful information to the consumer. Such information can range from assisting patients in selecting practitioners to helping them understand their health conditions. The following pages on consumers leveling the playing field by cruising the information superhighway are excerpted from the chapter "Management and the Educated Consumer" in my textbook *Principles of Health Care Management, Second Edition.*

## ✍ Cruising the Highway for Doctors

To begin, we might ask the following question: How much can a patient find out about a potential doctor? At one level, people seem to know more about institutions than individual physicians, and thus the institution can play a role in connecting the patient with a doctor.

How does a healthcare organization assist the consumer in finding a doctor? Consider the following three websites servicing the same general community. On the Plantation, Florida, Westside Regional Medical Center site, there is a Resource tab that brings the user to a Find a Physician page where one can list as much or as little information as possible. For my "experiment," I acted the part of a consumer looking for a cardiologist. I clicked on Cardiology under the Specialty tab and was presented with a long list of physicians. The only information available on any of these physicians was their name, their medical degree (some were MDs and others DOs), their office addresses, and the language(s) they speak. My next web stop was Holy Cross Hospital in Fort Lauderdale. Their website was similar to that of Westside and equally uninformative. If I were handing out stars, they would each get one star. In contrast, the Cleveland Clinic in Weston, Florida, would get five stars for its website. Once again, I was able to find a cardiologist. But this time when I clicked on his name I found pages of information on the physician, including the following: a four-paragraph biographical sketch; his picture; the languages he speaks; professional highlights of his career; his education and fellowships; and his certifications, specialty interest, awards, honors, and memberships. In other words, I had all the information I needed to decide whether I was interested in potentially using him.

In Florida (and many other states), the interested consumer has another important resource: the government. Through a state website, www.floridashealth.com, considerable information about any practitioner can be obtained. For example, there is information about the doctor's education and training, academic appointments, specialty certification, financial responsibility, and any proceedings or actions taken against him or her. This website is continually updated and provides the public with enough information to make the basic decision: Do I see this particular physician or find another one?

There are also two private companies that pop up when searching the web. One of these, HealthGrades (www.healthgrades.com), provides useful general information in sidebars on its site. For example, if the consumer arrives at this website when doing an online search for "hand surgeon Florida," the core of the webpage has a list of cities where there are hand surgeons. Selecting a particular area, such as Fort Lauderdale, will bring up a page with the names and addresses of the local hand surgeons. Selecting a particular surgeon brings up another screen with a map of his or her location and additional information (self-reported) about the group or practice he or she is a member of, the specialties within the practice, insurance plans accepted, conditions treated, and languages supported. At no charge, HealthGrades provides information about the physician's education and training, any disciplinary action, specialty certifications, hospital affiliations, and a patient rating profile based on consumer surveys.

An alternative site is UCompareHealthCare (www.ucompare-healthcare.com), which offers consumers similar information to that presented by HealthGrades. However, neither of these sites tells the consumer much about the doctor's experience, personality, or bedside manner. The smart consumer always simply Googles the doctor of interest and often comes up with surprising (and sometimes disturbing information). For example, I ran a Google search on a doctor and found a website full of criticism as well as an official sanction from another state. None of this was available from the other sites! Caveat emptor!

## Cruising the Highway for Hospitals

Thanks to the U.S. Department of Health and Human Services (HHS), there is a relatively user-friendly website for comparing hospitals: www.hospitalcompare.hhs.gov/. The site is a good educational tool for consumers; it explains subjects such as the hospital process-of-care measures and hospital outcome measures. Users of this site can compare up to three hospitals at a time and examine how the hospitals did with a range of medical conditions and surgical procedures. Overall, the data available covers six medical conditions: heart attack, heart failure, chronic lung disease, pneumonia, diabetes in adults, and chest pain. The data can also be used to compare how well hospitals handle 22 surgical procedures such as those involving the heart and blood vessels (angioplasty, pacemaker implants, and heart valve operations); abdominal procedures for removal of the gallbladder or hernia repairs; procedures involving the neck, back, and extremities (neck or back fusions or other bone-related surgeries); bladder and prostate surgery; and finally, surgery related to the female reproductive organs. Depending on the condition or surgery selected, the report will compare processes and outcomes across the hospitals. The following are illustrative questions on various conditions and procedures: (1) percentage of surgery patients who were given an antibiotic at the right time (within 1 hour before surgery) to help prevent infection; (2) percentage of surgery patients whose preventive antibiotics were stopped at the right time (within 24 hours after surgery); (3) percentage of surgery patients whose blood sugar (blood glucose) is kept under control in the days right after surgery; (4) percentage of heart attack patients given aspirin at arrival; (5) percentage of heart attack patients given a beta blocker at discharge; (6) percentage of pneumonia patients given oxygenation assessment; and (7) percentage of pneumonia patients assessed and given pneumococcal vaccination. These reports also contain a fascinating section on a survey of patients' experiences with the hospitals in question. Here the consumer states how well the hospital doctors and nurses responded to his or her needs, rates the cleanliness of the facility, and finally, gives a recommendation.

Of considerable importance to all managers are three questions: First, do consumers really look at these sites? Second, is the site providing accurate information about your institution? Third, what do you do about it? The answer to the first question is simple: we don't know, but we should assume that some percentage of consumers and perhaps healthcare insurers and other providers are looking at the site for information and competitive comparisons. The data is likely reasonably accurate because it comes from a variety of sources including the Online Survey, Certification, and Reporting data system (OSCAR), managed by the Centers for Medicare and Medicaid Services. A problem is that this data, which is from recent survey results, is merely a snapshot in time and, although likely reasonably correct, does not account for changes since the time of the snapshot. Other data comes from The Joint Commission (TJC), formerly known as the Joint Commission on the Accreditation of Healthcare Organizations (JCAHO) as well as from ongoing surveys and other regular submissions. Hospitals have the responsibility of updating basic characteristic information, and the website for this project acknowledges the issue of time lag.

For the healthcare manager, the bottom line is what to do about this public information. In a joint effort, the American Hospital Association, the Federation of American Hospitals, and the Association of American Medical Colleges publish a quality advisory that makes suggestions to health providers on how to deal with the Hospital Compare release. The August 15, 2008, advisory offered providers a set of likely questions and answers that could be expected from the media and the public subsequent to the government's data release. Some of the answers were merely technical such as explaining the meaning of the statistic confidence level. Other answers might be considered mild spin, with statements pointing out the problem with the data (primarily Medicare data) or data on mortality not allowing for the decisions made by patients or their families. So while the message put forth is always, "We love quality and want to always improve quality," the second message is that what the government says doesn't really hold much water—so trust your doctor, and certainly trust us!

## Cruising the Highway for Nursing Homes

Once again, the government is providing consumers with a wealth of data—this time to help them select a nursing home (information on this subject can be found in my book *Choosing a Nursing Home*.) The website www.medicare.gov/NHcompare/ is similar to the HHS hospital site but specific to nursing homes, for which the government has developed a five-star quality rating system. The homepage of this site discusses the various elements within the rating scale and allows the consumer to find a home based on state, zip code, and star ratings. Once several homes are selected, they can be compared. Initially, these comparisons are shown by star ratings, but the user of the website can get behind the star ratings and can find more detailed data on fire inspections, health inspections, quality care deficiencies, resident assessment deficiencies, nutrition and dietary deficiencies, pharmacy deficiencies, staffing, 14 quality measures for long-stay residents, and 5 quality measures for short-stay residents. For all these measures, the tables present the date of the inspection, the date of correction, the level of harm associated with the deficiency (least to most), the number of residents affected by the problem (useful to see if widespread or isolated), contact phone numbers for the state long-term care ombudsman, the state survey agency, and the state quality improvement agency.

Some states, such as New York, make life for the consumer particularly easy. For example, in New York if a consumer merely searches the name of the nursing home, he or she will retrieve a New York State Health Department website that provides an overview of the nursing home, report on its quality, inspection reports, complaints, and any enforcement activities.

As with the hospital compare site, administrators are typically not happy with consumers having such easy access to this information, particularly when their institution has fewer than four stars. The explanations one hears for these low ratings are usually that the data is old, that the snapshot was taken last year, that the government is measuring the wrong thing, and finally that the surveyors "had it in" for the nursing home. Regardless of the validity of any of these claims, these reports are potentially helpful or harmful, or perhaps a useful signal for self-improvement!

## Cruising the Highway for Self-Doctoring and Self-Medication

Interested in practicing medicine on the side? Or perhaps in simply avoiding a doctor's visit? Or, better yet, securing a prescription drug without visiting a doctor? All of this is now possible thanks to the Internet. Name practically any disease or even symptoms—Google it and the consumer will find a treasure trove of information. Try searching something as simple as "backache." You will find millions of websites. In addition, a consumer will find scores of web advertisements. In a sample search, on one webpage for backaches, there are eight sidebar advertisements and one sponsored ad that leads the webpage and sells all manner of merchandise for improving the back—chairs to cushions and everything in between. Another site provides ads plus a range of home remedies. A third site, medicinenet.com, although having some advertisements, does provide a significant amount of substantive physician-authored information on low-back pain. Other sites include, among others, self-help, dictionary definitions, and holistic health.

For the most traditional and clinically substantive information, the consumer can learn a great deal at medical center sites such as www.mayoclinic.com (the site of the Mayo Clinic in Rochester, Minnesota), www.hss.edu (the site of the Hospital for Special Surgery in New York City), or www.ninds.nih.gov (the site of the National Institute of Neurological Disorders and Stroke, a division of the National Institutes of Health).

Securing a prescription on the Internet is fairly easy. For example, www.controlleddrugs.com is a site from which a range of drugs can be ordered, including the anti-anxiety medications Ativan, Valium, and Xanax; the antidepressants Prozac and Zoloft; and the erectile dysfunction medications Cialis and Viagra. To order, you need a credit card and must agree to a disclaimer that states that you have had a recent physical and understand the terms of the transaction and the costs and benefits of the medications. The website then requires you to fill out some basic medical information. In fact, the site's customer service representative said that in many cases it was unnecessary to even fill out that information. Drugs are shipped from outside the United States to the customer. Essentially, a consumer who wants to bypass the medical system can enter a gray market of drugs purchasing and, assuming the legitimacy of the quality of the drugs, self-medicate. If a person has a legal prescription, it can also be transmitted to online pharmacies for fulfillment; but, in those instances, the transaction is really about cost and convenience.

Although patients and their care are discussed in numerous cases throughout this book, this chapter presents five unique perspectives. The first case, set in a nursing home, demonstrates the various players involved in decision making, including the federal government. The second case is particularly interesting because it is primarily written by a former nursing home resident whose unique perspective should prove to be of value to all managers. The third case again visits the dynamic triangle of patient, staff, and family. The fourth case focuses on hospitals, doctors, and effective communication with patients. The last case explores the ethical obligation of the medical community with regard to impaired driving by senior patients. Changes are clearly afoot. The challenge is dealing effectively with these changes.

## CASE 1-1  The Unwanted Resident

Mr. and Mrs. Jack Ross investigated nursing homes for their elderly and impoverished aunt, Ms. Janet Horner, who was living with them. On their visit to California's College Valley Home, they met with its administrator, Mr. Albert Press, who explained to them that even though Ms. Horner would be on MediCal, prior to and as a condition of admission, Mr. Ross (who was known as a wealthy man in the community) would have to make a donation of $10,000 to the home.

Mr. Ross made the donation, and Ms. Horner was admitted. A few weeks after her admission, Mr. Ross called the home to tell Mr. Press that he was quite dissatisfied with the care at the home, particularly the quality of nursing care, which he found disrespectful and unresponsive to Ms. Horner's needs. Mr. Press then wrote Mr. Ross the following letter.

*November 1, 20__*
*College Valley Home*
*Prentice Hill Southern, California*

*Dear Mr. Ross:*

*I am sorry to hear that you are unhappy with the care that we are providing to your aunt, who actually seems perfectly happy, particularly with our food. However, in light of your dissatisfaction, we have decided to discharge her on November 10, 20__. Please make the appropriate arrangements to pick her up on that date.*
*Finally, because of your negative attitude toward the home, I hereby bar you from visiting Ms. Horner at any time prior to her discharge.*

*Sincerely,*

*Albert Press, Administrator*

* * *

QUESTIONS

1. What options does Mr. Ross have?
2. Who has the power to make a decision about staying or leaving? Ms. Horner? Mr. Ross? Mr. Press?
3. What Omnibus Budget Reconciliation Act (OBRA) compliance issues are raised by this case?

## CASE 1-2  The Residents Speak Out

By *Seth B. Goldsmith* and *Roberta Bergman*

> *Note: Roberta Bergman (of blessed memory), my sister,*
> *was a teacher, mother, and devoted friend who suffered*
> *from multiple sclerosis and spent the last 11 years of*
> *her life in a nursing home. During this period, she*
> *was an inspiration to everyone she met and remains a*
> *special spirit in our lives.*

An increasing number of complaints from the families of residents as well as an informal meeting with the ombudsman from the state department of elder affairs led the administrator of the Green Meadow Home to hire Gary Newman as an outside consultant to clarify the problems residents and their families were having with the home. Newman met with a number of residents and their families and felt the following four situations exemplified the state of affairs at the home.

1. Miss Fish, a 74-year-old woman who was never married, was admitted to the home 6 months before the meeting with Newman. Prior to her admission, which was precipitated by two massive strokes, she had lived independently and for 35 years had been an active volunteer at the Green Meadow Home. Her two sisters attended the meeting with Newman and told him that their formerly vivacious sister was now very withdrawn. After some probing by Newman, it came out that the sisters were quite frustrated because none of the staff seemed to have the time to deal with Miss Fish. In their opinion, this appeared to be because Miss Fish had lost her ability to communicate verbally. One sister said she was particularly disappointed because it seemed that everyone in the home was just interested in forcing Miss Fish to "become part of the system, you know what I mean: getting up when the nurses or aides want you up, eating when they want you to eat, going to the bathroom when it is convenient for the aides, sitting around the nurses' station 10 hours a day, and going to sleep like a baby at 6:30 PM even in the summer when the sun is still shining!" The sister added that Miss Fish "deserves much better treatment, particularly in light of her years of contributions to the home."

2. Mr. Lester Mead is an 88-year-old man who has been a resident of the home for 2 years. In his meeting with Newman, he stated, "Forty years ago I was a pretty well-off business-man in this town, and in fact I was one of the guys who raised the money to build this home. I frankly never thought I would ever live here. And when my wife and I moved to Sun City in Arizona, I never thought I would ever move back here to Metropolis. But here I am—my wife is dead, and my only son lives 100 miles away. I look around and see many people who I used to associate with and see what they have become, and it is a scary sight! The thing I hate about this place is that there are many staff who don't respect old people. This is our home and we should be treated accordingly, and we are not. And particularly me—I'm private pay, not one of those Medicaid patients."

3. Mrs. Meg Douglas also had some things that she wanted to share with Gary Newman: "I have been a resident of the home for 4 years. As you can see, I have had one leg ampu-tated because of my diabetes. A few weeks ago I cut my index finger and told the aide that it looked like it was getting infected and asked her to tell the nurse. The nurse told her to tell me not to worry—so I didn't, until a few days later when my son came to visit and saw it and made a whole big stink on the floor about my care. He also called the administrator, and finally I was taken care of, but what could have been a small problem now took weeks to clear up, and because of my diabetes it might have had to be cut off. When the nurse was asked about it, she said she was never informed, so she sided with the aide. I wish I could get out of this place!"

4. Mr. Max Stein is an 81-year-old man who has been a resident of the home for 5 years. He is one of ten Jewish residents in the home. Still ambulatory, Mr. Stein is one of the most physically active residents in the home. He met with Gary Newman to express his anger and outrage at the anti-Semitism displayed by some of the other residents, who he said have called him a range of offensive names. Mr. Stein said he handles these slurs by occasionally "smacking the bastard," but he added that he only does this if no one is look-ing. He also stated that he does not like to take the law into his own hands, "but nobody is doing anything about this problem

here because we are such a small minority." Mr. Stein would not provide Newman with the names of the residents who had insulted him. In checking with the director of nursing and the administrator, Newman found no recollection of any resident complaining of being hit by another resident.

\* \* \*

QUESTIONS

1. What problems are likely to be identified by Newman at the nursing home?
2. To what extent do the problems reported by the consultant relate to the issues discussed in this chapter?
3. What steps can administration take to correct or minimize the problems presented in these situations?

---

## CASE 1-3 | Mother and Son Case

Mrs. Gigi Noir is a 72-year-old widow who has been a resident of the Greenway Nursing Home in Miami, Florida, for the past 2 years. Unfortunately Mrs. Noir has multiple sclerosis, which is an autoimmune disease affecting the brain and spinal cord. Until moving into the nursing home, she was able to function in her Florida condominium with some outside help. Now in addition to her having very slurred speech, she has occasional muscle spasms and needs help eating, bathing, transferring, toileting, and taking her medications.

When she moved into Greenway, she brought with her two personal items, a 32-inch flat-screen TV and a 25-year-old La-Z-Boy-type recliner. Every morning after the staff cleans, feeds, and dresses Mrs. Noir, they help her into her chair and turn the TV to her favorite channel. The staff typically checks in with her every 2 hours and provides whatever care is needed.

Over the past several months, the recliner chair mechanism has broken several times and in each instance, except the last, the nursing home's maintenance staff has been able to fix it. The last breakdown determined that the chair was beyond repair. At the behest of the nursing staff (who are quite fond of Mrs. Noir), the maintenance staff searched the nursing home's warehouse and found another recliner that was in decent shape and could, with some work, become functional. This recliner differed from the first by having an electrical system for positioning and also having a lift assistance capability whereby the chair tilted forward. The chair was given to Mrs. Noir, who greatly appreciated the concern of the staff.

Once again, Mrs. Noir was positioned each morning to watch her TV shows. One day, she had a spasm and accidentally hit the armrest button that tilted the chair forward, resulting in her being ejected from the chair. She was discovered 30 minutes later on the floor, taken to the hospital where they found two broken legs, casted her, and returned her to the nursing home. The nursing home Executive Director, Malcolm Contento, immediately called her son, who lives in Charlotte, North Carolina, informed him of the situation, and told him that she would have around-the-clock aides sitting with her for the next several weeks to ensure that everything was okay. The son, Guy Noir, seemed appeased by the conversation. Six weeks later, the casts were removed, everything seemed to have healed satisfactorily, and the orthopedist stated that there was no need for the around-the-clock aides. Mr. Contento decided to keep aides on for the 7 AM to 7 PM shift for another month, as a precaution.

The day after the evening aides were dismissed, Mr. Contento received a call from Guy Noir demanding that the aides watch his mother 24/7, stating that otherwise he would see a lawyer. Contento then called his social services department to see if they knew anything about Mr. Noir. The response from the head social worker was, "I'm no private eye but I know that this Noir guy is no loving son. Since his mother has been in the home, he hasn't visited her once in 2 years, despite the fact that there are plenty of flights between here and Charlotte. Also, I know that even after the accident he didn't visit despite the fact that he was 30 minutes away in Fort Lauderdale going out on a Caribbean cruise on the *Allure of the Sea*."

\* \* \*

QUESTIONS

1. How relevant to this case is the relationship between Mrs. Noir and her son?
2. Is it the home's business that Mr. Noir went on a cruise and did not visit his mother?
3. What options does Mr. Contento have? What are the costs and benefits of these options?
4. Should anyone else be involved in the decision process?
5. What type of documentation should be kept? Why?
6. Is there a policy issue about the role of maintenance and nursing staff in providing for resident amenities?

---

## CASE 1-4 | Community General Hospital

| | |
|---|---|
| MEMO | |
| From: | Kip Kipling, MD, Medical Director |
| To: | Medical Staff |
| Subject: | Patient Interaction |

In the 4 years since I joined the staff of this institution, I have become increasingly convinced that, in general, we provide an excellent quality of care here. Our hospitalists are well trained and our attendings are both well trained and experienced. Unfortunately, as you all well know, our patient census has declined as an increasing number of patients are migrating to some of our newer neighboring facilities. Additionally, malpractice claims and awards against us, both personally and organizationally, have skyrocketed.

Although I cannot pinpoint the exact causes of either the loss of patients or the malpractice activity, I have heard enough complaints from patients and their families to know that we need to improve our patient interaction and communication skills. As has been pointed out numerous times, patients don't sue when they feel connected to their MD and when they feel they are being listened to.

Let me give you an example of a communication issue we recently encountered. A patient with esophageal cancer who was being seen by one of our staff came in and mentioned a therapy that is being used in NYC but is not available here. She was rudely dismissed with the comment, "Why bother? You probably don't have more than a year to live, so what you really need is palliative care." Although the MD might have been technically correct, he was emotionally wrong in both dismissing her and stealing her hope. In another case brought to my attention, one of our specialists dismissed a patient who he felt was ready for hospice. The patient went across town and was treated by another specialist, and now, 3 years later, she is still ill but ambulatory, functional, living at home, and certainly more hopeful. Frankly, we don't have the Bucksbaum Institute that they do at the University of Chicago (where many of you have trained), but even without that money, we need to find ways to better interact with our patients. I welcome your suggestions about improving patient interactions as well as what penalties might be applied to staff who do not assist in this critical effort.

* * *

QUESTIONS

1. What is the Bucksbaum Institute, and what are they trying to accomplish?
2. Is there evidence that better communication between practitioners and patients results in better outcomes?
3. Is Dr. Kipling being too aggressive in this memo? Is the threat of penalties appropriate?
4. Is there a better way to encourage good patient interaction?

---

### CASE 1-5 | Elderly Drivers

The Luxtown Medical Center (LMC) is a 73-physician multi-specialty group practice located in southern New England. The following is a memo from its CEO to staff:

---

MEMO

From:      Bob Rudyard, CEO, Luxtown Medical Center
To:        All physicians, nurses, and professional staff
Subject:   Impaired drivers

---

Last week this community experienced the tragedy of a 91-year-old man who lost control of his car and hit a group of children at a school crossing. As you might have heard, the man was visiting from out of state and was visually impaired and had been diagnosed with early Alzheimer's disease. Despite these medical issues, he was able to rent a car at the airport—with an unrestricted license!

You might be aware that our neighboring state of New Hampshire now has some of the strictest laws for senior driving, requiring, among other things, a pre-license-renewal road test after age 75. Here the legislature has failed to act, so our seniors generally have no problems renewing their licenses. The data from New Hampshire now shows a dramatic decline in accidents involving seniors.

In my own family we had a major-league hassle when we tried to get my 88-year-old father to stop driving. He finally agreed, after two fender-benders—followed by a big hike in his insurance premiums!

As physicians and other healthcare professionals, we have an ethical responsibility to be aware of when our patients' health is so compromised that they should not be driving. Although at this moment we do not have a legal responsibility to report people we suspect of being impaired to the Department of Motor Vehicles or to the police, we do have an ethical obligation to protect them and the public.

All of this brings me to an issue that I would like your thoughts about. Specifically, almost 30% of our patients are over 65 years of age, and we have a large number of people we care for who are over 75 and 80. What can we do to both help them be safer drivers and, when the time comes, make the transition to nondriver status smoother? I look forward to hearing from you!

* * *

QUESTIONS

1. Is the CEO of Luxtown exaggerating the problem?
2. What ideas exist to make seniors better drivers?
3. What strategies can be used to prevent someone with a license from driving?
4. What specifically can or should the medical center be doing? Is it a good idea for the medical center to be involved in this or is this a public health issue?

## CHAPTER 2

# CORPORATE GOVERNANCE

 ## INTRODUCTION

This chapter explores a range of issues that are affected by the relationship between managers and their boards. Although the settings for the cases differ, the principles of the cases tend to be universal simply because boards of directors are a fact of life for managers of corporations, in both health care and other industries. State statutes usually set some requirements for corporate boards, such as age or number of members on the board. These same statutes then enfranchise the board with the legal responsibility and authority for the operation of the enterprise. The board, in turn, normally delegates significant amounts of their powers to a full-time managerial staff headed by a chief executive officer (CEO).

Although problems with boards are not a new issue, the last few years have seen considerable controversy over the role and functioning of boards of both for-profit and nonprofit corporations in and out of the health sector. This controversy has led to increasing literature about boards, CEOs, and governmental over-sight, including the passage of the Sarbanes–Oxley Act of 2002, a landmark piece of corporate reform legislation directed at the accountability of public corporations. The reality is that managers almost invariably work with the board they find in place when they are hired, leaving us with the fundamental question: How can a manager have an effective relationship with a board? At one extreme, the manager must cope with what some perceive as a necessary evil; at another, the manager is able to utilize the resources that a board can offer.

Many managers view their relationship with the board as somewhat adversarial. This was well articulated by one chief executive who claimed to work more than 400 hours per month and who said that his board couldn't be smarter than him on any issue simply because they had not put in the time that he had. And although this executive claimed to keep his board fully informed, they simply did not have the volume of material or assistance that he had for examining any given situation. At the other extreme was an organization in which I worked where the board chairman refused to share any meaningful information with the board, thus concentrating all power in his own hands. Most boards operate with digests or summaries of information, which are often poor substitutes for the full scope of information.

In my experience, even well-meaning boards and managers often have difficulty managing their information. For example, I once served on a board of a foundation grant program. Our 15-person board was responsible for allocating $50 million to community hospitals that were developing hospital-based group practices. Our job involved reviewing scores of complex applications plus staff-written field visit reports about the applicants. The typical package per applicant was an inch thick. At any given board meeting, we reviewed 7 to 10 applications, and those documents usually arrived at the board members' offices about 3 days before the meeting. Frankly, I doubt if all the members carefully reviewed the hundreds of pages presented to them. I suspect most of us instead turned to the executive summary and listened to the staff presentations and recommendations at the board meeting. In the course of the 3 years of this program, not one staff recommendation was disapproved. Although we did have a top-flight staff, it must also be acknowledged that the essential decision-making power truly resided with staff because they were in control of the information.

Effective relationships are of major concern in healthcare organizations. On the one hand, the board is necessary for fund-raising and community contacts, while on the other hand, the board can rarely match the professional expertise or time invested in the organization by its professionals. From a managerial perspective, boards become problematic in a variety of ways. First, they simply do not do their homework. If a manager sends out material for a board to review prior to a meeting, he or she expects the board member to review the material and be able to discuss the subject intelligently. As a board member and CEO, I have too often attended meetings where one or more board members were sitting reviewing the material while the discussion was in progress and would then ask questions that were profoundly stupid.

A second problem is those board members whose success in one industry gives them the sense that they could run the health facility or programs with their eyes closed. This arrogance of board members often translates into disrespect for the management and second-guessing of managerial decisions. My favorite example is that of a board member who owned a pizza franchise and wasted 30 minutes at a board meeting belaboring a managerial decision to hire a new snow removal company to clear the hospital grounds.

A third problem involves board members who directly or indirectly use their positions for personal gain. When this occurs, the manager is often put into the position of walking on eggshells. Over the years, I have seen board members insist on jobs for their family members, use institutional monies for essentially private parties, promote their businesses through the institution, insist that the institution use their companies as a primary purveyor, hire the board members for professional services, or use suppliers that would benefit a board member. For example, at one medical center, the owner of a large restaurant was also treasurer of the board. He demanded that certain food service suppliers be used by the medical center—the same ones he used for his restaurant, who then provided him with much better prices because of the deal he could deliver with the medical center.

The question is as follows: Why does management go along with a board that cannot behave in a professional manner? The answer is probably ego and job security. In my own experience as CEO, I found that I had a board that, while personally quite congenial, was also quite dysfunctional. When I joined the organization, there were 200 people on my board. Most of them liked being on the board, but few had any clue as to their responsibility or authority. When I was hired, it was agreed that I could reshape the board into a smaller, more effective group, that the longtime chairman would retire, and that we would have a board with a rotating executive group.

In the first few months of my tenure, I learned that all board meetings were essentially Sunday morning breakfasts with 60-minute show-and-tell reports scripted by the public relations department. The social nature of these board meetings was emphasized by the tradition of bringing family and friends to the breakfasts and the total lack of any financial reporting. Occasionally a vote on an issue was taken, and all of those votes were unanimous. Hundreds of bagels, Danish, omelets, cups of coffee, and pounds of halvah later, the meeting was over and no real business had been transacted. All of the major decisions were made in smaller meetings of the board chairman, board president, and a handful of trusted advisors.

My ego told me that I could change this system. So shortly after I arrived, I began educating the board with mailings about current issues, including various reports about board functioning from the American Hospital Association. I also made myself available to board members for meetings on a variety of subjects. Finally, I made it a point to attend all of the meetings of the various board committees. I thought that I could change a 40-year-old system by the power of education and my personality. I, like many other CEOs, found that it is not very easy to change what are essentially the board habits of a lifetime. In this case it was a board that had learned to go to the party and neither pay the bill nor clean up afterward. As a group they had long ago ceded their power to an inner circle, and now they were coasting. It did not take long before I went from the white knight to the intruder; the next step was for me to leave. While there were a few board members who wanted to see the organization change, they were clearly in the minority and were unwilling to speak up in public for even the simplest of changes, such as board reports on the organization's finances.

Clearly, many managers continue to work for years with less-than-optimal boards. Some do it simply for the money; a job is a job, and most boards are problematic, so why trade the devil you know for the devil you don't know? Others persist with a spirit of hope for the future. Over the course of years, the fortunate few are able to influence the selection of board members with whom they can work successfully, while others live with the vagaries of the board selection process. In one midwestern city, I met with the CEO of a nonprofit geriatric system who was pleased with his new board chairman. I had lunch with the chairman, a young self-made millionaire, and concluded that his arrogance and lack of respect for nonprofit organizational managers boded poorly for this CEO. Within a year he was out of a job. If there is an analogy, management board relationships are like boating: the wind, the currents, and unexpected weather all affect the outcome at the end of the day. The smart manager realizes that board management relationships change constantly and that the most he or she can do is act professionally and competently and offer his or her best judgments on the issues of the day.

A final thought: despite the high salaries, perks, and titles, the board does not forget that management works for them. A medical center CEO I am friendly with is an avid golfer. I once asked him whether he was a member of the country club in his community. He told me that it was a perquisite available to him with the job but he hadn't joined. He preferred to play at the local municipal course because that way he never confused himself; that is, he reminded himself that he was an employee of the medical center.

## A Final Thought Before the Cases: The Business Judgment Rule

Nothing is more important for board members and managers to understand than the business judgment rule. In 2006, the Brooklyn Hospital Center and Caledonian Health Center, Inc., which had filed for bankruptcy protection in 2005, found itself in the U.S. Bankruptcy Court in New York on an issue involving an attempt by the hospital's directors and others to implement a key employee retention plan (KERP) to ensure that key staff remained with the organization as it tried to dig its way out of bankruptcy (which it later did). In analyzing the facts in this case, the court adopted the business judgment rule as its standard. In essence, this rule asks whether the board has acted in the best interests of the corporation, which means that they followed a process that is based on good faith and rational decision making and that the issues have been fully and fairly aired; that is, due care has been used in the decision making.

Part of that due care involves no abuse of discretion and loyalty to the organization for which the director is a fiduciary— that is, no self-serving behavior, in particular, trading on non-public information. Just as insider trading is clearly illegal in public companies, such behavior is also an issue in nonprofits. For example, if a board member knows from meetings that the medical center is planning an expansion into a certain neighborhood (and the information has not been released to the public), the duty of loyalty would, like the insider-trading rule, preclude him or her from buying up property in that neighborhood with the goal of later selling it to the institution at an inflated price.

Thus, when considering how well a board member is carrying out his or her job, one should keep the following keywords and phrases in mind: good faith, conflict of interest, duty of loyalty, duty to disclose, affirmative misrepresentations, due care, self-dealing, and due diligence. It all boils down not to whether the decision of the director or directors was correct (based on 20-20 hindsight), but rather to whether the directors acted with care and in the best interest of the organization.

## CASE 2-1 | Board Restructuring

Since its founding just after World War II, the Watergate Home and Hospital for the Aged has been structured with a two-tiered board. The executive committee, which is the de facto power group, consists of Wayne Brewster, chairman of the Watergate's board; Pete Johnson, the president of the board; John Peterson, the vice president of the board; Wylie Foxx, the treasurer of the board; and Huey Duckman, the board secretary. Each of these five people has served on the board for more than 30 years and has never been in danger of not being reelected to his post. The chairman has served in that capacity for close to 40 years.

The second tier is the theoretical board of directors, which is made up of 125 people. They are all initially appointed by the executive committee and subject to reappointment every year based on the recommendation of the executive committee. The entire board meets eight times per year, always on a Sunday morning for a breakfast meeting, and they are always invited to bring along spouses or friends. Typically, reports that speak to new developments in the organization and upcoming events are presented at these meetings. No financial reports are ever presented, and when votes are taken, they are simply to ratify decisions made by the executive committee. Rarely are any dissenting voices heard. Indeed, it is rumored that if anyone offers any dissent during one of these board breakfasts, he or she will not be reappointed the following year.

Although this system is clearly autocratic, it did work rather effectively for many years. However, in the past 12 months there have been two major changes in the organization. First,

Chairman of the Board Wayne Brewster died, and his cousin Robin Brewster, who is a longtime board member, has replaced him. Unfortunately she simply does not have the time to devote to Watergate as did Wayne. Second, Watergate CEO Dean Johnson left, and his deputy, Nix Dickson, has become Acting CEO. Dickson has proposed a number of changes to the board, including the following:

1. Cutting the board size from 125 to 18
2. Educating the board
3. Providing the board with a broad range of financial decisions
4. Making the board responsible for annually reviewing and approving the operating and capital budget of the organization
5. Having the board involved in all major policy discussions
6. Eliminating the social nature of board meetings
7. Moving ultimate power from the executive committee to the board

\* \* \*

QUESTIONS

1. In light of the history of this organization, do Dickson's suggestions make sense? Why? Why not?
2. From an organizational politics standpoint, is the proposal feasible?
3. Is there anything inherently wrong with the way Watergate is doing business?
4. Assume you are a consultant. What type of educational program would you develop for the board? How could this program be effectively delivered?

---

## CASE 2-2   Gelt and Jeffe

For most of the 4 months prior to his being fired, Ira M. Gelt, CFO of the Mercury Medical Center (MMC), had been having a testy relationship with Len Jeffe, chairman of the board of trustees of MMC. Allie Baker, the CEO, although usually agreeing with

Gelt, always tried to be the organizational peacemaker. This generally meant that Baker would spend her time first trying to appease Gelt and then trying to appease Jeffe.

The ostensible basis of the conflict was the financial shape of MMC. Gelt's view was that the operating funds were too reliant on the growth of the endowment and its income. Jeffe's attitude was that it was not Gelt's concern. That is, as chair of the board, money was his exclusive concern. Gelt, he said in not so many words, was merely the chief bookkeeper. Baker told Gelt to ignore Jeffe, that he was just a full-of-himself bigmouth who was born with a silver spoon in his mouth and knew nothing about healthcare management. To Jeffe she would say that Gelt was a bit compulsive but a solid man who was needed by MMC.

Gelt's view was that the board was too involved in spending the money. Jeffe actually had total control of one of the MMC operating accounts. Some have speculated that the conflict ran deeper since they were both football players on rival schools at the same time.

Gelt's firing resulted from an altercation at a board meeting. Although there are conflicting opinions about what occurred, the following is certain. Jeffe was sitting between Gelt and Baker while Baker was pushing through a minimal agenda for the meeting that included eliminating Gelt's financial report. In response to Jeffe's comment, "I think we will skip the finance report tonight because nothing much is happening," Gelt stood up and said, "Just a minute, Len. There is some important financial business to discuss, including your proposal to purchase the naming rights of the new ambulatory care center so that you might name it for your wife. In my judgment, we need to discuss the donation you will make and whether we can raise more money with an auction or at least by soliciting other donors."

Jeffe was obviously embarrassed and told Gelt to sit down and that he would handle the matter. Gelt said that he would not sit down and that it was his fiduciary responsibility to bring this matter to the attention of the board. At this point Jeffe put his hand on Gelt's shoulder and was heard to say, "When I say sit down, you sit down." Gelt responded by saying, "Take your hand off of me. As long as I am CFO here, I will make my report." Jeffe replied, "That's easy to deal with, you blockhead! You're fired." As he said this, he still had his hand on Gelt's shoulder. Gelt then brushed aside Jeffe's hand and shoved him away. Next, Jeffe took a swing at Gelt. Gelt ducked and punched Jeffe in the face, knocking him down. Gelt then turned away and walked out. The board meeting was immediately terminated.

* * *

QUESTIONS

1. What are the issues in this case?
2. Has Baker been operating appropriately?
3. What about Gelt? What about Jeffe?
4. What should Baker do about Gelt's firing?

---

## CASE 2-3 | Organizational Tragedy

As the board of directors sat down for their emergency meeting, a profound sense of sadness and gloom permeated the room. Less than 24 hours earlier, JP Jones had been their dynamic CEO on the third year of his second 5-year contract, and Bobbi Ann Jones (no relation) had been their equally dynamic 47-year-old CFO.

Now Bobbi Ann was dead, and JP was in the intensive care unit as a result of a drunk driver hitting them as they were returning from a chamber of commerce dinner. The board chairman, Commander Matt Perry, U.S. Navy (Ret.), opened the meeting.

*Perry:*

Let us begin with a moment of silent prayer for the soul of our dearly departed Bobbi Ann, and let us also pray for the recovery of JP.

After a minute of silence, Perry opened the meeting.

*Perry:*

Folks, we have a serious problem. Obviously it could be months, perhaps longer or maybe not at all, before JP can return, and Bobbi needs to be replaced as soon as possible.

*Board member #1:*

   Do we have anyone in the bullpen?

*Perry:*

   Not really for the long haul. Right now Myron Appel-
   baum is the assistant VP, but he is still too young and
   has no leadership experience. In finance, basically
   everyone there is a technician—in fact, Bobbi was the
   only CPA.

*Board member #1:*

   So why not start a search for Bobbi's job?

*Board member # 2:*

   Might as well search for both jobs.

*Board member # 3:*

   It seems to me we are in a pickle because we don't want
   to hire a CFO without the CEO recommending it. Basically we would wind up selecting a CFO who would
   report to the CEO. I think that could be a problem.

*Perry:*

   Folks, I have a proposal. Why don't we use an interim
   management firm for both jobs until we can sort out
   what is happening?

* * *

QUESTIONS

   1. What are the costs and benefits of using an interim firm
      for both jobs?
   2. Are there other alternatives that make sense?
   3. Has this board dropped the ball by not having a succes-
      sion plan?
   4. Is this just an example of an unpredictable organizational
      tragedy, or are there organizational rules that could pre-
      vent such a situation?
   5. Does it matter whether the organization in this case is a
      not-for-profit or for-profit corporation?
   6. This case does not state the type of organization where
      the tragedy happened. Does the analysis change if this
      is a medical center, hospital, nursing home, home care
      agency, or medical group practice?

## CASE 2-4 | Board Fees

At a recent meeting between Nancy Jones, CEO of Community Medical Center (a 501[c] 3 corporation), and Charlene White, chairperson of the board, the following conversation occurred:

*White:*

Nancy, I am interested in your thoughts about providing our board members an annual honorarium.

*Jones:*

Are you serious? Why would you want to do this? We've never paid board members before. Why start now?

*White:*

Several reasons. First, I think our board members put in a lot of time and we should recognize their effort by something more than our monthly dinner meetings. Second, if we gave them some money, I would feel more comfortable asking them to work. Finally, I think it would increase our pool of potential board members.

*Jones:*

Interesting thought. What kind of honorarium are you thinking about?

*White:*

Not much, maybe $3,000 per year. For our entire board of 12 people, that works out to $36,000 a year, and I bet we get some of that back in contributions. So what do you think?

*Jones:*

This is certainly a fascinating idea. Let me do some research and thinking. I will get back to you on this next week.

*White:*

Great! I look forward to your report.

* * *

QUESTIONS

1. What is a 501(c) 3 corporation?
2. Is paying a fee (no matter what you call it) to the board of a 501(c) 3 company legal?

3. Other than the discussed issues, what other issues might arise from paying board members?
4. Assuming you are going ahead with paying the board members, do the annual fee and the proposed amount make sense? Any other options?
5. What is your recommendation? Why?

---

| CASE 2-5 | **Firing The CEO** |

On the morning of November 1, Paul Blackman, administrator of the Crescent City Nursing Center for the past 23 months, received a call from Roger Johnson, former president of the nursing home's board, who told him that, on behalf of the other former presidents of the board, Johnson was asking for Blackman's resignation by the end of the year. Blackman was stunned by this call and immediately telephoned Angela Fisher, the home's board president, and received assurances from her that, despite the fact that he had no employment contract, his job was secure.

The Crescent City Nursing Center is a 250-bed skilled nursing home that has a reputation for being the finest in the region. Since its founding shortly after World War II, the home has been under the direction of a 24-member self-perpetuating board of trustees. The original board comprised a number of people who were instrumental in the founding of the home, including members of the Johnson family, who were not only involved in the home's founding but also provided close to $3 million of the home's total $5 million endowment. The most important of the Johnson family members were two brothers, Roger and William. The 24 members of the present board consist of 7 former presidents and at least 10 other people who have been involved with the home for over 15 years. The board is now dominated by Roger's son Kenneth and William's son John. In addition, five other Johnson family members are on the board, along with several board members who have significant business involvement with the Johnson family.

Since the home opened, there have been three administrators. The first administrator also served as director of nursing and held the job until 1965, when she was replaced by

Mac Davidson, who administered the home for the next 30 years. Davidson's training was in social work, and he came to the home at a crucial time in its evolution. He was responsible for its growth from a 100-bed old-age home to the high-quality home it is today. Davidson and his wife Leslie were intimately involved in all aspects of the home. Although Leslie was only a part-time receptionist, she made her presence felt throughout the home by being there a significant part of each day, visiting the residents daily, participating in the various resident shows, and socializing with many of the volunteers and board members. Mac Davidson also kept a very high profile in the home through various means, including early morning rounds of all the resident units, close contact with family members, and an active series of social engagements with many of the board members, especially the Johnson clan. In contrast, Paul Blackman has spent more time in his office and less time visiting with residents or socializing with the board. Mrs. Blackman, who is an accountant with a certified public accounting firm, has also been quite uninvolved with the home, in sharp contrast to Leslie Davidson.

The last few years of Davidson's tenure were both professionally and personally difficult for him. On the professional side, he faced a broad range of challenges, including an attempted unionization at the nursing home, a decrease in the home's ability to raise funds, and a decrease in income from residents due to a declining private-pay census as well as Medicaid cutbacks. On the personal side, Davidson had a series of medical problems, including a heart attack, bypass surgery, and a bout with prostate cancer. After enduring these problems for 3 years, the board prevailed on Davidson to retire. Because of Davidson's health problems, he retired in January and his longtime assistant, Alvin Jakes, who for 27 years was the home's personnel manager, took over as the acting administrator.

The board recognized Jakes's limitations and agreed among themselves to increase their supervision of the home, particularly in the area of finances. The increased supervision provided the board with some unexpected and unpleasant information about the facility's fiscal health, such as an undisclosed (by management) deficit of close to $1 million. They also learned that the home was overstaffed and that its salary and benefit structure was exceedingly problematic.

The board decided to find a new CEO to solve the problems and bring the home's finances into line. After a 6-month search, they hired Paul Blackman, a 39-year-old experienced nursing home administrator with an MBA in health administration. On January 1, Blackman took over the job and set about identifying and rectifying the problems. The first of these involved low morale among the staff, largely due to Davidson's long history of favoritism, which had resulted in inequitable pay and fringe benefits. For example, in the food service department, a cook with 20 years of seniority was paid less than another cook who had been with the home only 7 years. Also, the 20-year veteran was entitled to only 3 weeks of paid vacation, whereas Davidson had negotiated a 4-week vacation package for the new cook after 5 years of service. The food service example was not an isolated case. There were numerous inequities throughout the organization, many of which apparently resulted from Davidson's desire to control staff through a series of private negotiations. The individual staff member would thus become beholden to Davidson because he had bent the personnel rules to accommodate the employee's desires.

Other problems included the huge deficit resulting from overstaffing and state Medicaid cutbacks. Blackman dealt with these problems by undertaking a thorough review of personnel policies and actions as well as staffing levels. In addition, Blackman decided to replace a number of senior management personnel with people loyal to him. In one conversation with Angela Fisher, he stated that the home was still full of Davidson loyalists who ran to him with every complaint or controversy. A further problem was that many of those who were likely to lose from Blackman's policies had cordial relationships with the board. This was another legacy of the Davidson years, when the CEO often hired people at the suggestion of board members, particularly the Johnson family.

In pursuing his policies, Blackman felt considerable pressure to get things in order as soon as possible. He also felt that every change he made reflected poorly on his predecessor, and that frequently either Davidson or one of his friends on the board would react to a proposed change with the question, "How come we never had this problem when Mac ran the home?"

Blackman's analysis of the situation was that Mac Davidson was an out-of-touch and manipulative manager who ran the home by keeping the board in the dark, and that the board was complicit by choosing to stay in the dark. John and Kenneth Johnson, both former board presidents, viewed Blackman as the key problem. From their perspective, Blackman was doing a respectable job of dealing with the home's fiscal problems but was making a mess of the staff situation. Specifically, they believed he was wrong to fire or force into retirement so many top management staff, including the director of nursing, the director of the physical plant, the food service director, the personnel manager, and the purchasing agent. In addition, while they applauded his efforts at developing a more equitable system of wages and benefits, they were concerned about its costs as well as its potential for labor strife. Other matters that concerned these board members included Blackman's active participation on the state nursing home association's board of trustees and his lack of time to socialize with the residents.

Angela Fisher found herself in the middle of this dispute. On the one hand, she personally liked Paul Blackman and respected what he was trying to accomplish. On the other hand, she felt that he should probably spend more time at the home and perhaps be more diplomatic about board relationships. Her main concern, however, was how to deal with the powerful group of former board presidents who had announced that they were going to fire Paul Blackman.

* * *

QUESTIONS

1. In light of Roger Johnson's personal and financial involvement with the nursing center, was it wrong for him to fire Paul Blackman?
2. What does this case imply about the structure and operation of the board of directors of the nursing home?
3. Assuming Angela Fisher will have a talk about this matter with Mr. Johnson, what responses should she be prepared to handle?

4. If Ms. Fisher were to bring in a consultant to deal with the conflicts on the board, as exemplified by this case scenario, what issues should the consultant be prepared to tackle?

---

## CASE 2-6 | Luke Mackenzie

Luke Mackenzie is being considered for the position of CEO of the Scott Vista Home Health Center for the Elderly, a 300-bed facility located in a suburb of a major metropolitan area. The facility has had decent but not great managerial leadership for a number of years, but the untimely death of the 59-year-old CEO has resulted in the availability of the position.

The board's executive committee, consisting of seven individuals, decided to hire an executive search firm to find candidates for the job. Mackenzie, an experienced nursing home administrator, presently working for a private nonprofit foundation, was one of the three they recommended for the position. The preliminary interview was positive, and now Mackenzie has been invited back to Scott Vista for a second interview.

In preparation for the interview, he has asked for and received the organization's financial statements and various documents related to the strategic plan.

Mackenzie is quite interested in the job for a variety of professional and personal reasons (he has school-age children and Scott Vista is located in one of the best school districts in the country), but based on his analyses, he feels that the organization is at a crossroads financially. In his opinion, it is significantly overstaffed, many of its programs are running at significant deficits, and with the way these programs are structured, it would be extremely difficult to turn them around. Additionally, fund-raising, which has been able to cover the deficit in the past, has diminished more than 70% in the past decade. Finally, based on his first trip to the health center, he found a board that was living in the past and was quite poorly educated about the challenges facing both the industry and the Scott Vista Home.

\* \* \*

QUESTIONS

1. What options does Mackenzie have in approaching the second interview?
2. Would Mackenzie be wise to present the board with his bad news analysis of the organization?
   a. If yes, how should this be presented?
   b. If no, what should he say about the problems?

---

## CASE 2-7 | Cardiac Innovation

The Metropolitan University and Medical Center is one of three medical schools and university-based hospitals in the city. Ostensibly, the relationship between all three organizations is cordial, but in many ways they are quite competitive, with Metropolitan usually perceived as being in third place.

Three weeks ago, Franklin Benjamin, MD, chairman of the Cardiac Surgery Division, met with Jeff Thompson, the CEO, to continue discussions about the possibility of Metropolitan becoming a provider of care using the Edwards Life Sciences Sapien Heart Valve. The conversation between them went as follows:

*Benjamin:*

Jeff, I think we need to go ahead and get the Sapien system. This will be our opportunity to take the lead in the region in cardiac surgery.

*Thompson:*

Frank, I would certainly like to be the leader in your area of work. But frankly they make it quite hard to get into their system. I would have a team of people pulling data together for months for them to peruse, and then, if accepted, we have site visits and oversight in the OR. Also, we would have to do some upgrading of one of our OR suites, and we just don't have the money.

*Benjamin:*

I hear you, but we have a golden opportunity to take the leadership role. We will be helping patients who otherwise might not get help.

*Thompson:*

> Frank, I am definitely sympathetic to your concerns, but other similar products are coming down the road, and it doesn't appear that the other companies are going to make us jump through as many hoops as Edwards. And don't forget one of those hoops is selection of patients for the valves. I think the uptick we would get for being innovative might be offset by the downside of raising hope for some patients and not being able to deliver.

*Benjamin:*

> So, what is your decision?

*Thompson:*

> I've thought long and hard about this. In fact, I was up most of last night thinking about it and searching the Internet for any data. My conclusion is that we should not pursue it. I don't think the costs are worth the benefits at the present time. Let's revisit this in 6 months.

Dr. Benjamin left the meeting totally frustrated. That evening at the Metroplex Country Club he ran into the chairman and the treasurer of the Metropolitan University and Medical Center board and started telling them of his frustration over this matter. The next morning, the chairman called Mr. Thompson and said the following:

"Jeff, I ran into Frank Benjamin last night and he told me about your decision regarding the Sapien system. It sounds to me like this is our shot at becoming the leading center in the region for cardiac surgery. Why are you so against it? You are not afraid of taking a chance are you?"

\* \* \*

QUESTIONS

1. Is this a board or a management issue?
2. Is this board member acting responsibly?
3. What should Thompson do about Dr. Benjamin going to the board?

4. What are the costs and benefits of going with the Sapien system?
5. Is Thompson's conclusion reasonable?

---

| CASE 2-8 | Board Breakfasts |

At the State Hospital Association's annual meeting, June Bookman, the CEO of the 130-bed MacIntosh Memorial Hospital, located 47 miles from a major metropolitan area, heard a presentation from JJ Kimberly, a hospital consultant. The consultant was speaking about the importance of an educated board and presented examples from hospitals with which he worked. Bookman spoke with Kimberly and arranged for him to visit the hospital with the idea of developing such a program.

A week later, Kimberly visited and toured the facility. What he found was a small community hospital with 600 employees. According to Bookman, the hospital served a growing exurban community that was rapidly developing its own hi-tech industry center around Josephs Robotics. This, she thought, would result in a major expansion of the hospital, which she was already planning. Bookman also told him that she thought the board was out of touch with what was happening in health care and was not prepared for the challenges and changes she foresaw. For example, she was very disappointed that the board was strident about staying independent of any of the three regional medical school networks. Bookman thought this was because of the physicians on the board who were concerned that any network affiliations might hamper their long-standing referral connections. She was also concerned that the board was not ready for a major expansion and all that it implied, particularly in terms of fund-raising. Kimberly agreed to undertake a series of bi-monthly 90-minute breakfast seminars for the board.

At the first seminar, Kimberly was introduced by Bookman, who, after making some introductory remarks, excused herself, saying that she had a schedule conflict. Kimberly began by telling the board members of his background and then went around the room asking each of the members to introduce themselves and say something about their own businesses. He was particularly interested in listening to Juan Josephs, whom Bookman had told him about. Josephs, an inventor and entrepreneur, had moved to the area 12 years earlier and had begun a small company that made robots that were used in certain limited areas of surgery. As the robots proved themselves, the company grew, went public, and became the largest employer in the region, with close to 1,300 staff, many of whom were technicians and engineers. All of the Josephs Robotics employees were insured through a generous indemnity plan.

Juan introduced himself in a very modest way as an executive with the local robotic company. Kimberly asked him why he had picked the MacIntosh community for his company. He answered that he liked the school system for his kids, the cost of living was dramatically less than in the city, and he felt that if his company ever took off, he wouldn't have trouble recruiting engineers or technicians to work on the robots. Then he dropped the bombshell that he was going to be sorry that the company was moving most of its manufacturing operations to another state because of taxes, the need to expand, and the desire of his major stockholders to start mining the South American market from a better location. Kimberly asked how many jobs were staying and how many leaving. Rather casually, Josephs answered, "Just the executive and marketing group are staying . . . probably 25 to 30 people. The rest will move, or at least have the opportunity to move, to Texas as soon as the factory is finished, in about 14 months." Kimberly was stunned but soldiered on with his first presentation.

After the breakfast, he waited for Bookman to have a break and then shared with her what he had learned from Mr. Josephs. Bookman sat quietly, thanked him, and said, "See you next week."

\* \* \*

QUESTIONS

1. What does this case say about June Bookman? Why?
2. What should Ms. Bookman do with this information?
3. Assume the board president also just learned at the breakfast about the Josephs Robotics plan. What should the president do?
4. What does this incident say about board administration relations at MacIntosh?
5. Are the problems in this case remediable?

---

**CASE 2-9** | **The Bad Barber**

Subsequent to a scandal that focused on the poor quality of physician care at a neighboring hospital, the chairman of the board of directors asked the CEO at Tober-Mory Community Hospital to undertake a study of their own quality of care in order to find out if they had any rotten eggs.

The CEO and the chief of the medical staff met privately and identified five physicians about whom they had concerns. They went ahead and hired the Yithro Group, a nationally recognized independent medical review organization, to examine the cases of these physicians. The reviewers were empowered to do a thorough medical records-based analysis on each physician under review.

The conclusion of the Yithro Group was that four of the physicians were functioning within acceptable parameters, but with regard to the fifth, Dr. Jarad Barber, his clinical management, professional conduct, and medical record keeping were below par. Specifically, they noted that Dr. Barber was performing numerous high-risk procedures, he was often disruptive by screaming at staff and patients, occasionally using profane language, and he typically refused to function as a member of the patient care team (all documented in nursing and social worker notes).

Unknown to the reviewers was the additional information that Dr. Barber admitted more patients per year to the hospital than other doctors—indeed more than the next four highest-admitting physicians combined. Although he behaved in the manner that the group identified, he could also be quite charming and generous with the staff (bringing in candy and donuts and giving generous Christmas presents).

\* \* \*

QUESTIONS

1. What does the CEO tell the chairman of the board?
2. Assume the CEO wants to get rid of Barber. What does he have to do?
3. What message is sent to the staff if Dr. Barber is not reappointed? What message is sent if he is reappointed?
4. Are there any good options?

**CHAPTER 3**

# HUMAN RESOURCES MANAGEMENT

 INTRODUCTION

The single largest budget category for virtually all healthcare providers is the expenditures related to staffing the organization— that is, salaries, salary-related expenses such as social security or pension contributions, and other fringe benefits, most notably health benefits. It would not be unusual for an organization's operating budget to have more than two-thirds of its expenditures in this human resources (HR) category.

Similarly, the success or failure of an organization can often-times be traced to the quality of its staff. The nature of many health enterprises presents special challenges because of the large number of unskilled people who work in health care at low salaries. For example, it would not be unusual for 50% of a nursing home's staff to be nurses' aides. These people typically are high school graduates with no additional education other than a mandatory state training program of a duration of between 50 and 100 hours. Many medical office assistants who do everything from administering electrocardiograms to giving injections have, at best, limited vocational school education. Compounding this HR situation, in my experience, is that a fair number of these low-paid staff also have second full-time or part-time jobs. This situation is truly a conundrum for organizations that usually cannot afford to raise wages but have staff coming to work who are often too tired to effectively and efficiently do their job.

In this chapter the reader will be faced with a variety of problems that administrators must deal with on a regular basis. For example, in our multicultural society, cultural competence is required by virtually all staff, from clinician to housekeeper, and two of these cases focus directly on that issue. Living in health-care organizations also means living with myriad governmental regulations as well as self-generated employee manuals that frequently have the force of contracts. This chapter provides opportunities to study this type of document. A final dimension of this chapter relates to specific HR activities that management is called on to handle, such as strike preparation, whistle-blowing, and sexual harassment. As noted in the introductory chapter, HR management is in many ways the heart and soul of an organization. Thus, although this chapter might highlight the HR management function, the reality is that almost every case in this book is an HR case.

## CASE 3-1 | Paid Time Off

CONFIDENTIAL MEMO

From:  Harry O. Dini, HR Consultant
To:       Wilbur Jones, Executive Director, The Cinco Cities
             Health and Medical Center
Subj:  Personnel Audit

I have just finished the audit of all the personnel files and related documents. In my 17 years as a personnel management consultant, I have never seen so many inconsistencies in HR policies. Frankly, I have to assume that your organization is in violation of some state and federal labor laws.

To be specific, nonmanagerial staff seem to have a broad range of vacation days. For example, there are some people who work in your engineering department who have been there for 10 years and get as much as 6 weeks of paid vacation per year, while there are those with more than 20 years of service who are getting 4 weeks of vacation per year. New hires are getting between 1 and 3 weeks of paid vacation, and it is not dependent on department or anything else I can discern.

Additionally, it appears that some staff have accumulated hundreds of days of sick leave over as many as 20 years, while others during that same period have no sick leave accumulated. Based on conversations with a number of staff people who preceded both of us here, it appears that your predecessors were using the personal time off and vacation system as a way of awarding bonuses—that is, gifts of time and not money.

This mess must be cleaned up! I suggest Cinco go on a paid-time-off (PTO) system for ALL its staff: clinicians, management, and other employees. My suggestion is to lump sick leave together with vacation time and holiday time. Also, I suggest that PTO should be related to years of service, regardless of rank. Such a system is clear and equitable.

I am available to discuss this further.

\* \* \*

QUESTIONS

1. Theoretically, is PTO a good idea?
2. How would you handle the backlog of inequities to get people into a PTO system?
3. Is total equity in the organization possible? Expected? Necessary?
4. What are the costs and benefits of following the consultant's advice?
5. Is this memo "confidential"? That is, is it subject to discovery in case of a lawsuit?

## CASE 3-2 | Cultural Competency

The CEO of Community Medical Center recently read an article about a teaching hospital in Mason City, Iowa, that has a monthly series of "cultural competency" lectures designed for foreign medical staff. For example, among the topics covered in the well-regarded program are Topics for Small Talk With Iowans and An Intro to Working Effectively With White Europeans. The CEO has asked you to design a curriculum for the Community Medical Center that will assist its coterie of 30 foreign medical graduates (FMGs) and general staff (about 40% of whom are not locals) to become more "culturally competent" with regard to dealing with the community's patient population. Included in this grouping is a large community mental health center. In preparing the curriculum, it is anticipated that you will state all your assumptions about the demographics of the population served by the medical center.

* * *

QUESTIONS

1. How will your demographic assumptions affect the curriculum?
2. What will be your basic strategy for designing the curriculum? Specifically what steps will you take in writing up the curriculum?
3. Will you have a different curriculum for the FMGs and general staff? Why?
4. How will the curriculum be delivered? Why?

## CASE 3-3 | General Nudnik

Less than a year ago Maxwell Nudnik, a retired three-star Marine general, was appointed to the board of trustees of the holding company of Our Lady of Good Deeds Health System (OLGD). During his time on the board, General Nudnik has been relatively quiet, asking few questions and never casting a dissenting vote. The flagship of the system is a 478-bed hospital. Additionally, the system has a 200-bed skilled nursing home, a 135-bed hospital in the rural part of the county, and a 100-unit assisted living center.

For years the system has been running at a deficit, which was easily covered by the system's endowment and various fund-raising activities. In December the board held its annual budget session to look at the system's operating and capital budget for the following year. After Casper (Cap) Ghostly, the system's longtime CEO, made his presentation, Nudnik started peppering him with questions about the budget. His primary focus was the staffing. Finally, after a heated exchange, Nudnik said the following, "I'm new to this outfit, but I can smell indulgence and inefficiency a mile away. We have more staff per bed than any other facility in the region, our budget is higher per bed than the other places, and, frankly, we deal with our inefficiencies by raising money. In my opinion, the world is changing and we are not going to be so able to pay our bills through endowment income or fund-raising. In fact, look at how the interest rates have dropped over the last 3 years. We need more productivity and more efficiency. I don't know what you guys are doing, but I've run everything from small platoons to entire brigades and I can tell you if you want to lead men, you need to kick butt and take names. That's what I did, and it works. I think you guys are operating like a bunch of candy stripers. It's time to step up to the plate and manage this show!"

There was a profound silence in the room until Ghostly politely said, "Thank you, General, I will take your remarks under consideration." A few minutes later, the meeting ended and Ghostly returned to his office where his administrative resident (AR) and the associate director (AD) were waiting for a post-meeting recap. After composing himself, he related to the two other people what had just happened. He then asked them for their impression of the general's remarks. They replied as follows:

*AD:*

> Boss, the general sounds like a general. Just like the officers I knew in the Army. You know what I mean, "Do it my way or the highway." He doesn't get what goes on here, the excess staff we need because of our

teaching activities, the issues we have with unionization, and, frankly, our civic responsibility to try to keep people in our community employed. Face it—we are the biggest employer, the employer of last resort, and to a limited extent our employees are part of the political patronage system that ensures our support from the community.

*AR:*

The general reminds me of the Theory X managers we read about in our motivation class. He thinks everyone is lazy and not trying. I think we should try to educate him.

*CEO:*

I doubt if he is capable of being educated. And, he may have a point that we have been a bit too easy on our employees, Theory Y-like. Maybe we need to stir stuff up, make the employees more insecure, use money to motivate people. I am frustrated!

\* \* \*

ASSIGNMENT

1. In his moment of frustration, the CEO hit on an idea. Have the AR put together a presentation for him on how the theories of motivation such as Theory X and Y, Maslow's hierarchy of needs, and Herzberg's motivation/hygiene theory can help better run the organization.

2. Are these theories applicable in light of the diverse employment goals articulated by the associate director?

---

| CASE 3-4 | **Medical Group Locums** |

The medical director of Algonquin and Rogers Medical Group, a 21-physician multispecialty group practice in Iowa, has recently learned from a fellow radiologist about the 2006 case in Missouri of *Cravens v. Smith*. In this case a physicians group that was similar to that of the Algonquin and Rogers Group hired an interim radiologist through a temporary staffing firm that Algonquin and Rogers often uses to employ locum tenens when the group is experiencing shortages.

\* \* \*

ASSIGNMENT

Assume you are the administrator of the group practice and the medical director has asked you to prepare a memo about the case and its implications for the group, including recommendations that are in the group's best interest.

---

## CASE 3-5 | Painful Hands

While in her last semester at a community college where she was studying ultrasonography in an associate of arts program, Jean Autreo was diagnosed with carpal tunnel syndrome. After graduation, Ms. Autreo spent 6 months traveling and another 5 months searching for a job. Finally, almost a year after graduation, the Calder Cardiology Group hired her as an ultrasound sonographer. The work required her to hold a probe for 95% of the workday. Three months after beginning her new job, she started experiencing tingling and numbness in her hands. Although her MD felt the recurrence of the carpal tunnel syndrome was work related, he did not place her on any work restrictions.

During the next 2 years, she continued having problems with her hand until one day the pain was so great she felt she had to report it to her employer. The HR department immediately filed a Report of Injury to the State Workers' Compensation Agency. Several days later, Ms. Autreo filed a Workers' Compensation claim against the Calder Cardiology Group. Calder then sent Ms. Autreo to a specialist who also diagnosed her as having carpal tunnel syndrome. In the consultation with Ms. Autreo, the specialist suggested that she not grip the probes for more than 7 minutes per patient—a situation that would severely limit her ability to be an effective employee.

Ms. Autreo returned to work, met with the HR department, and orally reported what the MD had told her (all of this without the HR department receiving a written report from the physician consultant). In response to what Autreo told HR, the head of the benefits section suggested to Autreo that she go on leave under the FMLA for 12 weeks because of a "serious health condition that makes you unable to perform the essential functions of your job." Autreo was also told that before she could come back, she would need a "fitness for duty certificate." At the end of Ms. Autreo's 12-week leave, her physical condition remained unchanged and she was discharged.

\* \* \*

QUESTIONS

1. Could this entire situation have been avoided through better hiring practices?
2. What do you expect that Ms. Autreo will do?
3. What is FMLA?
4. Is this a retaliatory discharge because Ms. Autreo filed under Workers' Compensation?
5. What should Calder do to ensure that they are dealing fairly with all employees?

---

| CASE 3-6 | **Strategic Dismissal**

For 27 years, Homer DuLac, MD, has been the medical director of the Rouge Valley Geriatric System, a multifacility system consisting of two 170-bed nursing homes, a home health service, a 75-unit assisted living facility, an Alzheimer's day-care center that services 24 people a day, and a geriatric clinic. In addition to his part-time position at Rouge Valley (for which he is paid $100,000 per year), he is also professor of geriatrics at the local medical school and serves as the physician of record for approximately 40% of the nursing home residents.

DuLac became medical director when the organization was a single 100-bed nursing home founded by several wealthy families in the Rouge Valley as a home for the poor. Over the last three decades, it has grown to become the largest geriatric facility in the state and one of the most respected nonprofit facilities in the country.

Several years ago, in response to increased pressure from the state and federal Departments of Labor, Rouge Valley hired a consultant to prepare job descriptions for every position in the organization. DuLac was perhaps the most uncooperative person on the staff with the consultant, complaining to the chairman of the board by saying: "Why the hell are you wasting money on this guy? I do my job and that's that! I've been here for almost 30 years, my family gave the money to build the conference room and the coffee shop, and I don't need any outsider telling me what to do." Finally, he demanded that the CEO be told to keep that "idiot consultant" away from him. To avoid stirring up Dr. DuLac (who was also the chairman's personal physician), the consultant was asked to develop a job description for medical director without discussing it with DuLac or any of his staff of three part-time physicians and three geriatric nurse practitioners.

The consultant used the federal regulations that established the requirements for long-term care facilities (42CFR483.5), as well as a survey of medical directors, to outline the various responsibilities of this position. From the Code of Federal Regulations, he found that the facility must have a "designated medical director who is responsible for implementing care policies and coordinating medical care, and who is directly accountable to the management of the institution of which it is a distinct part." He went on to learn that, in practice, most effective medical directors were actively engaged in quality improvement activities, patient services, residents' rights, and administration. For example, in the area of quality improvement, medical directors were generally expected to review and revise medical and clinical policies, provide leadership in quality of care, and engage in other activities that enhanced quality. In the area of patient services, medical directors were expected to work with attending physicians to ensure that the patients received the appropriate services. Similarly, the medical director was expected to work with the nurses and other staff on medical-related issues. Part of this category and the residents' rights category was related to ensuring that the range of services a patient receives is appropriate, whether it involves restraints, medications, or even nutrition. Finally, the job was found to require close coordination with administration and considerable liaison work between all parties. Based on the information gathered, the consultant submitted his job description to the CEO.

The CEO received the report, discussed it with his deputies, and came to the conclusion that, based on the new job description as well as certain inappropriate behaviors of Dr. DuLac, it was time for DuLac to resign as medical director. The CEO approached the chairman of the board with his proposal. The conversation went as follows:

*CEO:*

After considerable analysis, I think the time has come for Homer to either resign or retire.

*Chairman:*

Wait a minute. Homer's been here almost as long as I have, and I consider him to be integral to our system. Why, I remember back 20 years ago when a tornado came through this community and we were on emergency power for 3 days and Homer slept here and worked night and day. No, he needs to stay.

*CEO:*

I understand what you are saying, but we recently had a consultant put together a job description for the medical director's position and, to be blunt, Homer doesn't do what needs to be done.

*Chairman:*

Well then, rewrite the job description to reflect what Homer is presently doing. We need him. He is our link to the medical school, and the staff love him.

*CEO:*

I don't doubt what you say, but may I be frank?

*Chairman:*

Sure go ahead.

*CEO:*

I realize that Homer is an old and dear friend. And, I also recognize his many contributions to the system. But, since you said I could be frank, I will. Homer is more liability than asset. Obviously, he costs us over $100,000 plus benefits, but that is not the issue. The real problem is that he is incredibly undermining and destructive to the system.

*Chairman:*

Those are strong words; do you have facts to back them up?

*CEO:*

Certainly. Here are two examples. First, 6 months ago we had a Joint Commission accreditation visit. As you know, 5 years ago we adopted a smoke-free policy within the facility, and 2 years ago the state passed a law requiring that all long-term facilities be smoke free. Anyway, as you also know, Homer loves his cigars, and although it is okay for him to smoke in the confines of his office, it violates both our policy and state law for him to smoke elsewhere. So, in defiance of this, during the accreditation visit, he made it a point to wander the halls and patient units smoking his cigar. Frankly, this behavior caused us much grief with the accreditors and only through my begging, telling them some untruths about Homer's health and likely short tenure, did we manage to escape relatively unscathed by the accreditors. We are also lucky that Homer did not behave this way in front of the state inspectors. If that had happened, we would have had some real problems.

The second example has to do with the rehabilitation department. I met with them last week and they are furious because Homer has taken the position that none of our residents can benefit from rehabilitation. He is not sending any of his patients to rehab, and he is advising the other physicians to not use rehab.

*Chairman:*

Does he have a point?

*CEO:*

In some cases he is probably right. But to make a blanket policy like that is harmful to the residents who will definitely lose strength and mobility, and to us because we will lose revenue.

*Chairman:*

I'm still not convinced. Let me think about it for a few days.

A week passed and the CEO again met with the chairman.

*CEO:*

> Look, sir, Homer has to go. He is getting worse, and I am going to have a revolt on my hands. Every single person on the executive teams agrees with me.

*Chairman:*

> If Homer left, do you have an immediate replacement?

*CEO:*

> My plan is to have Rachel O'Hara fill in on an interim basis and then begin a national search for a superstar.

*Chairman:*

> Okay. You've warned me now. Tentatively, I'm going along, but I want a replacement ASAP. Don't do anything without the replacement, and I don't mean Rachel!

*CEO:*

> Okay.

Over the next few weeks, the CEO began an extensive search for a replacement. Although he identified several candidates, none would be available for at least 6 months. When he brought, or rather tried to bring the subject up with the chairman, he was brushed aside with three comments: (1) Be careful, Homer's my friend; (2) a replacement before Homer leaves, and not Rachel; and (3) stop bothering me about this!

The CEO also feared that once he put the dismissal of Homer into action he might get a backlash from the chairman and Homer's friends. He further felt he would have only a single opportunity to get rid of Homer.

A month later, the chairman announced that he and his wife were going on a 10-day cruise to Alaska. A couple days after he had left, the CEO called his executive management team together and told them of his plan to ask for DuLac's resignation that day and to install Rachel as interim medical director. When the CEO asked if anyone disagreed, they all stated that, quite the contrary, they all agreed.

\* \* \*

QUESTIONS

1. Why was the CEO going ahead with the dismissal when he did?
2. How should he actually handle the dismissal? Is there anyone that he should consult before dismissing DuLac?
3. Are there any documents that he should review or have on hand before the meeting?
4. What backlash can he anticipate from his action?
5. Is this a career-making or career-breaking action?

---

## CASE 3-7   Firing at Sunrise Hill

A year after Francine Owen accepted a position as a staff nurse at the 100-bed Sunrise Hill Nursing Home, she was promoted to the position of assistant supervisor. Several weeks later she had an argument with her immediate superior, Audrey Jeffers, over the vacation schedules of aides on the night shift. At the conclusion of the argument, Jeffers said to Owen, "I feel that your arguing with me is disrespectful, and I consider it insubordination. You're fired!"

After Owen recovered from the shock of being told she was fired, she went home and reviewed her records, including a copy of her employment application, which included the following statements:

> I understand that the first 3 months of employment will be considered as a period of probation and that my employment and compensation may be terminated with or without notice at any time, at the option of Sunrise Hill Nursing Home or myself.

> I understand that no representative, employee, or resident of the Sunrise Hill Nursing Home has authority to enter into an agreement with me for employment for any specified period of time or to make any agreement with me contrary to the foregoing.

Ms. Owen then took out her Sunrise Hill employee manual and reviewed the sections presented in the accompanying Exhibit.

---

| Exhibit | Sunrise Hill Nursing Home Personnel Manual (Excerpts) |

## INTRODUCTION

This manual has been prepared so that all employees will understand their responsibilities and rights as employees of the Sunrise Hill Nursing Home.

In this manual we set forth our policies regarding employee behavior, the relationship between employees and residents, and the disciplinary procedures to be followed at Sunrise Hill.

## PROBATIONARY PERIOD

To allow all employees to adapt to professional life at Sunrise Hill and to allow supervisors to make appropriate evaluations of your performance, the first 3 months of employment are considered probationary. During this 3-month period, you are considered a temporary employee, and at the conclusion of that period, you will be evaluated by your supervisor. If the evaluation is satisfactory, you will become a regular employee, and if not, your employment will be terminated.

## DISCIPLINARY PROCEDURES

The rules and regulations of Sunrise Hill Nursing Home are designed to be fair yet to ensure the efficiency and effectiveness of the organization and the ultimate well-being of the residents. Toward that end, we have established three levels of employee offenses and appropriate disciplinary action for each offense:

### Level I: Minor Offenses

1. Inappropriate dress or poor appearance
2. Loitering, wasting time, or horseplay on job
3. Leaving work premises during working hours without permission
4. Absenteeism
5. Violation of common safety procedures, such as smoking in unauthorized areas

6. Failure to record work time activity
7. Negligence in performance of duty
8. Failure to report to work on time
9. Other minor offenses not included above

## Disciplinary Action for Level-I Minor Offenses

These offenses are normally corrected through discussion and a simple reminder. A brief notation of this offense will be placed in the employee's file. The seriousness of Minor Offenses comes with repeated occurrences of the same incident or multiple offenses of a minor nature. A fourth Minor Offense will be regarded as a second Major Offense.

## Level II: Major Offenses

1. Falsification of any personnel record
2. Neglect of duties, insubordination, disobedience
3. Absence for 3 days without notification or reasonable cause
4. Fighting on nursing home property
5. Unauthorized use or removal of nursing home property
6. Discourteous treatment of resident
7. Use of any unauthorized drugs at work
8. Reporting to work under the influence of drugs or alcohol
9. Discriminatory action or harassment of one employee against another because of age, sex, race, physical disability, or religion
10. Other Major Offenses not included above

## Disciplinary Action for Level-II Major Offenses

An employee found to have committed a Major Offense will receive counseling and formal written warnings, which will be signed by the employee and the department head. A copy of this document will also be sent to the home's executive director. A second Major Offense will result in a disciplinary suspension— the rest of the shift and up to 5 scheduled work days upon approval of the executive director.

A third Major Offense will result in the dismissal of the employee.

## Level III: Intolerable Offenses

1. Incompetency in resident care
2. Unauthorized possession of firearms, knives, or explosives
3. Stealing from other employees, residents, or others
4. Immoral or indecent conduct on home premises
5. Conviction of a felony
6. Flagrant abuse of home policies or standards
7. Repeated infractions of minor violations or as many as three (3) Major Offenses
8. Other Intolerable Offenses not included above

## Disciplinary Action for Level-III Intolerable Offenses

An Intolerable Offense is the most serious offense and results in immediate temporary suspension until the offense can be reviewed by the department head and the executive director. Dismissal without notice or severance pay is the penalty for Intolerable Offenses. However, dismissal is viewed as the last resort. The disciplinary review of an Intolerable Offense includes consideration being given to an employee's past record, to the circumstances surrounding the incident, and to the effects of the offense on the departments of the nursing home.

* * *

QUESTIONS

1. What responses to her firing should an administrator expect from Nurse Owen?
2. Did Nurse Supervisor Jeffers handle this situation in accord with the personnel manual?
3. Does the manual appear clear, unbiased, and defensible?
4. How can problems such as arose with Ms. Owen be avoided in the future?

## CASE 3-8 | Barbara Jones, RN

During the 3 years before her license to practice nursing was revoked, Barbara Jones had worked at the Clearview Nursing Center as a registered nurse. Some of the specific charges brought against Jones were that, during the 3 years she worked at Clearview, she had on 17 occasions failed to administer medication, treatment, and feedings to residents; 14 times she had made false entries into the residents' records concerning medications, feedings, and treatment; she had slept while on duty; she had removed residents' call bells so that she would not be called in the middle of the night; she had abused patients, including the forced feeding of residents and hitting the stumps of two amputees against their bed rails; and she had failed to make rounds in accordance with the home's policies and the good practice of nursing.

After 8 days of hearings, a hearing officer recommended that Ms. Jones's license to practice nursing be revoked. The State Board of Nursing agreed and revoked the license. Ms. Jones appealed the decision to the State Supreme Court, which upheld the decision.

A week after the State Supreme Court upheld the revocation, Ralph Robinson, the home's recently appointed administrator, was contacted by the administrator of a home in another state asking for a recommendation for Ms. Jones.

\* \* \*

QUESTIONS

1. What response should Mr. Robinson send to the nursing home that asked for a recommendation for Ms. Jones?
2. Why would the egregious behavior of Ms. Jones be tolerated for 3 years?
3. Is it possible that the behavior of Ms. Jones was unknown to her supervisor?

## CASE 3-9 | Hospital Housekeeping

The housekeeping department at the 330-bed Jewish Hospital of Philadelphia is managed by Mrs. Ethel Greenburg, a 55-year-old widow who is a Russian immigrant. Prior to working at this hospital, Mrs. Greenburg spent 8 years as the assistant executive housekeeper at Central General Hospital in Philadelphia, a 550-bed government hospital. Mrs. Greenburg's background includes 1 year of nurse's training in Moscow and graduation from a 2-year post–high school training program at the Soviet National School of Hotel Management in Moscow. In the Soviet Union, Mrs. Greenburg worked in various administrative capacities in different hotels. Prior to leaving her country, she was one of four assistant managers at a 300-room modern "intercontinental" hotel. Since arriving in the United States 10 years ago, Mrs. Greenburg has been active in hospital housekeeping circles, attending seminars and professional meetings.

In Mrs. Greenburg's present assignment as executive housekeeper of the Jewish Hospital of Philadelphia, she is responsible for a staff of 20 men and 25 women, as well as for the administration of a budget of close to $2 million. Approximately half of the employees in the department are Hispanic, and the other half are black, including several from Haiti. The department is organized with Mrs. Greenburg as the head and Mr. Iglesiada, a Puerto Rican, as assistant head. All staff assignments are approved by Mrs. Greenburg weekly after Mr. Iglesiada submits to her a schedule of activities for each cleaner, maid, and janitor. Both Mrs. Greenburg and Mr. Iglesiada interview each prospective employee. Mr. Iglesiada has been at the hospital for 9 years and has worked his way up from janitor to assistant department head. Prior to Mrs. Greenburg's arrival, he functioned adequately as acting department head for 3 months after the previous department head retired from the position after 37 years at the hospital. He was generally well regarded by the employees but viewed as unprofessional and a poor manager by the management.

Since Mrs. Greenburg's arrival, the quality of housekeeping in the institution has improved slightly. Relations between the department heads of housekeeping, dietetics, laundry, maintenance, and nursing have become markedly better, but the morale among the staff has deteriorated. Turnover and absenteeism have increased dramatically, and it appears that union activity has increased in this unit.

The assistant administrator has discussed the morale problem with Mrs. Greenburg, who feels that Mr. Iglesiada is undermining her efforts to professionalize the housekeeping service. Mr. Iglesiada, she contends, is making it difficult to install new mechanized cleaning equipment, develop more efficient work schedules, and run an effective in-service training program. Mrs. Greenburg's analysis is that the department had been loosely run and that treatment based on favoritism had been the norm under the previous department head.

Mr. Iglesiada argues that Mrs. Greenburg was a bad choice for the job because she is insensitive to the needs of the workers and is only interested in "her own ego trip," not in the best interests of the hospital. Mr. Iglesiada has threatened to quit unless Mrs. Greenburg is dismissed, and he says that half the department will leave if he does.

The assistant administrator thinks that about 10 or 15 employees might quit if Mr. Iglesiada leaves. Although he believes that he did an adequate job as acting department head, he does not think that Mr. Iglesiada has the managerial experience and perhaps the potential (although there is uncertainty about this) to be the department head.

\* \* \*

## QUESTIONS

1. What are the probable points of conflict between Mrs. Greenburg and Mr. Iglesiada? Between Mrs. Greenburg and the staff?

2. What options are available for resolution? What might be the costs and benefits of these possible resolutions?

## CASE 3-10 | Death at Bondville

On a cold Tuesday morning in January, probably between the hours of midnight and 3:00 AM, Max Morse, a resident of the Bondville Geriatric Center, left his room, went outside the center, and died of exposure in the frigid night air. Mr. Morse's body was found between 8:00 and 8:30 AM, after the morning shift discovered that Mr. Morse was missing.

On the Monday evening before this incident, at approximately 5:30 PM, Richard Albertson, the center's administrator, had left work after checking with the evening supervisor on the overnight (11:00 PM to 7:00 AM) staffing pattern, which called for a total of two aides and one nurse for the 200 residents in the three-story building. At approximately midnight, one of the aides put Max Morse to bed. The nurse's records indicated that the side rails on Morse's bed were put up and that he was checked every 2 hours and passed an uneventful night.

\* \* \*

QUESTIONS

1. With regard to Max Morse's safety, what was the duty of the night supervisor? Of the administrator?
2. How could this incident have been prevented?
3. Was there any staff negligence?
4. Was there any criminal behavior involved in this case?

## CASE 3-11 | Retaliatory Discharge

On February 10, 2010, the United States Court of Appeals for the Tenth Circuit affirmed the judgment of a Federal District Court in a case involving an alleged retaliatory discharge, *Rohrbough v. University of Colorado Hospital Authority* 596 F. 3rd 741 (2010). In the case, the plaintiff, a nurse and heart transplant coordinator who was a 13-year employee of the hospital, claimed she was fired because she had spoken up to her supervisors as well as various levels of management concerning a staffing crisis in her area, as well as poor-quality care being given to patients. Additionally, after meeting with staff from the hospital's risk management group, she started filing incident reports about her perception of what was happening in the transplant unit.

* * *

## QUESTIONS

1. What is a retaliatory discharge?
2. Do the bare facts here seem to indicate a retaliatory discharge?
3. Under what circumstances could this discharge be unrelated to the actions of the plaintiff?
4. What must management do to avoid any discharge from being perceived as either retaliatory or discriminatory?
5. What do you think happened in this case and why?

---

## CASE 3-12  Whistle-Blower

Barry Jenkins was a nurse who liked to play the horses and paid for his $100,000 losses by claiming extensive overtime at the Mountain Valley Hospital. When the hospital learned of his behavior of falsifying his time sheets, they fired him and reported him to the state licensing board for nurses. The board temporarily suspended his license for 90 days. Six years after his license was reinstated, he got a job at another diagnosis-related group (DRG) hospital about 30 miles away from Mountain Valley, where, in response to the question of whether his license had ever been suspended or revoked, he checked "no." Over the course of the next several years, he rose to the position of associate director of nursing. About a year after taking this position, he was again fired, this time for falsifying records concerning his training other nurses in CPR as well as his failing to inform the director of nursing about two errors that occurred in the operating room suites that were his responsibility. Eight months after this second firing, he was hired by a third hospital that later claimed it had no knowledge of Jenkins's firings.

During his tenure at the DRG hospital, he fired Darla Day, an RN who recognized that he had falsified the CPR training records and complained to Jenkins and the director of nursing. Two weeks later she was terminated.

Ms. Day is now engaged in a whistle-blower suit against the DRG hospital, claiming $70,000 in lost wages, $300,000 in future lost wages, and $150,000 for pain and suffering.

\* \* \*

QUESTIONS

1. What do you think will happen with this lawsuit and why?
2. Is the hospital's position compromised by its lack of knowledge about what happened at Mountain View?
3. Why is someone with Barry Jenkins's history able to escape his past?

---

## CASE 3-13 | Sexual Harassment

Shortly after Jane Robinson started her new job as an accountant in the business office of the Green Tree Valley Medical Center, she was approached by her supervisor, Bill Post, who asked whether she wanted to hear a joke. She agreed, and Post told a short but rather sexually explicit joke. Robinson laughed politely and then went on with her work. The following Friday, Post again approached Robinson and suggested that they have lunch together at a local restaurant. The luncheon conversation began with a discussion of the center's cash-flow problems and continued with more conversation about several financial issues related to the employee benefits program. As they were concluding lunch, Post reached across the table, touched Robinson's arm, and said, "How about continuing this conversation over dinner tonight and breakfast in the morning?" Robinson said, "No, thanks. I have other plans."

Post got quite angry and responded, "Jane, I hope you understand that I run this department, and nobody is approved for a regular position unless I approve. I trust you remember that you are a probationary employee and that if you really want this job I need to give the word. So, let's not play games. You take care of my needs and I'll take great care of you." Jane glared at Post, got up from the table, and walked out.

Over the weekend, she thought more and more about the conversation with Bill Post and decided that it was important that she meet with Ms. Gail Page, the medical center's HR director of 15 years. Ms. Page responded to Robinson's story by saying, "Look Jane, in this organization you have to learn to roll with the punches. Bill is a bit of a lecher, but he really is harmless, and he is a terrific business manager. My best advice is just to ignore him and not go out to lunch with him any more."

Robinson said nothing to Page at that time, but as she left the HR office she decided that her situation in the medical center was simply untenable. However, she needed the work and enjoyed her coworkers, so she decided to stay and vowed to steer clear of Post. At the end of the 3-month probationary period, she was terminated based on Post's evaluation that she was not competent to fulfill her duties. Ms. Robinson has consulted an attorney who has contacted the medical center with an informal complaint.

| Exhibit | Definition of Sexual Harassment From Code of Massachusetts Regulations (151 B CMR 1.8) |

The term "sexual harassment" shall mean sexual advances, requests for sexual favors, and other verbal or physical conduct of a sexual nature when (a) submission to or rejection of such advances, requests or conduct is made either explicitly or implicitly a term or condition of employment or as a basis for employment decisions; (b) such advances, requests or conduct have the purpose or effect of unreasonably interfering with an individual's work performance by creating an intimidating, hostile, humiliating or sexually offensive work environment. Discrimination on the basis of sex shall include, but not be limited to, sexual harassment.

---

**Exhibit** | **Code of Federal Regulations: §1604.11 (Sexual Harassment)**

(a) Harassment on the basis of sex is a violation of section 703 of title VII. Unwelcome sexual advances, requests for sexual favors, and other verbal or physical conduct of a sexual nature constitute sexual harassment when (1) submission to such conduct is made either explicitly or implicitly a term or condition of an individual's employment, (2) submission to or rejection of such conduct by an individual is used as the basis for employment decisions affecting such individual, or (3) such conduct has the purpose or effect of unreasonably interfering with an individual's work performance or creating an intimidating, hostile, or offensive working environment.

(b) In determining whether alleged conduct constitutes sexual harassment, the Commission [the Equal Employment Opportunity Commission] will look at the record as a whole and at the totality of the circumstances, such as the nature of the sexual advances and the context in which the alleged incidents occurred. The determination of the legality of a particular action will be made from the facts, on a case by case basis.

(c) Applying general title VII principles, an employer, employment agency, joint apprenticeship committee or labor organization (hereinafter collectively referred to as "employer") is responsible for its acts and those of its agents and supervisory employees with respect to sexual harassment regardless of whether the specific acts complained of were authorized or even forbidden by the employer and regardless of whether the employer knew or should have known of their occurrence. The Commission will examine the circumstances of the particular employment relationship and the job functions performed by the individual in determining whether an individual acts in either a supervisory or agency capacity.

(d) With respect to conduct between fellow employees, an employer is responsible for acts of sexual harassment in the workplace where the employer (or its agents or supervisory employees) knows or should have known of the conduct, unless it can show that it took immediate and appropriate corrective action.

(e) An employer may also be responsible for the acts of non-employees, with respect to sexual harassment of employees in the workplace, where the employer (or its agents or supervisory employees) knows or should have known of the conduct and fails to take immediate and appropriate corrective action. In reviewing these cases the Commission will consider the extent of the employer's control and any other legal responsibility which the employer may have with respect to the conduct of such non-employees. The principles involved here continue to apply to race, color, religion, or national origin.

\* \* \*

QUESTIONS

1. Does the action by Post constitute sexual harassment? (See Exhibits.)
2. What further actions can be expected from Robinson?
3. To what extent does Ms. Page's attitude affect sexual harassment in the organization?
4. If you were a consultant to the medical center, what would you propose the medical center do to become a sexual-harassment-free facility?

---

| CASE 3-14 | A Management Development Dilemma |

By *Alex Szafran*

Jim Tudball, an assistant vice president at Specialty Surgical Hospital has four department heads who report to him. Each is responsible for leading and directing his or her department to achieve clinical, service delivery, and financial goals. Each department head has subordinate managers and supervisors who manage the day-to-day work. In order to be successful, department heads at Specialty Surgical must demonstrate competence in a diverse skills set including HR management, management of clinical services, billing, and finance.

A major challenge presently facing Tudball is changing an information system strategy that the hospital has followed for more than decade. This best-of-breed purchasing has resulted in a wide array of information systems from a large variety of vendors, each considered the best in its specialty niche. These systems are connected to one another through complex custom interfaces. Because of new financial incentives offered by the federal government, Specialty Surgical has recently decided to embark upon a wholesale replacement of these disparate systems with a single vendor system. The new system will also better enable the hospital to implement upcoming regulatory changes related to coding and billing for hospital services. The upcoming information system changes, and billing/coding changes are enormously complex, and there are very few people within the organization who have the in-depth technical knowledge and skills to properly design the system and implement the regulatory changes.

In order to implement this new system, Jim will have to decide what to do about Mark Conway, who is one of his department heads. Conway is the only one of the department heads with the technical skills and knowledge required to help design the new system so that it is in compliance with the upcoming mandated coding and billing changes. Mark has reported to Jim for 6 years, and, in general, they have a good working relationship, particularly when it comes to issues related to information systems. For example, Mark has been instrumental in creating work processes that overcome many of the technical limitations of the old collection of information systems that are planned for replacement. During annual performance reviews, Mark has consistently scored at a very high level on the sections of his review related to teamwork and achievement of financial and he teamwork goals, and he has received high praise from other department heads because of his ability to manage complexity.

Historically, however, Mark has not done nearly as well in managing his own staff. His direct-report managers and supervisors complain that he is inconsistent and unclear in his directions, tends to micromanage his staff, and is unable to appreciate the impact these traits have on morale within his department. These people feel unsupported by Mark and complain that he becomes punitive when they ask for clarity of direction and help in solving problems. In a recent situation, one of Mark's managers turned to another department head for help in solving an acute staffing problem when Mark was away on vacation. When Mark returned, he scolded the manager for embarrassing him by discussing internal departmental problems outside of the department. The manager responded by asking for guidance on how she could have better handled the situation and received only negative blaming responses from Mark.

Jim has long been aware of Mark's deficiencies in managing staff. Jim has worked with Mark for the last 3 years on improving Mark's skills in managing and motivating people. Jim has even arranged for a training and organizational development mentor to work closely with Mark with the hope that Mark could achieve in HR management what he has been able to achieve in financial, information systems, and billing management. After much effort to improve Mark's skills, little progress has been made. In fact, the situation has worsened in that Mark no longer recognizes his own role in these failures. All recent attempts at discussion result in Mark becoming defensive of his own actions. Mark also finds ways to divert attention from his own failures by redirecting attention to failures, some perceived, some real, of his own staff and other department heads. Some other department heads have also made comments about Mark's challenges.

Jim is clearly faced with a dilemma: Mark's exceptional skills are invaluable and will be critical to the success of the upcoming implementation of the new information systems and the conversion to the new billing and coding schema. These projects have a multiple year timetable. It is clear, though, that further efforts to improve Mark's general management skills are unlikely to result in any meaningful improvement. At this moment, Jim sees only two alternatives: either tolerate Mark's poor performance in order to maintain access to Mark's exceptional technical skill, or recommend to Mark that he seek other employment, even though this would have a significant unfavorable impact on the critical projects.

\* \* \*

QUESTIONS

1. What, if any, alternative solutions does Jim have?
2. What could Jim have done earlier that might have eliminated this dilemma?
3. If Jim decides that losing Mark at this critical point is intolerable, what should Jim's next steps be in working with Mark?
4. What mistakes has Jim made in the way he has managed Mark?
5. If you were performing Jim's annual performance review, how would you rate his efforts and skill in dealing with Mark?

---

## CASE 3-15 | Strike

> VALLEY HEALTH AND MEDICAL SYSTEM MEMO
>
> From:  CEO
> To:      All Clinical and Nonclinical Department Heads
> Subj:   Strike Preparation

As most of you know, the contract with our nurses' union expires in 90 days. Unfortunately, so far we have been unable to negotiate an acceptable contract with the nurses' union. We will, in the next 90 days, continue with our good-faith bargaining efforts in hopes of satisfactorily resolving our differences.

However, I wish to be prepared in the event that a strike takes place. Toward that end, I wish to meet with all of you on Friday at noon to discuss strike preparations.

See you Friday!

\* \* \*

ASSIGNMENT

Prepare the agenda for the Friday meeting. What are the most critical items on the agenda and why?

---

## CASE 3-16 | New NLRB Ruling

The following notice was received from the National Labor Relations Board (NLRB) at the Clearwater Heights Nursing Home, a facility without a union and one that has won two past union-organizing elections.

---

## Exhibit | Fact Sheet From NLRB

### Final Rule for Notification of Employee Rights

Background

The National Labor Relations Board (NLRB) has issued a Final Rule [1] requiring most private-sector employers to notify employees of their rights under the National Labor Relations Act by posting a notice. The rule is scheduled to be posted in the Federal Register on August 30, 2011, and will take effect 75 days later.

Employers should begin posting the notice on November 14, 2011. Copies of the notice will be available on the NLRB website and from NLRB regional offices by November 1.

Similar postings of workplace rights are required under other federal workplace laws. The 11-by-17-inch notice is similar in content and design to a notice of NLRA rights that must be posted by federal contractors under a Department of Labor rule.

The notice of rights will be provided at no charge by NLRB regional offices [2] or can be downloaded from the Board's website and printed in color or black and white. Translated versions will be available and must be posted at workplaces where at least 20% of employees are not proficient in English. Employers must also post the notice on an intranet or an Internet site if personnel rules and policies are customarily posted there.

Questions and Answers

**Does my company have to post the notice?**
The posting requirement applies to all private-sector employers (including labor unions) subject to the National Labor Relations Act, which excludes agricultural, railroad, and airline employers. In response to comments received after the proposed rule was announced, the Board has agreed to exempt the U.S. Postal Service for the time being because of that organization's unique rules under the act.

**When will the notice posting be required?**
The final rule takes effect 75 days after it is posted in the Federal Register, or on November 14, 2011.

**There is no union in my workplace; will I still have to post the notice?**
Yes. Because NLRA rights apply to union and non-union workplaces, all employers subject to the Board's jurisdiction (aside from the USPS) will be required to post the notice.

**I am a federal contractor. Will I have to post the notice?**
The Board's notice posting rule will apply to federal contractors, who already are required by the Department of Labor to post a similar notice of employee rights [3]. A contractor will be regarded as complying with the Board's notice posting rule if it posts the Department of Labor's notice.

**I operate a small business. Will I have to post the Board's notice?**
The rule applies to all employers subject to the Board's jurisdiction, other than the U.S. Postal Service. The Board has chosen not to assert its jurisdiction over very small employers whose annual volume of business is not large enough to have more than a slight effect on interstate commerce. The jurisdictional standards are summarized in the rule.

**How will I get the notice?**
The Board will provide copies of the notice on request at no cost to the employer beginning on or before November 1, 2011. These can be obtained by contacting the NLRB at its headquarters or its regional, sub-regional, or resident offices. Employers can also download the notice from the Board's website and print it out in color or black and white on one 11-by-17-inch paper or two 8-by-11-inch papers taped

together. Finally, employers can satisfy the rule by purchasing and posting a set of workplace posters from a commercial supplier.

## What if I communicate with employees electronically?

In addition to the physical posting, the rule requires every covered employer to post the notice on an Internet or intranet site if personnel rules and policies are customarily posted there. Employers are not required to distribute the posting by email, Twitter, or other electronic means.

## Many of my employees speak a language other than English. Will I still have to post the notice?

Yes. The notice must be posted in English and in another language if at least 20% of employees are not proficient in English and speak the other language. The Board will provide translations of the notice, and of the required link to the Board's website, in the appropriate languages.

## Will I have to maintain records or submit reports under the Board's rule?

No, the rule has no record-keeping or reporting requirements.

## How will the Board enforce the rule?

Failure to post the notice may be treated as an unfair labor practice under the National Labor Relations Act. The Board investigates allegations of unfair labor practices made by employees, unions, employers, or other persons, but does not initiate enforcement action on its own.

## What will be the consequences for failing to post the notice?

The Board expects that, in most cases, employers who fail to post the notice are unaware of the rule and will comply when requested by a Board agent. In such cases, the unfair labor practice case will typically be closed without further action. The Board also may extend the 6-month statute of limitations for filing a charge involving other unfair labor practice allegations against the employer. If an employer knowingly and willfully fails to post the notice, the failure may be considered evidence of unlawful motive in an unfair labor practice case involving other alleged violations of the NLRA.

## Can an employer be fined for failing to post the notice?

No, the Board does not have the authority to levy fines.

Was there a public comment period? What was the response?
The Board received more than 7,000 public comments after
posting a notice of the proposed rule in the Federal Register. A
detailed description of the comments and the Board's response
to them, including responsive modifications to the rule, may
be found in the Preamble to the Final Rule.

[1] Source URL: https://www.nlrb.gov/news-media/fact-sheets/final-rule-notification-
employee-rights
Links:
[2] https://www.nlrb.gov/who-we-are/regional-offices
[3] http://www.dol.gov/olms/regs/compliance/EO13496.htm
Published on NLRB: https://www.nlrb.gov

\* \* \*

QUESTIONS

1. What must the administration do after November 2011?
2. Is there anything the nursing home can now do to limit its
   vulnerability to a union organizing drive? The successful
   outcome of such a drive?

---

## CASE 3-17 | Salary Advance

Although the Delta Green Hospital was a small facility with
only 98 beds and a staff of slightly more than 400 employees,
Jake Smith, the CEO since January 1 (3 months), still did not
know all the employees of the facility or their back stories.
One staff member he did know, though, was Edie White, the
chief telephone operator and receptionist. Every day as Smith
walked in through the front entrance, Ms. White, whose desk
faced the entrance, would offer him a cheery greeting and
exchange a few words about the weather.

On the first Monday in March, Smith trudged in through
the snow that had accumulated from a weekend storm and
found Ms. White sitting at her desk with tears in her eyes.
Their conversation went as follows:

*Smith:*

Edie, what's wrong?

*White:*

Oh, Mr. Smith, good morning. Sorry.

*Smith:*

Are you okay?

*White:*

I've had better days and certainly better weekends. Yesterday I had a car accident.

*Smith:*

Oh, my! Are you okay? Anyone hurt?

*White:*

No, I'm okay but my car needs work and I have to come up with the $1,000 deductible, and I just used my savings to pay for a root canal.

*Smith:*

So sorry to hear this!

*White:*

I wonder if I could ask a favor. Do you think it possible that I get an advance on my pay so I can pay my bills?

*Smith:*

I don't know. Let me look into this.

Smith went to his office and called Kelly Jimson, the director of the HR department, and asked both about the hospital's policy for pay advances as well as White's record. First he learned that White was a stellar employee with 17 years of excellent service to the hospital. He also learned that on three other occasions she had requested a pay advance, and in all three instances the request had been denied. Additionally, he learned that the hospital had a very strict policy about payroll advances. This policy set up a series of hurdles including a written request with approval by the supervisor, the HR director, and the CEO. Smith then went to Jimson's office to have a private discussion with her about this policy. After hashing it out, they decided that the policy made sense. Finally, in discussing the White situation, Jimson offered her observation that because White had requested advances before that had been denied she was simply trying to circumvent the system by speaking directly to Smith.

Smith returned to his office to mull over what he should do.

\* \* \*

QUESTIONS

1. What should Smith do? Why?
2. What are the implications of any decision Smith makes?
3. Should this advance pay policy be revised?

---

| CASE 3-18 | **The Prima Donna** |

By *James S. Davis, MD*

Dr. Kyle Lucas Mason was one of the more prominent surgeons on staff at the hospital. His peers all agreed that he was accomplished and possessed superior technical and clinical skill. Dr. Mason had come on staff a decade ago and had built up a thriving practice of some local renown. He possessed a large referral base from the surrounding community due to his reputation and skill. Within the last few years, he had mastered a range of minimally invasive techniques that he offered patients. These techniques were advertised on the radio and further strengthened his practice. Within the Surgery Department, it was widely acknowledged that Dr. Mason generated significant revenue—both for himself and for the hospital. Additionally, it was equally clear that his public persona generated positive marketing for the hospital.

Despite his obvious material and professional successes, Dr. Mason occasionally acted in a manner that was cause for concern. Although amicable with patients and coworkers alike, he was known to have a temper that flared during stressful moments in the operating room. Usually, he worked a designated operating room staff, and this regular crew downplayed his actions. However, substitute nurses and technicians often (privately) requested that they be assigned to other surgeons after working in his room. The doctors who entered Dr. Mason's operating room to discuss cases were treated to his verbal salvos and had even seen him throw instruments on the floor. Both male and female residents routinely grumbled about his verbal abuse. Once, a new nurse left his room in tears but declined to discuss the

matter or file an incident report. Nothing came of these incidents and observations despite his behavior being an open
secret in the institution. Dr. Mason's friends were unwilling
to jeopardize their friendship by speaking to him in private.
Residents assumed that their experiences were simply part
of old-school training and that recourse did not exist for
addressing behavioral issues. Others pointed to Dr. Mason's
status within the hospital, which was such that they would
not be protected when lodging complaints.

* * *

QUESTIONS

1. What hospital policies should exist to censor/discipline
   those who perpetrate verbal abuse?
2. Is the Mason situation a hopeless case?
3. Does the hospital put itself at risk by failing to act?
4. Is the hospital accreditation at risk because of Mason's
   behavior? Why or why not?
5. Who would be the best people to have a conversation with
   Mason? What should be the setting, tone, and focus of the
   meeting?

---

## CASE 3-19 | The Harassed MD

The Vickery Medical Center is a complex health system that
includes one 400-bed tertiary care hospital, two 100-bed rural
hospitals, one large multispecialty group practice, and seven
hospital-owned primary care practices. All of these primary
care practices had at one time been solo or small group practices that were purchased by the hospital over the past decade.

One condition of each practice purchase was that the original owner or partners would remain with the practice and
that the practice would continue to be run by the partners or
solo practitioner for a period of 7 years. The agreement stated
that at the expiration of the 7 year period the hospital would
have the authority to manage the practice in what manner it
deemed appropriate. Essentially then, the practices that were

purchased were allowed to run in a manner not very dissimilar to how they had been run prior to their being acquired by the hospital. The single major change was that all the staff, including medical and professional, became employees of the hospital and were subject to the same rules and regulations governing other employees of the Vickery system.

This case stems from a meeting that Mr. Hugo Santiago, the HR director, had with Viola Sartell, an MD and a hospital employee for 13 months as a result of the practice she worked in being acquired by Vickery. Subsequent to the meeting, Mr. Santiago prepared the following document.

---

This document is a record of the meeting I held today with Dr. Viola Sartell, a physician employee of the Lake Westerly Primary Care Center (LW). Dr. Sartell has been an employee of LW for the past 3 years. For the last 13 months, LW has been owned by Vickery and since that acquisition Sartell has been a full-time employee of the Vickery system.

Dr. Sartell claims that since she has worked at LW she has been sexually harassed on a regular basis by Dr. Ted Grodno, who founded the center 17 years ago and as per the contract with Vickery, Dr. Grodno now functions as its chief executive officer.

Dr. Sartell told me about the following incidents:

1. Shortly after Dr. Sartell began working at the clinic, Dr. Grodno appeared in her office, saying he wished to show her an x-ray of his hip that showed a deformity. The x-ray also showed a shadowy image of his penis that he called Mr. Happy. Dr. Sartell felt quite uncomfortable about this interchange. Over the next few weeks, Dr. Grodno would see her and again say something about Mr. Happy. Dr. Grodno also left the x-ray hanging on the wall and showed it to most of the staff as well as drug representatives.
2. A second incident occurred at a staff meeting where Dr. Grodno commented that he was happy that his wife had a c-section so that her "vagina was still tight." Several times in the months after that, Dr. Grodno brought up with Dr. Sartell the tightness of his wife's vagina.
3. On another occasion, he asked to speak with Dr. Sartell in his office, and he told her a male colleague had remarked to him what a nice set of breasts she had. Dr. Sartell was totally

embarrassed and stated that she always dressed in a conservative, professional manner.

4. After a scuba diving trip to Costa Rica, Dr. Grodno insisted on showing Dr. Sartell his photos of himself in tight-fitting and quite revealing Speedos and his wife topless. Dr. Sartell turned away and left.

Dr. Sartell also opined that Dr. Grodno's sexual remarks, crude sexual jokes, and sexual innuendos were not directed just at Dr. Sartell but also at the other women in the primary care practice and even visiting female drug representatives. Overall, Dr. Sartell felt she was consistently either harassed or on the verge of being harassed.

* * *

## QUESTIONS

1. What should Mr. Santiago do with this information?
2. Does this sound like Dr. Grodno's behavior is severe and pervasive enough to create a hostile work environment?
3. Could this be the basis of an Equal Employment Opportunity Commission (EEOC) claim under Title VII of the Civil Rights Act of 1964?

**CHAPTER 4**

# ORGANIZATIONAL MANAGEMENT

 **INTRODUCTION**

For most healthcare managers, no two days are the same, and generally every day brings a least one crisis! This section presents a broad range of cases that challenge the professional life of every administrator. The cases range from those involving the nexus between clinical and managerial issues and others that are purely managerial in nature.

In my judgment, management might best be viewed as both an art and a science. On the one hand, it deals with sharply defined areas such as productivity and efficiency, areas best exemplified by the operations research/management science approach to problem solving. On the other hand, it also deals in more diffuse areas such as leadership and motivation.

This sets up a challenge for the manager. How does he or she construct or reconstruct organizations so that they maximize efficiency and effectiveness to their various external constituencies and simultaneously minimize stress, disaffection, and unhappiness to their internal constituencies? It should be recognized that this problem or challenge is a value-laden statement, as are most definitions of management and concepts of the manager's role. The emphasis in this statement is on satisfying external constituencies, performing efficiently in economic and financial terms, being effective, and, finally, respecting the human dignity of workers. If, for example, workers are considered drones, peasants, or simply inputs for a resource system, this challenge might be restated to eliminate concern with the disaffected workers. Indeed, the manager's concept of the meaning of work can dramatically shift his or her perspective.

The goal of most young managers is to someday become the CEO, and the cases in this chapter demonstrate a broad range of issues that senior management must learn to handle. Certainly the desire to be a CEO is a worthy and honorable goal if the reasoning behind it is that by being the organizational leader you can run, develop, and implement programs and services that will be positive for both the organization and its constituencies. A bad reason for wanting the job is greed and self-aggrandizement! Yes, the job of CEO does often come with a large salary and perks. But, as a good friend of mine who was CEO of a billion-dollar company told me, "When someone pays you a great deal of money, they also want a great deal of your soul." So, in a nutshell that is the trade—you get the money, the power, and the office, but you also get the headaches and possibly the ulcer. Indeed, one of the best students I ever had decided early in his career that he did not wish to ever be a CEO and would be content to always play a minor role in the enterprise. Today, 20 years later, he has had a very good career as a manager of a clinical support department where he is responsible for a $20 million budget and more than 200 employees. His salary is a third of that of the CEO, yet he is also quite comfortable, enjoys his job, his leisure time, and his family, and views himself as a valuable contributing member of a major medical center.

As you read and work through the cases in this chapter, indeed in this entire text, you might want to consider the following advice I offer about taking senior management jobs in the healthcare field:

- *Do your own organizational due diligence.* Oftentimes, an executive search firm manages the senior positions, and their focus is to find the right person for the job. They will frequently be quite helpful in providing information about the organization and its key players. But it is imperative that a job aspirant uses his or her own network to learn about the organization. It is also imperative to believe organizational history. If an organization has a history of turning over CEOs, do not assume that your tenure will be any different. If an organization has a history of being corrupt, do not assume that your being a person of integrity will change everything. Unfortunately, decay is often quite deep and covered over by a thin veneer. In practical terms, this means examine the organization's books (and, if necessary, hire your own experts). Talk to people. Do not become so enamored of the CEO job that you forget to ask the right questions.

- *Forget the oral tradition.* Too often, a potential CEO will negotiate a job based on meetings and discussions with headhunters or boards. It is imperative to reduce important points to writing. These points are usually not found in employment contracts but can find their ways into a memorandum of understanding. This comes directly from my own experience when I took the CEO job discussed previously. Before agreeing to take the job, I had several meetings with key board members about various subjects, one of which was the size, structure, and functioning of the board. They all solemnly nodded their heads in agreement when I told them that the 200-person board was too large and the 54-person executive board was also cumbersome and that there was a need for more focused and decision-oriented board meetings. But my mistake was not committing that discussion to writing with some agreement to change, because when the time came to implement changes, I simply had no support or leverage.

- *Get a contract and/or generous severance package.* Never take a CEO job without a contract with at least several years' tenure or at the minimum a generous severance package. CEO jobs are high profile and high risk, and it is imperative that the CEO be protected, both personally and professionally. A contract and/or severance package ensures that the organization will not treat the CEO as an employee at will. In essence, this means that the CEO will have the time to develop and implement his or her agenda for the future.

- *If you have the responsibility, make sure you have the explicit authority.* A friend of mine who was CEO of an organization in New England assumed that he ran the show. When his first winter came around, he sought bids for snowplowing. He was about to award a contract when he received a call from an irate board member, demanding to know why Jim Brown was not being given the contract as he had been for the last 10 years. The CEO explained that Brown's bid was $3500 more than the lowest bidder and, in checking around, he had found that the lowest bidder had an excellent reputation and Brown's work in the past decade had become barely satisfactory. The board member dismissed the complaints and insisted that Brown be rehired. A few minutes later, the board president called the CEO and tried to smooth things over between the CEO and the board member by saying that the board member was a bit of a hothead but really cared about the organization. In the end, though, he urged that Brown be hired just to calm down the board member, who was said to be a very generous donor. The CEO gave in and hired Brown, who did a lousy job. The staff lost some respect for the CEO, who they thought was coming in to change things around, and the board member's donation never came close to compensating the organization for the extra money paid out for plowing. Also, the CEO never found out why a snowplowing contract was so important to these board members.

Obviously, there are always areas where a CEO should negotiate and compromise with the board. But it is imperative that if the CEO is expected to run the organization, he or she should have the authority to do the job. In my own experience, the good news was I was immediately given authority to spend up to $25,000 without board approval. The bad news, though, was that the board had many more sacred cows than I had anticipated, and when I tried to reshape the organization through terminations, reassignments, or reorganizations, I immediately learned why I had been warned away from this organization: the micromanagement of its board. My favorite example was that of Pete the baker. Pete had worked in the kitchen of one of the constituent corporations for more than three decades and was earning almost as much as the department head. Pete was a nice man, well past retirement age, and if he collected his pension he would make about the same as if he were working. By way of work, Pete would only bake Danish pastries from frozen packages. Because of various deficits, Pete's name came up on the proposals for cutbacks. I saw no harm in Pete being terminated since his departure would mean a considerable savings to the department, he personally would not suffer economically, and others could easily accomplish the Danish baking. When word got out that Pete might be involuntarily retired, the board president, who was fond of Pete for a variety of reasons, told me that he would rather fire me than Pete. So, there it was, a sacred baker and a CEO without the authority to reduce expenses but with the responsibility of bringing the organization into fiscal balance. It can't be done!

An unfortunate risk of being in management is that of being unemployed. As noted earlier, a manager can try to mitigate the damage of unemployment through a contract or severance package, but rarely will anyone other than the most senior managers be able to negotiate such organizational commitments. In the last several years, I have met more and more senior executives who have become unemployed and stayed that way for extended periods of time. Based on these experiences, I think those who have the most success in finding their next jobs have followed the following strategies.

First, several people I know smelled the unemployment coming and immediately got busy, not trying to politic to keep their job but rather finding a new job. They recognized the old maxim that it is easiest to find a job when you have a job, not when you are unemployed. These people did not get into the frame of thinking that 3 months off with a severance package makes for a great paid vacation. Rather, they immediately started networking with professional colleagues and exploring job options that often did not pay as well as the job they were leaving. In one case, a senior finance person found a job that paid 15% less than the job he was losing, with considerably fewer fringe benefits. He took it and within 2 years had passed his previous salary and was in line for a major promotion. In contrast, a well-paid experienced senior hospital executive held out for a job and salary at his current level and 3 years later was still unemployed, was forced to sell his house, and was considering personal bankruptcy.

Another strategy some have chosen is to consider related and alternative careers, such as sales in the health industry. For example, one former CEO now works as a sales representative for a nursing temp agency. According to his reports, it is a great job with good earning potential and without the pressures of being a CEO.

Going into business for oneself is a different, perhaps risky, and sometimes quite rewarding option. One friend pursued that option by opening a healthcare case management business for seniors. Despite good marketing and reasonable capitalization, however, the operation was simply not able to become financially viable. Another friend bought an executive search franchise, focused his efforts on the health field, and retired at the age of 60 as a wealthy man. A third friend opened a consulting business, promoted his operation on the Internet, and is well on his way to financial independence and professional success. These vignettes suggest that unemployment or the threat of unemployment will definitely be a challenge that managers might face in their personal lives, but it is a challenge that, if met, may well be the opportunity of a lifetime.

Each case in this chapter in some way illustrates both the demands on management as well as the tightrope that management is oftentimes forced to walk. Managerial life would likely be easier if most situations were either black or white. As these cases show, most situations fall into the murky gray zone (also known as the managerial twilight zone). Finally, some of these cases exemplify the frustrations inherent in simply trying to do the right thing.

## CASE 4-1 | Hospital-Acquired Infection

On a snowy winter afternoon, State Senator Millicent White was crossing the street in front of the State Capitol when she was hit by a speeding taxicab. Bystanders and Capitol police rushed to her side to offer aid and support. Within 5 minutes of the accident, EMS personnel arrived and followed their standard protocol for trauma victims, which included a check for lacerations, abrasions, fluid (including blood) loss, pain, and shock. Senator White was breathing easily but having pain in her neck and back. Following a neurologic assessment that found her awake and responsive, they immobilized her with a rigid cervical collar and placed her on a long backboard. Next they started a normal saline IV and transported her to the university hospital emergency room, where, upon further examination, it was determined that she had sustained a fractured hip, a broken leg, and a fractured wrist. Surgery followed. Prior to the surgery, she was catheterized and, within a day of the surgery, she developed a urinary tract infection that required her to extend her hospital stay by several days.

During her recovery and rehabilitation, it came to her attention that her infection was likely the result of a hospital-acquired infection. In fact, although she was not medically trained, she recalled that it appeared to her that the nurses were handling the catheter in a somewhat sloppy way, such as allowing it to sit on an unsterile tray. Senator White has decided to hold public hearings on hospital-acquired infections, which she claims generate unnecessary deaths, hospital days, and costs to the health system of the state.

* * *

## ASSIGNMENT

Assume you have been asked to make a presentation at Senator White's public hearing on the subject of hospital-acquired infections. (By way of background, this case has an appendix from the Pennsylvania Health Care Cost Containment Council. Assume that Pennsylvania and the state in this case study are similar.)

---

## CASE 4-2 | The Pressure Ulcer

Walter Cox, the CEO of the Southview Foundation (the largest component of which was the Southview Home for the Aged), was working on a speech he was to deliver that evening at the annual dinner/dance of the board of governors when Toni, his secretary, knocked on his door and asked to speak to him. Toni told him that Ms. Carla Furillo was in his waiting area, was quite upset about the care that her father was receiving at the Home, and wanted to discuss it with Cox. Toni also told Cox that Ms. Furillo had been active on the home's women's committee for more than 10 years and had been a regular, though not significant, donor to the home's foundation. Cox agreed to see her, left his desk, and went into his waiting room to greet Ms. Furillo.

Ms. Furillo stepped into the office and relayed the following story: Her father was 91 years old and had been a resident of the home's skilled nursing facility for 3.5 years. While he had some cognitive impairment, he still was a relatively active and conversant person. Because of a stroke 2 years earlier, he did have some limitations in his ability to get in and out of bed, take his medications on schedule, and bathe and toilet himself. He was, however, quite capable of feeding himself and, according to his daughter, he usually had a good appetite.

Ms. Furillo then told Mr. Cox the reason for her visit: "My Dad is presently across the road at River Run Medical Center where he is recovering from having his right leg amputated below the knee. The reason for the surgery was a pressure ulcer that he contracted here at the home and that was never treated properly. He is coming back to his room here tomorrow or the next day and I want your assurance that he will be properly cared for."

"Mr. Cox" she continued, "I don't know what's happening here, but in the last few months things have been going downhill and they need to change."

Cox looked at Ms. Furillo and saw a woman in great distress but was a bit uncertain as to her analysis of her situation. He also feared a lawsuit. He then said: "Ms. Furillo, I am truly sorry about this situation. I promise you that I will look into this immediately and take whatever action is necessary to ensure that your father and all the other residents of our nursing home get the care they need. Please call me anytime."

Shortly after Ms. Furillo left, Mr. Cox asked Toni to come in with a notepad; he needed to convene a meeting and review some materials.

* * *

QUESTIONS

1. How well did Cox handle the meeting?
2. When patients get pressure ulcers, is that a likely cause for litigation?
3. What do you think Ms. Furillo really wanted?
4. Who does Cox want to meet with and why?
5. What materials does Cox want to review?

## CASE 4-3 | FDA Warning

> COMMUNITY HOSPITAL MEMO
>
> From: CEO
> To: Chief, Medical Staff
> Subj: FDA warning

Jack:

I just read a very interesting article in the *New England Journal of Medicine* about the diabetes drug rosiglitazone and, as you probably know, how this drug is associated with a 43% increase in myocardial infarction. Additionally, the article went on to say that expert panels in the United States and Europe have recommended against the use of this drug in managing hyperglycemia; a few years ago the FDA decided to restrict access to this drug.

What is of interest to me is that the response to the use of this drug and its warnings has been less than adequate and varies significantly by geographic area. This leads me to a couple questions:

1. How do we diffuse important information to our medical staff?
2. How can we ensure that they are following best practices?

I think this drug makes for a good case study. That is, we can see where we are on the spectrum of being at the cutting edge. Let's meet to discuss this further. Thanks!

\* \* \*

QUESTIONS

1. Should the CEO have attached the article he had read?
2. What is the CEO's real agenda?
3. If a task force were to be established to look into this, who should be on it?
4. Is conflict with the medical staff a likely outcome of this memo? If so, how can it be mitigated or avoided?
5. Is the CEO behaving properly in the interests of the hospital? The community?

## CASE 4-4 | Medication Error

The following incident has recently occurred at Community General Hospital:

A 91-year-old man was admitted to the hospital following an acute coronary. The admitting physician prescribed a daily dose of warfarin, a drug that is often used subsequent to a heart attack to prevent blood clotting. Dr. Casey wrote the prescription for a 10-mg tablet daily rather than the more typical dose for an elderly person of a 1.0-mg tablet. About 12 hours after admission, the staff noticed that the patient was complaining of back pains, his fingers were turning purple, and he said he felt numb on his left side. Casey examined him and then looked back over the lab results and noticed that he had prescribed a dose of warfarin that was 10 times what he had meant to supply. He decided to sit with the patient for the next 12 hours to be certain that there would be no other adverse reactions. Fortunately, during the next day, the patient improved and he did not have other problems. Dr. Casey reported this incident to the patient safety coordinator and clearly admitted his error.

\* \* \*

QUESTIONS

1. What disciplinary action appears appropriate for Dr. Casey? Why?
2. Are others on the staff equally responsible, such as nursing?
3. What about the responsibility of the pharmacy?
4. How can such errors be avoided in the future?
5. Is this a classic example of the "trailing zero" issue?

## CASE 4-5 | Egg Crate Mattress

*Note: An egg crate mattress is actually a soft foam pad with bumps on it that make it look like an egg crate. Typically it is put on top of a mattress for either comfort or pressure ulcer prevention strategy. In nursing homes, physicians prescribe these egg crate mattresses when someone is at risk of pressure sores (also known as pressure ulcers). However, some nursing home residents have no clinical need for the egg crate mattresses but like the feel of them and can purchase the pads themselves or, as in this case, ask the nursing home to provide them.*

The Good Heart Nursing Center had a policy of providing egg crate mattresses to any resident who requested one. Typically, egg crates are covered with waterproof pads and then sheets. The Good Heart policy is to change these mattresses on an as-needed basis.

During the course of a Medicaid survey of the Five North nursing unit, the surveyor noticed that a used egg crate mattress was rolled up in the corner of a patient's room and that the patient's bed was completely made up. She walked over to the bed and found it did not have an egg crate pad on it. She then went to the nurse supervisor and asked why there was not a pad on the bed, but there was one rolled up in the corner. The supervisor replied, "I guess the aide forgot to get the new pad and put it on the bed." The surveyor said, "Okay, that's a survey deficiency." The supervisor then said, "Wait a moment. That mattress pad is given to the patient as a courtesy and isn't ordered by the physician. We can't be given a deficiency on that." The surveyor did not respond but again told the administrator that they would be given a deficiency for the missing egg crate mattress.

* * *

## QUESTIONS

1. What should the nurse supervisor do about the aide?
2. What should the nursing director do about the supervisor?
3. What should the administrator do about the survey deficiency?
4. Should the policy regarding the egg crate mattress and other hospitality policies be changed?

## CASE 4-6 | The Road to the Top

In the fall of 20__, Eliot Van Buren was engaged as an independent consultant by the president of the board of the Gatesville Health system. Van Buren, a retired U.S. Public Health Service officer who had risen to the position of deputy surgeon general of the United States, was one of three partners in a boutique healthcare consulting firm.

The project at Gatesville involved a 7-day-per-month commitment to assist the board in straightening out a host of personnel, financial, and regulatory issues. For Van Buren, the project turned out to be both interesting and financially rewarding. Within 3 months, he had become socially friendly with several members of the board, often dining with them on his visits to Gatesville.

One problem that Van Buren spotted was that of a lack of organizational leadership. Two years earlier, the board had fired Andy Jackson, who had served as CEO for 9 years. Jackson was a well-known administrator who was caught up in a series of financial irregularities.

Rather than replace Jackson, the board opted to allow the organization to be managed by a committee, at the president's suggestion. Ten people were appointed to the committee: the deputy CEO, the chief financial officer, the human resources director, the food services director, the director of the physical plant, the administrator of the extended care facility, the chief of the medical staff, the hospital director of nursing, the administrator of ambulatory care, and the director of development. Technically, the group was chaired by the board president (who rarely attended); in practice it was Calvin Pyle, the deputy CEO, who ran the meetings.

By the time Van Buren arrived, Pyle had been with the system for 15 years and had been promoted to his job several years earlier by Jackson. Many on the staff, including Pyle himself, had assumed that he would be promoted to the CEO position when Jackson was fired. Pyle was clearly disappointed, but in the following 2 years did everything he could to win the board president's confidence. Within weeks of arriving at Gatesville, it became evident to Van Buren that Pyle's sycophantic behavior toward the board president was part of his lobbying the president for the top job. Van Buren quickly became convinced that the management team approach was a mistake. He proposed to the board that his consulting assignment should be expanded to include an executive search. The board agreed, and for the next 5 months Van Buren searched for appropriate candidates, several of whom were brought in for interviews. In each instance, the board's executive committee rejected the candidate.

Eight months after the consulting project began, and subsequent to what he thought were visits from four candidates, Van Buren confronted the board about their difficulty in selecting a CEO. Out of frustration, he even suggested that Pyle be given the job. The board president responded by saying, "He would be a decent number two, maybe the best, but, as long as I'm board president, he will never be the CEO." Van Buren was surprised by the president's statement and even more shocked by the president's next statement: "Eliot, I think we can't select anyone because we all agree that we simply want you to be our CEO. Name your deal! You can do anything you want—hire or fire anyone!" Within a month, Van Buren agreed to the proposal, resigned from the consulting firm, and began planning his move to Gatesville.

Based on his experiences with the system, Van Buren expected problems with Pyle. First, he recognized that Pyle had wanted the CEO job and did not get it. Second, he had heard through the grapevine that Pyle had been denigrating his experience and background and that Pyle thought that Van Buren would be a disaster. Shortly after accepting the job, Van Buren telephoned the board president and suggested that Pyle be terminated. The president rejected this proposal and told Van Buren that he wanted Pyle as number two in the organization and that he had just given Pyle a significant pay increase.

Van Buren is now having second thoughts about having taken the job.

* * *

## QUESTIONS

1. Assume Niccolo Machiavelli is Eliot Van Buren's personal consultant. What advice would Machiavelli give Van Buren?
2. Assuming Van Buren stands by his decision to take the job, what can he expect from Pyle?
3. What should Van Buren do?

## CASE 4-7  The Shakedown

Alicia Meryl Brown, the CEO of the Jonestown Medical Center, is a preceptor for State University's graduate program in healthcare management. Her role as a preceptor primarily involves a commitment to annually accept a graduate student as an administrative resident and to ensure that the student has access to every level of the organization. Brown is considered one of the top preceptors because she is willing to let the student sit in on confidential meetings and then discuss the essence of those meetings. These discussions typically run into the early evening and cover a range of subjects from personalities to tactics and long-range strategies.

Three weeks after Joni Michelson began her residency, Brown suggested she sit in at her 1:00 PM meeting that was with three representatives of a major drug company. Also at the meeting was the chief of the medical staff, the head of the hospital pharmacy, the medical center's director of clinical research, and Hyman Walker, the hospital's chief operating officer. As reported by Michelson, the first 20 minutes of the meeting were a presentation by the drug representatives about a developmental drug that their company thought would be a breakthrough product for hospital inpatients. Then they stated that their reason for visiting Brown was to solicit her approval to use the drug in the hospital for the Phase II clinical trials that involve evaluation of the drug. Following their short presentation, several questions were asked and answered about the protocol for the research aspects of the program.

In recounting the meeting, Michelson told the director of her graduate program that she was asked to leave the meeting and wait in the adjoining receptionist's space until the next meeting that was scheduled to begin 15 minutes later. As she waited, Ms. Michelson reviewed her notes and jotted down some questions she wished to ask Ms. Brown. A few minutes before the meeting, the head of nursing and director of plant operations appeared in the reception area for the next meeting with Brown. At almost precisely 2:00 PM, the door to Brown's office opened and the three drug representatives exited. Michelson looked up at them and was startled by what she saw. All three, who had looked jovial and healthy 20 minutes earlier, appeared to be drained of color and were sweating profusely. They left the offices, never looking up. Curious about what had happened in the office, she asked Ms. Brown, "Are those men feeling okay?" The reply was, "They are just fine."

The next day Michelson had lunch with the chief operating officer, a graduate of State University's healthcare management program, and he asked her how the residency was going. She replied with a series of positive comments and ended by saying, "Usually Ms. Brown explains in some detail what is going on and often tells me her strategies for getting something done. So, this is a great experience. Frankly, the only time I feel she was a bit circumspect was yesterday when she asked me to leave the meeting. In fact, that was the first time she ever asked me to step out. And then those guys walked out like they had seen a ghost. I don't get it." Walker hesitated for a few seconds and then said, "I probably shouldn't tell you this, and please never repeat it, but what happened in that room was Brown was squeezing those guys for a sizeable donation to our educational foundation if they wanted to test the drug here. We knew they had been turned down at other hospitals and are desperate to use our facilities. Brown saw this as a great opportunity to replenish this foundation, which covers the travel and expenses to various conferences for our senior staff." Michelson was taken aback by this information and decided to not comment.

The next day she called the director of her program at State University and related what happened and ended with the following, "I'm not a lawyer, but I think I just witnessed something illegal. What should I do?"

\* \* \*

QUESTIONS

1. Was Ms. Brown's behavior illegal? Unethical? Tacky?
2. Did the chief operating officer cross any lines when he told Ms. Michelson what had transpired?
3. Was it appropriate for Ms. Brown to speak to her professor about this experience?
4. What should the professor do?

## CASE 4-8 | The Porn Shop

### BACKGROUND

The Bialystok Health System (BHS) is a large and complex organization with its headquarters based about 20 miles from Phoenix in an area that has a large percentage of retired people. The components of the organization include a 375-bed hospital, three separate 120-bed nursing homes, four ambulatory care clinics in communities that are within the city limits of Bialystok but still several miles from the hospital, a medical office building on the hospital campus, and two thrift shops that generate approximately $3 million per year for the system, which is a 501(c) 3 not-for-profit corporation.

The system's history began shortly after World War II when a large number of retirees started migrating to the Southwest in search of easy living, sunshine, and golf courses. Over the ensuing years, the original 40-bed hospital grew and developed into the system via a series of acquisitions and building projects. Originally named after the town in which it was located, the name was changed in 1985 to the Bialystok Health System in response to a $5 million gift from the Max Bialystok Foundation. The Foundation, which supports other charities in the communities, also continues to provide the health system between $1 million and $3 million per year. The chairman of the foundation, Max Bialystok Jr., is also chairman of the board of directors of the health system.

The Bialystok family members are accountants by profession, but they made their fortunes on Broadway with a series of fortuitous investments. To this day Junior (as he is known) still dabbles in theater productions in New York, London, and Toronto. However, his primary interest is in the health system, and over the years he has solidified his power over the system through a self-perpetuating board that is loyal to him. Of the 12 current board members, Junior has had a hand in selecting each one, and three are close relatives. One of Max's closest confidants is Ira Gershon, a retired Broadway producer whose connection with the family and Max Sr. goes back to their first Broadway hit, *Impala*, in 1968. Now in his mid-80s, Gershon keeps busy running the thrift shops that are in two different sections of town. The primary shop, Thrift Shop #1, is a 35,000-square foot stand-alone building located in the North Park community, which is one of the poorest parts of town. The second shop, Thrift Shop #2, is in South Park, a middle-class neighborhood. This shop is in a strip mall that was built by developer Ron Rump as a single building with six separate condominium units. BHS has owned the three units (total of 18,000 square feet) on the north side of the building since the facility was built, while the developer kept the other three units for himself. The developer's three units were rented to an auto parts business, a paint store, and an adult toy and video store that also offers Thai massages.

Heading the professional staff of the organization is CEO Charlie McCarthy, who was appointed to his position 9 months before the issue presented in this case occurred. McCarthy, although trained as a hospital administrator, had not been in an operating position for 25 years prior to joining BHS as the CEO. For 15 of those years, he was a health and hospital consultant with a large international firm. Then, 10 years ago, he and a partner formed a boutique executive search company focusing on senior management and medical staff positions. Junior heard of McCarthy's firm and hired them to search for a new CEO when the previous one retired. One of the candidates for the job was Gerald Mahoney, who, at the time, was chief operating officer (COO) of the BHS. Although McCarthy personally did not care for Mahoney's style, he felt that Mahoney, in light of his familiarity with the system and his years of experience, was a viable candidate for the CEO position. When he presented this analysis to the board, Junior looked at McCarthy and said, "Forget about Mahoney. He is simply a dummy. I need a smart guy like you to run this operation. Whaddaya say? You can name your price." McCarthy thought it over, discussed it with his partner and family, and decided to take the job. His instinct was to terminate Mahoney, but Junior said that Mahoney would be a good soldier and stay. So, instead, McCarthy met with Mahoney, told him he recognized the awkwardness of the situation but that he would like him to stay on, with a generous raise. Mahoney agreed.

## THE PROBLEM

Mr. Rump, the developer, has approached Ira Gershon about BHS purchasing his three condos in the strip mall where the second thrift shop is located. Gershon would like to expand that shop and thinks that the income from the shop justifies the condo purchase. He has a private discussion with Junior, who approves Gershon negotiating with Rump. The first time McCarthy hears about this potential deal is when Gershon calls to ask McCarthy to authorize the money for a deposit. McCarthy decides to investigate the deal and calls Rump, who tells him of the purchase price (which is fair in light of the market conditions) but also shares with the CEO the fact that the paint store and auto supply store will be moving out, but the adult toy and video store has a 20-year lease and refuses to move. So, Rump explains, after the deal goes through, the BHC will be the lessor of the property and will receive rent from the store for the next 20 years. This will also mean that the thrift shop will have not one large space, but the original three units at one end of the structure and two units at the other end. After thinking about this situation—that is, the BHC renting to a seedy business—McCarthy writes the following memo to Junior:

---

MEMO

From:   Charles W. McCarthy, CEO
To:      Max Bialystok Jr., Chairman of the Board
Cc:      Ira Gershon
Subj:   Rump condo purchases

---

Yesterday I was informed by Ira Gershon that you and he had decided to go ahead with the expansion of Thrift Shop #2 by purchasing the three condo units presently owned by Ron Rump so as to expand the shop into the entire building. As I trust you are aware, Mr. Rump is interested only in selling all three units as a package. Two of these units, the auto supply store and the paint store, have leases that expire within 3 months, and it is anticipated (by Rump) that they will be vacated by the time of a sale.

However, in my judgment, the third unit's status presents significant issues for our organization. This unit is under lease to a business that sells adult toys and videos, and has a back room for Thai massages. Frankly, this is a pornography operation that I believe is demeaning (and indeed, disgusting). The business owner has 20 more years left on his lease and is uninterested in moving for any price (according to Rump). Thus, if we close on this deal, we will be collecting monthly rent from a porn operator.

As you well know, some of our biggest supporters are people with close connections to religious institutions, and I believe they would become quite upset with us if they learned about our connection to a porn store. Further, I think that such a connection is morally offensive and not in keeping with the high ethical standards of the Bialystok Health System. I daresay any enterprising reporter could easily find out that we are the owners of the condo that rents to the porn store and expose us to unfavorable publicity.

Although I recognize that the thrift shop needs to expand, I think we need to look elsewhere. Finally, allow me to be perfectly clear that I do not support the purchase of the condos because of the lease with the porn shop.

After reviewing the memo, Junior immediately called Gerald Mahoney. The conversation was as follows:

*Junior:*

Gerry, what is with McCarthy? Is he some kind of moral majority?

*Mahoney:*

I don't know what you're talking about. Fill me in.

*Junior:*

Ira wants to buy the three other units at Thrift Shop #2 from Rump. The deal looks good to both Ira and me, but McCarthy sent me this moralistic memo that he won't go along with it because one of the condos has a 20-year lease with a porn shop.

*Mahoney:*

So, what's the problem?

*Junior:*

The problem is that he says that it is morally wrong for us to lease property to a porn shop and that when this is found out, our donations will be jeopardized. Is there a way around this crap?

*Mahoney:*

> Sure. Let's set up a couple of dummy corporations to hold the lease so if someone comes snooping, they really won't find BHC's fingerprints on the lease. How does that sound?

*Junior:*

> Sounds good to me. Why don't you go ahead and do it. Keep McCarthy out of the loop until it is a *fait accompli.*

*Mahoney:*

> It's as good as done, boss. You can count on me!

\* \* \*

QUESTIONS

1. What should Mahoney do to preserve his relationship with McCarthy?
2. What could Mahoney do to undermine McCarthy's position?
3. What should McCarthy do when he learns about the conversation between Junior and Mahoney?
4. What are the various implications of the courses of action that McCarthy could take?

---

## CASE 4-9  Trouble at Triangle

Dr. John Porter is one of 50 full-time physicians employed at Triangle Hospital, a 600-bed university teaching hospital in Metroplex. Porter's specialty is gastroenterology, and he is generally regarded as a competent physician. Indeed, in the 14 years that he has been at Triangle, not a single complaint has ever been lodged against him. He is clearly one of the informal social leaders of the medical staff. For example, he plays viola in a chamber music group that he founded 9 years ago, and he has numerous friends on the medical staff. Also, he has been happy to use his political connections (his father was once mayor of Metroplex) to benefit the hospital and its staff. Three years ago, Porter went through a traumatic divorce, in which he lost a bitter custody fight over his children.

Last year, a housekeeper making a routine Sunday evening check of the physicians' offices found Porter's office in disarray. She straightened it up and on Monday reported this unusual situation to the executive housekeeper. The following Sunday evening, the office was again in disarray, but this time an empty needle and syringe were found in the wastepaper basket. The housekeeper reported her findings to the executive housekeeper, who brought the situation to the attention of the assistant director and CEO of Triangle. After a few minutes of discussion, the executive housekeeper was told to have the housekeeper retrieve the needle and syringe if it happened again. Also, the hospital CEO asked for the emergency room roster for the previous 2 weekends and asked the medical records department for a rundown on Porter's cases for the past 2 weeks. Both sources indicated that he had not seen patients over the weekend. On a hunch that Porter may have seen a private patient during that period, he checked with Porter's business office, but that turned up nothing.

During the next week, the CEO casually asked Porter's colleagues about his general state of health, both physical and mental. Responses from the staff indicated no problems. The following Monday, another report was delivered about a "messed-up office," but this time the syringe and needle were retrieved. It was clearly a used, preloaded, morphine syringe. For confirmation, the CEO sent the items to the laboratory for examination. The CEO then briefed the hospital's chief of medical staff on the entire situation. The chief said he would talk to Porter. The following is the transcript of the conversation:

*Chief:*

John, how are you feeling?

*Porter:*

Fine, why do you ask?

*Chief:*

Well, you look tired lately, maybe even a bit depressed.

*Porter:*

Yes, I'm tired, but that's because I've been working my butt off. Just this week alone I had 10 colonoscopies.

*Chief:*

Are you depressed?

*Porter:*

No, why? What are you getting at?

*Chief:*

Okay, I won't beat around the bush. The housekeepers found a morphine syringe in your office wastebasket during the weekend, and your office has been messed up. What's going on?

*Porter:*

Oh, well, my pet golden retriever, you know, Lassie, has terminal cancer, so I've been giving her morphine to ease the pain. I apologize for not disposing of the syringe properly.

*Chief:*

Is that all?

*Porter:*

Yes.

The chief went back to the CEO with Porter's story, adding that, in his opinion, Porter was not telling the truth.

The CEO and the chief decided to put Porter under close surveillance for the next few weeks in order to see how he was dealing with his patients. No major problems were observed, although reports from the nursing staff indicated that he was more short-tempered than usual and, despite what he told the chief about being very busy, the business office indicated that his patient load seemed to be slowly decreasing. His appearance was generally neat, although he did come to the hospital on a few occasions without a shave and in badly wrinkled clothes. Only once during this 4-week period was another used morphine syringe found in his office. During this time, however, the housekeeper reported that another lock had been installed on the inside of the door.

The chief and the CEO met again and decided that Porter represented too great a threat and that he needed a sabbatical to straighten out his problem. The CEO called Porter in.

*CEO:*

John, how are you feeling?

*Porter:*

Fine, but why all this interest in my health lately?

*CEO:*

John, I'm concerned about you. Are you into drugs?

*Porter:*

No!

*CEO:*

So why morphine syringes in your office? Look, we want to help you.

*Porter:*

I told the chief my dog is dying of cancer, and you can help by just leaving me alone.

*CEO:*

Look, John, the chief and I think you need a rest. We want you to take a 2-month sabbatical, with pay, and get yourself together.

*Porter:*

I am together.

*CEO:*

We don't want a big hassle here. If you want to stay at Triangle, we want you to take a sabbatical and see a psychiatrist during that time.

*Porter:*

Do I have a choice?

*CEO:*

Not really.

*Porter:*

I'll go.

After Porter left, the CEO and the chief reviewed the situation. They both felt that Porter was involved with drugs, and their solution was reasonable. Two months later, the director received Porter's letter of resignation from the medical staff. Dr. Porter provided no explanation for his resignation. A year later, a letter came from a hospital in another state asking for a recommendation from the CEO and the chief of the medical staff for "Dr. John Porter, whom we wish to appoint as Chief of Gastroenterology at our hospital."

\* \* \*

QUESTIONS

1. What alternatives could the chief and the CEO have pursued?
2. What are the implications of these alternatives?
3. What should be the response of the chief and the CEO to the request for a recommendation?

---

## CASE 4-10 | The Successor

It was a 16-page special investigative report published in the *Leeward Island Daily News* that alerted Warren Polansky, the CEO of Southern District Health System in Florida, that he had problems with one of his newly hired senior executives. That executive, the man that Polansky envisioned succeeding him, Millard Jackson, had come to Florida a year earlier to assume the post of chief operating officer (COO) of the 718-bed District Health System at a salary of $370,000. Prior to joining the staff at District, he had been the CEO of the Leeward Island Medical Center (LIMC).

The report from the *Leeward Island Daily News* focused primarily on a recently released report from the region's inspector general that found massive mismanagement and fiscal irresponsibility on the part of the board and executive of the medical center where Jackson had served from 2002 until 2007. On page three of the special investigative report was the bombshell that led to Jackson's abrupt resignation. In 1993, while a hospital corpsman on active duty in the U.S. Army, Jackson had been court-martialed for stealing a credit card and related crimes. He was found guilty and served 9 months in at the Army's military prison in Ft. Leavenworth before being given a dishonorable discharge. None of this information was on Jackson's résumé, nor had it ever been disclosed during the COO hiring process.

According to Polansky, Jackson had failed to disclose the vital information about his Army arrest, conviction, imprisonment, and subsequent discharge. In a discussion about his initial decision to hire Jackson a year earlier, Mr. Polansky noted that the hospital had taken all the appropriate steps in hiring Jackson. First, they had used a national healthcare search firm before selecting Jackson. Second, Mr. Polansky had personally contacted several physicians at LIMC who had given Jackson positive reports. Third, standard criminal background checks were done. Polansky did state that no specific checks of military records were undertaken; however, Jackson had an outstanding reputation and was considered one of the top young healthcare administrators in the country.

* * *

QUESTIONS

1. Should Polansky ask for Jackson's resignation? Or should Jackson be fired?
2. If you were Polansky and Jackson refused to resign, what would you do?
3. How could this problem have been avoided?
4. How can similar problems be avoided in the future?

## CASE 4-11  The Grover

### BACKGROUND

The Grover (as it is known) has three components: a 272-bed skilled nursing facility, a 72-unit assisted living facility, and a 100-unit independent living apartment house. All three components are located on a 15-acre campus approximately 7 miles south of the central core of Grover, a city of 1.25 million people.

The Grover's location has always been one of its strengths and weaknesses. Because it is smack in the middle of one of the region's poorest neighborhoods, the administration, headed for the past 27 years by Albert Edwards, has never had trouble recruiting the vast majority of staff, whose average salaries are slightly higher than minimum wage. However, the location has some weaknesses, including the need for a 14-person (full-time equivalent) security staff, the occasional inability to recruit some professional staff who do not wish to come into the neighborhood, and the increasing difficulty of recruiting private-pay residents to the assisted living and independent living facility because of its location. (Most of the more affluent people come from North Grover about 8 miles north of the central core—about a 40-minute drive.)

In some ways, the neighborhood of the Grover has not changed much in the 30 years since the building was opened on land that was donated to the organization by one of its board members. Unfortunately, whereas in the past it was merely a neighborhood where poor people lived, it has now become one of the most crime ridden of the city. In response to these problems, 2 years ago Edwards augmented his security force by 8 people (from 10 to 18), but several months before the following incident occurred he downsized the security department to 14 because of budgetary complaints. Additionally, as far back as 4 years ago, he requested from the board a capital expenditure of $581,000 to build a wall around the property with a manned entrance gate to control access to the campus. His request has been denied five times, most recently 2 months before the incident.

## THE INCIDENT

Two days before Christmas, Edwards and his wife left on a planned 10-day vacation that included a flight to Ft. Lauderdale, Florida, an overnight stay at the Ritz-Carlton on Ft. Lauderdale Beach, and then an 8-day cruise to the Caribbean with a flight back to Grover from Barbados. On the fourth day of the trip, while at sea, Edwards received an email as well as an urgent phone message that three men had broken into the Grover the previous night, beaten up seven residents and the one security guard who had arrived a few minutes after the break-in, and stolen personal items from the rooms of ten residents, as well as several computers and television sets. Two of the residents were in critical condition, and one was not expected to live. The information that Edwards received was that the police had no suspects but were investigating. Edwards immediately called Jessica Stone, his deputy director, and learned that the one resident who was in critical condition had died, that the facility had been broken into through glass patio doors in the early evening while the residents were watching television, and that the news had traveled around the entire facility and everyone was petrified. Stone also told Edwards that the entire board had been notified.

After this call, Edwards and his wife discussed whether they should immediately return to Grover or finish the cruise and then go home. They decided to finish the cruise. Twice daily, Edwards spoke to Stone for an update, and twice he spoke to Mark Nansen, chairman of the board.

When he returned to his office on January 2, his secretary told him that Nansen was coming over to see him at noon. When he arrived, Nansen looked at Edwards and said, "Al, I'm not going to beat around the bush. You've done a great job for us for more than 25 years. In fact, without you the Grover wouldn't be what it is today. But this incident is totally unacceptable. As you know, I am a retired Navy officer and we had a saying in the Navy that a collision at sea can ruin your whole day. Well, Al, you have had a collision at sea, and the board met last night and decided to terminate you immediately. We will honor all the terms of your contract and your pension is secure. I'm sorry."

\* \* \*

## QUESTIONS

1. Begin by reconstructing the board conversation that led to the Edwards termination. What arguments could be made to terminate Edwards? What arguments against his termination?
2. Should Edwards be held responsible for an incident that happened while he was on vacation?
3. Is it likely that the board would have acted differently if Edwards had cut short his vacation and flown home?
4. Is the board culpable in this incident?
5. If you were a consultant to the board, what recommendations would you make?

## CASE 4-12 | The Cabinet Meeting

Every Tuesday and Thursday morning, the senior management of the Central Valley Medical Center, a 411-bed hospital, meet to discuss a broad range of managerial issues. A major subject of concern for the past several weeks has been the declining Medicare census, and discussions have revolved around strategies to increase the census. At today's meeting, the following conversation takes place:

*CEO:*

Any progress on the census initiatives?

*COO:*

One new thing we are exploring is a telemedicine initiative that may develop better relationships with practitioners in rural areas and result in their sending us patients.

*CFO:*

Have you costed the project yet?

*COO:*

No, but we are working on it. Besides, if it smells viable, I am going over to development and seeing if they can get some state, federal, or foundation money to pay for the deal.

*CEO:*

Anything else?

*COO:*

Yes, I've been approached by the Revere brothers, who are interested in doing a deal with us.

*CFO:*

Who are they?

*COO:*

They are two guys who own and run two private nursing homes with a total of 500 beds, mostly Medicare. Anyway, they want to work a deal whereby we would be their only referral hospital. I suspect they could put between 10 and 20 patients a day into the hospital.

*CEO:*

Sounds good, but what's the deal?

*COO:*

They want a guaranteed $75,000 per year for the referrals.

*CFO:*

It's certainly worth it, but we don't want to run afoul of the Medicare regs. Maybe we could give them a job or responsibilities for the money?

*CEO:*

Right! See if they would be interested in being Chief of Gerontology.

*COO:*

I doubt if they want to do anything, but I'll talk to them.

*CEO:*

Great!

\* \* \*

QUESTIONS

1. What is wrong with this picture?
2. What type of moral and intellectual leadership is being offered by the CEO?
3. What do you suspect will be the likely scenarios in this case?

---

## CASE 4-13 | Kosher for Passover

Every spring the food services department of the Mount Sinai Hospital faced the daunting task of preparing the hospital's dietary operation for the Jewish holiday of Passover. Because Mount Sinai was a kosher facility, and operated under the supervision of an orthodox rabbi, it was necessary to go through an extensive process of preparing for the 8-day holiday. Some of the activities involved a very extensive cleaning process of all the utensils that were to be used during the holiday. And, because certain utensils, such as those made from ceramic, couldn't be used during the holiday, they were replaced. In recent years, the hospital saved time and storage space by extensive use of paper and plastic for patients' meals and the staff cafeteria. Additionally stoves, dishwashers, sinks, and microwaves throughout the facility needed to be cleaned to the satisfaction of the rabbinical authority. Finally, special foods needed to be used during the holiday.

For the 8 days of Passover, plus the 2 days before the holiday, employees were asked to not bring in any food to the hospital, and all meals were provided in the cafeteria at 50% of the regular cafeteria charges. The food itself, though, was different from that available during the year. For example, the popular dessert bar that normally offered soft-serve frozen yogurt with a variety of toppings was not available. There was no bread or bread products available because it was a prohibited food during Passover. Many soft drinks, particularly some popular sodas, were not available because they were sweetened with corn syrup that is not considered kosher for Passover.

Every year during this period, management hears a fair amount of grumbling from the staff concerning the quality of food in the cafeteria as well as the lack of availability of traditional breakfast and snack foods such as bagels and donuts (also not kosher for Passover). This year the CEO has decided that she would like to do something to avoid the rumblings and has asked for your assistance in "doing something so that the staff isn't complaining for 2 weeks."

\* \* \*

QUESTIONS

1. What research will you have to do before making your recommendations?
2. What options would you recommend to ameliorate this problem?

---

## CASE 4-14 | Clowning Around

After a 2-week trip to Israel, Spencer Greene, a vice president of the board of Windsor Regional Medical Center, asked to meet with Sheila Jones, the Medical Center's CEO. The conversation was as follows:

*Jones:*

Welcome back. How was your trip?

*Greene:*

Great. In fact, that's why I wanted to meet with you. During my stay, I toured through the Hadassah

University Medical Center, and while on the pediatric floor I met two of the hospital's five clowns. I was mesmerized by them. They had the patients and staff smiling and laughing. Later on I met the chief of pediatrics and asked about the clowns. He told me they were a tremendous asset to the patient care. In fact, he said that one of the clowns, Dudie, a former Parisian street performer who now lives near Tel Aviv, actually has come in on his day off to help feed some kids who won't eat for anyone but him. What do you think?

*Jones:*

I think it's wonderful, but what are you asking me?

*Greene:*

Well, what about a clown program right here at Windsor?

*Jones:*

Spencer, I think it's an interesting idea, but I see a lot of problems making it happen, and the cost may not be worth the benefit.

*Greene:*

Well, they wouldn't agree with you in Israel.

*Jones:*

I'm sorry. I'm not making myself clear. What I am trying to say is that it may be possible here, and on the other hand, it may not be possible. For example, it sounds like the Hadassah medical staff is supportive of these clowns and also that there is some funding for them . . .

*Greene:*

Don't worry about the money—I'll take care of that.

*Jones:*

Look, Spencer, I think it is a very interesting idea, but can you give me a few weeks and let me look into it?

With Mr. Greene's agreement to rediscuss the clown program with her in 3 weeks, Jones prepares to send out a memo directing that one of her assistant directors investigate the feasibility of a clown program.

\* \* \*

ASSIGNMENT

Prepare a memo to an assistant for Ms. Jones's signature. The substance of the memo should identify the issue likely to be associated with developing a clown program at Windsor. Be sure to include the costs and benefits of such a program, whether staffed by volunteers or employees.

---

## CASE 4-15 | Computer Use Policy

COMMUNITY HOSPITAL MEMO

From:   Director of IT Services
To:      CEO
Subj:   Employee Computer Use

Chief:

As you know, we have hundreds of computer terminals and desktops throughout our facility. As I walk around, I often get the impression that there is a great deal of personal activity happening on these computers—particularly in the nonclinical office spaces. I am certain that I have seen people on Twitter and Facebook, and last week I observed someone ordering theater tickets at 10:30 AM. My impression is that there is plenty of time being wasted. Although we already have some filters and firewalls to prevent people from going onto certain sites, I would like us to have a clear policy on monitoring employees' computer use as well as personal time-wasting activities. *Do you want me to go ahead and develop a policy?*

Sid

-----------------------------------

Response from CEO: "Go for it."

* * *

ASSIGNMENT

Write the policy for the hospital.

---

## CASE 4-16 | Mistakes Not Corrected

By *Sheila H. Szafran*

### BACKGROUND

Eastern Valley Hospital is a 609-bed Level-I trauma center consistently rated among top-performing hospitals recognized by reputable and well-known organizations. The hospital is located in a city of 200,000 residents but represents a service area of 400,000 people. Three smaller community hospitals also serve the area. Because of its trauma designation and inner city location, a significant percentage of patients treated at Eastern Valley lack sufficient insurance coverage. Last year, more than 40% of the patients treated in the outpatient rehabilitation department were uninsured. Despite access to highly educated medical personnel, Eastern Valley has been slow to adopt electronic health records and internal policies and procedures that improve safety and quality across all departments.

### SITUATION

Mr. Lopez is a 23-year-old male who sustained a flexor tendon injury to his dominant right forearm from a knife wound that occurred during a street fight. He was brought to the emergency department at Eastern Valley and was admitted for a surgical repair by a board-certified hand surgeon. Mr. Lopez was discharged the following day with orders for immediate outpatient therapy. He was told to go to Eastern Valley because this is the only facility that accepts patients without insurance.

The usual practice is for the physician's office to fax an order to the rehabilitation department with the specifics, including physical therapy or occupational therapy, splinting specifications, and type of therapy. When Mr. Lopez's order arrived, office personnel noted that the circle marked by the physician surrounded both physical therapy and occupational therapy. Additional information included flexor tendon protocol, which, in the case of Mr. Lopez, meant that the splint should not be removed for several weeks.

At Eastern Valley, the occupational therapists possess the advanced practices skills necessary for this situation. Unfortunately, Mr. Lopez was added to the physical therapy schedule instead of the more appropriate occupational therapy schedule. Although hand therapy patients are usually treated at a group table, the physical therapist, a contracted travel therapist, took Mr. Lopez behind closed curtains, removed his splint, and asked the patient to show her how much active movement he could perform. After observing Mr. Lopez's range of motion, the physical therapist came from behind the curtain and asked the occupational therapist for splinting assistance, a skill that she did not possess. The occupational therapist immediately recognized that flexor protocol had been broken, replaced the surgeon's splint, and called the surgeon. Mr. Lopez was sent back to the surgeon's office for further assessment. The occupational therapist reported the incident to the department manager and encouraged the physical therapist to fill out an incident report.

\* \* \*

QUESTIONS

1. Should Western Valley initiate an accountability or disciplinary process? Who needs to be addressed: office personnel, contract physical therapist, the company through which this therapist works, or the department manager?
2. How should referrals be clarified to prevent errors?
3. Should the outpatient rehabilitation culture tolerate behind-curtains treatment of upper extremity patients?
4. Should Mr. Lopez be informed that errors were made in his treatment?
5. What steps should the rehabilitation administrators take to ensure safety of all patients?
6. Is there a broader issue such as use of contract therapists?
7. Is the hospital now looking at a potential lawsuit?

---

**CASE 4-17** | **Interrupted by Facebook**

By *Ilya Shekhter* and *Jill Sanko*

An 82-year-old man with a history of chronic obstructive pulmonary disease (COPD) came by ambulance to an academic medical center; he was complaining of increasing shortness of breath and chest pain. His glucose level on admission was 324 mg/dL (a normal level ranges from 70 to 145 mg/dL). Subsequent to the emergency treatment, he was admitted to the intensive care unit (ICU) with orders for long-acting insulin (Lantus) and sliding-scale coverage. That is a dosing system for the Lantus based on finger-stick glucose values greater than 200 mg/dL.

On the first day of hospitalization, a myocardial infarction was ruled out and his respiratory status was improving with treatment. On the third day, he was transferred from the ICU to a medicine floor for continued observation and additional respiratory treatments. Medication orders from the ICU were continued on the floor.

On the sixth day, during rounds, the medical team evaluated the patient and reviewed his progress. They noted that, while glucose values in the ICU ranged from 200 to 300 mg/dL, they currently ranged from 110 to 140 mg/dL (essentially normal). Therefore, reasoning that the patient's glycemic control had improved, the attending physician asked the junior resident on the team to discontinue the Lantus, glucose finger-stick checks, and insulin sliding-scale orders.

When the attending stated that they should stop the orders, the resident began to enter them into the computer physician order entry (CPOE) system via his smartphone. As he was entering the order, the resident received a Facebook message regarding an upcoming bachelor party for a friend, and he confirmed attendance through text messaging. The team then moved on to the next patient.

Two days later, the patient was found unresponsive. The resident ordered stat blood cultures, electrolytes, and a head CT scan. As staff prepared to transport the patient to radiology, the lab called to report a critical value—a glucose level of 26 mg/dL. The resident immediately ordered intravenous dextrose followed by an infusion, which led to a rapid improvement in the patient's mental status. Luckily, the patient suffered no subsequent events. His Lantus was discontinued, and he continued his rehabilitation at home.

Root cause analysis of this incident revealed that the resident never completed the order to discontinue the Lantus, and the patient continued to receive 10 units each day. Because everyone on the team thought the medication had been stopped, no one checked the patient's glucose level. In addition, because of the robust CPOE system, neither the resident nor the attending was reviewing the medication list for the next few days, so no one recognized that the patient was still receiving the Lantus.

The policy of the medical center is that when clinical incidents occur whereby patients are harmed or potentially harmed, the incident must be reported to the CEO. This incident was reported.

\* \* \*

QUESTIONS

1. What are the advantages and disadvantages of using mobile devices such as smartphones in the hospital?
2. What are the potential legal consequences of this incident?
3. Should any of the members of the team be disciplined? If so, how?
4. Is this a failure of the CPOE system?
5. What policy changes are recommended in order to lessen the likelihood of similar problems in the future?

---

## CASE 4-18 The Distracted Nurse

By *Alex Szafran*

### BACKGROUND

Memorial Hospital is a 350-bed general hospital serving a city with a population of about 150,000 people. There are two other slightly smaller general hospitals also serving the community. Even though it is a general hospital, Memorial has chosen to develop centers of excellence in neurosciences and oncology and enjoys a 60% market share in each of those service lines. As a result of this focus, oncologists in the community have come to heavily rely on Memorial's expertise in performing minimally invasive workups. Memorial has developed a strong reputation among patients because of its focus on patient comfort and pain management during these procedures.

## SITUATION

Mr. Longfellow, a 59-year-old patient, recently had a chest x-ray because he had a persistent cough. The chest x-ray revealed a small nodule in his right lung that required further workup to determine whether the nodule was cancerous. The oncologists determined that a minimally invasive image-guided needle biopsy in the operating room (OR) was the safest and most accurate procedure. The anesthesia for such a procedure is typically moderate sedation administered and managed by a critical care nurse. Because of the location of the nodule, Mr. Longfellow was positioned facedown on the operating table, with his face directed away from the side where the physician and other staff were located.

Staff in the room included the physician, the nurse responsible for managing the sedation and caring for the patient, an OR technologist responsible for assisting the physician, and an x-ray technologist responsible for operating the fluoroscopy machine used by the physician to help guide the needle to the proper place in Mr. Longfellow's lung. Because of the number of people and amount of equipment required, the room was crowded and access to both sides of the patient was possible but difficult.

Sedation was administered and the procedure performed without complication. However, during the procedure, the nurse became distracted by another nurse in the doorway who had questions about how much longer the procedure might take, the next patient scheduled for the room, and work schedules for the rest of the week. When the nurse refocused on Mr. Longfellow, the procedure was finished, and as she was taking a final set of vital signs (oxygenation level, blood pressure, respiration level, pulse), she discovered that Mr. Longfellow's oxygenation level was low and he was not breathing well. Medication to reverse the effects of the narcotic sedation was given, but Mr. Longfellow did not wake up. He was then admitted to the ICU. A few days later it was determined that Mr. Longfellow was most likely in a permanent comatose state caused by overmedication during the procedure. He eventually was discharged to a nursing home specializing in brain injuries where he died 3 months later.

Following such unexpected events, Memorial Hospital's standard practice is to perform a root cause analysis to determine what went wrong, determine the effectiveness and safety of standard work processes, and determine what, if anything, needs to be changed to reduce or eliminate the possibility of such events recurring. During the root cause analysis of Mr. Longfellow's case, it was discovered that the distractions caused the nurse to miss vital sign checks that were required by written policy to be performed every 5 minutes. During the time of the distractions, three such checks were missed. It was also discovered during the analysis that although the nurse claimed to have performed all vital sign checks during the procedure except during the time she was distracted, the medical record showed that she had also missed required checks periodically throughout the procedure. It was further noted that due to the crowded conditions in the room, it was difficult for the nurse to position herself on the side of the table toward which the patient's face was turned, and she was therefore not able to regularly observe the patient for signs of pain, overmedication, undermedication, or overall distress. She had adapted to this condition by relying on the x-ray technologist who was positioned on the side of the table to observe the patient. Although this was not an authorized practice, the nurse stated that it was a common practice. The x-ray technologist denied having any communication with the nurse during the procedure and denied having accepted responsibility for patient observation. It was noted that patient observation was not within the scope of practice for an x-ray technologist as defined by state licensure regulations.

\* \* \*

QUESTIONS

1. Should Memorial Hospital take disciplinary action against any of the staff members involved? Which staff members? What action might be taken?
2. Based on the findings of the root cause analysis, what, if any, changes to procedures should be made to prevent similar events in the future?
3. What features of the culture in the operating room contributed to the events?
4. What steps should Memorial Hospital take to change the culture of the operating room? Why?
5. Should Memorial Hospital allow similar procedures to be performed in the room that has size constraints that contributed to this problem? Why?

**CHAPTER 5**

# MANAGING CHANGE

 **INTRODUCTION**

Changes occur in organizations for a variety of reasons. Some are imposed from the outside because of economics, politics, or social factors. For example, trouble in the Middle East might result in higher costs for gas and other products that are derived from petroleum or related to oil prices. For a large institution, such a change can easily result in unanticipated cost increases for everything ranging from a gallon of gas for the hospital's vehicles to the cost of plastic forks and the heating or cooling bills. Change might come from a range of social issues such as drug abuse or the frustration that many people are facing in getting primary care—leading to a rise in concierge medicine.

In this chapter, cases are representative of those issues managers often face. Some are related to public health issues whereas others are driven by economics and social issues. Central to all of the cases is the responsibility of the administrator to be the change agent and not the guardian of the status quo.

---
**CASE 5-1** | **Smoking**

---

Dr. Sheila Atkins, the health officer of the city of Louisburg, is in the process of proposing a citywide ordinance that would totally ban smoking in all public spaces such as restaurants, hotel and hospital lobbies, trains, trolleys and buses, supermarkets, and any other establishment that employs more than three staff. Louisburg is a city of 100,000 people and is located in a state that has vehemently opposed smoking bans. If this ordinance is enacted, it will be the first in the state. A public hearing on the ordinance is being planned for the beginning of the following month.

Ever since her appointment as health officer, Dr. Atkins has worked assiduously to educate and legislate on a wide variety of health issues such as obesity, diabetes, and drunk driving. The few times she has proposed health-related laws they have been greeted with indifference and have not been enacted. Although recognizing that a ban on smoking may be quite unpopular among the citizens of Louisburg, Dr. Atkins is firm in her belief that such a ban will be in the best interests of the Louisburg residents. Indeed, her view on this matter was reinforced by a study by the Harvard School of Public Health and released by the Massachusetts Department of Public Health, which found that 600 fewer people in the state had fatal heart attacks, and which traced the decrease in fatalities directly to a state-wide ban on smoking.

\* \* \*

ASSIGNMENT

Dr. Atkins is responsible for organizing the public hearing in front of the city council on her proposed ordinance. What suggestions do you have in terms of speakers who could strengthen her position, and what opposition should she expect?

---

**CASE 5-2** | **Children Can't Fly**

---

After reviewing information collected from the city's emergency rooms, police department, fire-rescue squad, and ambulance services, the High City Health Department has concluded that there is a mini-epidemic of children falling out of windows. This problem seems to be seasonal and strongly correlated with the socioeconomic status of the victims. In general, the injured or dead children are poor and live either in city projects or in low-rent, high-rise buildings, with most of the problems occurring from late April through mid-October. Additionally, the city has experienced several teenagers making successful suicide jumps from bedroom windows.

High City's health commissioner, Peter Expressario, MD, has decided to follow the example of Lowell Bellin, MD, MPH, the late distinguished health commissioner of New York City, who initiated a program call Children Can't Fly. The New York City program required that landlords provide window guards in apartments where children 10 years or younger reside. However, Expressario wants to go further and pass an ordinance that requires every window above the second floor of any building, residential or commercial, to have window guards. He believes the public will be best served from a financial and healthcare perspective if such an ordinance is enacted.

* * *

QUESTIONS

1. What constituencies are likely to be in favor of such an ordinance? What constituencies will likely oppose it?
2. What arguments could be made to support the ordinance?
3. What arguments could be made against the ordinance?

---

## CASE 5-3 | Drug Problems

| MEMO | |
|---|---|
| From: | CEO, River City Health System |
| To: | Director, Pharmacy Services; Associate Director, Community Services; Director, ER Services |
| Subject: | Prescription drug abuse |

I just had a meeting with the County Health Officer, who was recently on a conference call with officials from CMS about questionable access to prescription drugs.

It seems there is a population of Medicare Part D beneficiaries, the majority of whom are beneficiaries because of disabilities, who go doctor shopping or perhaps doctor hopping to accumulate prescriptions for a range of controlled and noncontrolled painkillers, including hydrocodone and oxycodone. In many cases these drugs are accumulated and sold on the black market. I am concerned that, because of our demographics and the location of our five community health centers, we could be part of the problem.

I would like to meet with all of you next Tuesday to discuss two items. First, to what extent are we part of the problem? Second, what can we do to minimize this situation?

* * *

QUESTIONS

1. For each of these three services positions, explain how you can research the issue of being part of the problem.
2. For each position, explain how you can minimize the situation.
3. Based on comparing and contrasting what each area is capable of doing, what should the CEO do about this situation?
4. What are the risks if the CEO chooses to do nothing?

---

## CASE 5-4  Concierge Medicine

For the past 5 years your sister-in-law, Ming Lee, has been a hospitalist in the department of medicine at the University Hospital where she works 12-hour shifts 14 days per month. Her salary in 2012 was $195,000 plus a package of excellent fringe benefits including health insurance, a 10% contribution to a 401(k) pension plan, vacation and sick pay, a $3,000 allowance for continuing medical education, dues for two professional societies, reimbursement for license fees, and full malpractice coverage. One benefit she does not yet take advantage of is full tuition reimbursement at the hospital's college for all her children or 50% tuition at any other college. At the moment, Dr. Lee is not married, but she has recently become engaged and will likely marry in the next 12 months.

Dr. Lee has been approached by one of her classmates to join her and another physician in a three-person concierge medicine group that will focus on women patients.

* * *

QUESTIONS

1. What business questions should Dr. Lee consider in deciding about the costs and benefits of becoming a concierge MD? How can you assist in analyzing this issue?
2. What professional questions should be considered and why?
3. What personal/lifestyle questions should Dr. Lee consider?
4. Is concierge medicine an approach that should be encouraged or discouraged by the health system?
5. Is the patient-centered medical home approach the poor man's concierge medicine?

---

| CASE 5-5 | **Group Practice Consultation** |

COMMUNITY MEDICAL CENTER MEMO

From:    CEO
To:      CFO and Director of Planning
Subject: Online primary care

A 2010 study about providing online care in a primary care setting recently came to my attention (*Mayo Clin Proc.* 2010:85[8]). Based on my reading of this paper, the Mayo Clinic (at its Rochester, MN, site) signed up about 4,200 patients for a project whereby they would use online services presumably as a substitute for seeing the doctor. Apparently they used free text entries that led to branching questions.

Generally, the physicians responded within 24 hours. According to the article, about 55% of these online visits resulted in a prescription or refill. About 10% resulted in an x-ray or other procedure, and 5% resulted in lab studies.

In economic terms, I am uncertain whether this approach is viable because neither Medicare nor Medicaid reimbursed for these online visits, and the only reimbursement came from Mayo's own insurer (for those patients who were Mayo Clinic employees).

Frankly, my interest in such a system is related to the following goals: (1) taking pressure off our medical staff; (2) generating money for services that we already provide gratis; (3) increasing patient satisfaction with our system.

* * *

ASSIGNMENT

Prepare a response to this memo. Review the Mayo Clinic article and any other relevant articles and let the CEO know (1) what assumptions you are making about the center's need/ ability to implement such a system; (2) what issues the center would have to address if such a system were to be implemented for primary care; and (3) your opinion of whether successfully implementing such a system would be of significance in reaching the CEO's previously articulated goals.

---

## CASE 5-6 | The John Paul Jones Medical Center

The John Paul Jones Medical Center is a 47-physician multispecialty group practice located in an affluent suburb of a major city. The clinic's management team is led by John Paul Jones III, who is both the grandson of the founder and a well-trained manager with experience in ambulatory as well as hospital care.

Because the group's partners want to ensure the financial viability of the group, they have become extremely careful about recruiting new MDs whose starting salary demands are often close to the incomes of established partners, particularly in the specialty areas of pediatrics, psychiatry, and general internal medicine. Another problem faced by the group is the constant pressure of reimbursement from their insurers.

Recently one of their largest insurers met with John Paul Jones III and essentially told him that they want to implement a telephone care management system to enhance quality and control costs. It is not likely that such a system could be limited solely to patients of that insurer.

\* \* \*

## ASSIGNMENT

The medical staff has gotten wind of the insurer's interests and demands about telephone care management. Virtually every physician believes that such a system would not be in the interests of the patient's health or the financial well-being of the group. They have asked you to come to their next staff meeting to discuss the insurer's request.

Prepare a 25-minute speech for the clinic administrator that addresses the aforementioned concerns of the medical staff.

---

## CASE 5-7 | Organizational Angina

The city of Avion, with its three large hospitals, was thought to be a congenial healthcare community. Then, about a year ago, the Avion Cardiology Group (ACG) announced that they were seeking a closer affiliation with just one hospital. Since its inception 25 years ago, ACG has been an independent group practice with its physicians being on the active staff of all three facilities.

At the partners meeting last year, the decision was made to affiliate exclusively with one hospital, in light of the changing economics of health care. This resulted in a committee of five senior partners taking on the responsibility of negotiating a sale of the group to one of the hospitals. The terms of the sale would be that the buyer would purchase all of the group's assets and agree to employ all 25 physicians and 200 staff at salaries and benefits equal to that which they currently had.

Each of the three hospitals considered the proposal, and two of the three made a bid to buy the group. The 591-bed White Memorial Medical Center was the bid accepted by ACG. The unsuccessful bidder was the 517-bed Green Regional Hospital.

Now that the ACG is in the process of closing the sale of its two buildings and moving onto the White Memorial campus, the administration of Green Regional is quite concerned about the use of their cardiology service. In a recent press release, they indicated that the new ACG–White arrangement could prove detrimental to their patients. In response to this, the Medical Director of the ACG issued a joint press release with the CEO of White Memorial Medical Center stating that the ACG staff would continue to service the Green Regional patients for the foreseeable future.

\* \* \*

QUESTIONS

1. If you were CEO of Green Regional, would the press release from ACG and White give you comfort? Why?
2. What do you suspect is White Memorial's long-term plan?
3. What should be Green Regional's next move? How should it go about making its move?

---

| CASE 5-8 | **The Merger** |

On November 9, 1918, 2 days before Armistice Day ending World War I, the small western New England community of Oriole celebrated the opening of the 36-bed St. Anne's Hospital. Largely funded by Raymond McGee, a wealthy textile mill owner, the hospital was gifted to the Little Daughters of Perpetual Compassion, a Catholic order based in the state capital. The Little Daughters not only held the ownership of the hospital but also ran the institution for the next 80 years. The fortune of St. Anne's was in large measure a reflection of the fortunes of the Oriole community. As it struggled through the Depression, the hospital managed to stay afloat through the generosity of several wealthy Catholic families and some assistance from the Daughters of Perpetual Compassion. World War II brought considerable business to Oriole's four textile mills and tool-making shops. With that prosperity and subsequent increase in population, the hospital was expanded to 100 beds. Unfortunately, the end of the war, as well as threats of unionization, caused the mills to leave for North Carolina, and the town went into an economic tailspin from which it never recovered. By the late 1990s, the hospital had closed half of its beds, was running at 50% occupancy, and was flirting with bankruptcy.

Meanwhile, on the other side of the Oriole River, a mere 7 miles to the east, lies the town of Hawes. Since the end of World War II, Hawes has followed the course of retail and commercial development, eventually becoming the site of the state's first and largest Walmart. In the early 1950s, the town's mayor, a former state representative, was able to convince the government to route the interstate highway just east of the town, with two exits leading into Hawes. Several motels and restaurants were able to develop as a result. The most recent boost for the Hawes economy was the opening of the state regional office for motor vehicle licenses and registration. Overall, the local hospital in Hawes has done well, both because of the economy and because of aggressive leadership, which resulted in the hospital having one of the first general hospital-based inpatient psychiatric units in the state. By the late 1990s, the Hawes hospital was licensed for 190 beds, had an 80% occupancy rate, and usually ran in the black with the help of a modest endowment.

There was generally little overlap between the two medical staffs of Hawes and Oriole. In the last few years, the Hawes hospital has become closely affiliated with the regional medical school as a strategy for upgrading its staff and services. Because the two hospitals are in the same county and relatively physically close, there has often been talk of merger, particularly during the years when federally funded health planning agencies were active.

Once again, at the outset of the 21st century, there is new talk of a merger because of Oriole's difficult financial situation. The perspective of the Hawes board is that the merger will be good for the hospital and medical staff. The extra 20 inpatients per day would help build a solid financial situation for Hawes, and although the Oriole medical staff is generally not of the Hawes caliber, most of them are on the verge of retirement. Additionally, the Hawes property could be converted into a health center, perhaps some type of long-term care facility. While the Little Daughters of Perpetual Compassion are interested in relieving themselves of the financial burden of the hospital, they are deeply concerned about two issues. First, they are concerned about the legacy of St. Anne's in a subsumed organization, where there is a good chance that their name will be lost. Second, they are concerned that abortions are performed at Hawes Hospital and that there is an active family planning center.

\* \* \*

QUESTIONS

1. What are the exact objectives that each organization is seeking to attain in the merger?
2. Is there a way to accommodate their conflicting objectives?
3. How will the history of similar mergers affect their decision making?
4. What is likely to be more powerful, economics or ideology?
5. What do you anticipate is the likely outcome of this situation?

---

| CASE 5-9 | Identity Fraud |
|----------|----------------|

The following email was received by the CEO. She has forwarded it to you for your action.

| MEMO | |
|------|--|
| From: | CFO |
| To: | CEO |
| Cc: | VP, Ambulatory Services |
| Subject: | Losses from identity issues in ED and ACC |

Over the last 6 months we have lost close to $375,000 in our Emergency Department and Ambulatory Care Center due to identity issues. I believe some of this loss is a function of staff errors in names, numbers, etc. However, based on my analysis, the bulk of the problem is related to identity theft. Specifically, I think patients are passing around insurance and social security cards. We need to curb this behavior and at the same time avoid any PR or even EMTALA (Emergency Medical Treatment and Active Labor Act) problems.

\* \* \*

ASSIGNMENT

Prepare a plan-of-action memo for review by the CEO, CFO, and VP, Director of Ambulatory Services.

---

## CASE 5-10 | Citizens Hospital

The Citizens Hospital is a 176-bed community hospital that has recently celebrated its 100th anniversary. The relatively new CEO, Rose Flowers, has inherited an extremely traditional medical staff that still believes in the sanctity of private practices, abhors managed care, and thinks of the physician–patient relationship as essentially paternalistic.

Recently, Ms. Flowers became acquainted with the work of the Health Dialog Company in Boston, Massachusetts. Her reading as well as her experience has led her to conclude that many of the relationships between the medical staff at the hospital and the patients, particularly those under age 40, are deteriorating because of the attitudes of the medical staff. She believes they are simply not interested in any dialogue with the patients about their clinical choices. Since arriving at Citizens nearly 18 months ago, she has received about a dozen complaints (none formally) about the way the various specialists tend to push patients to make certain choices. Her belief is that the behavior of the medical staff is part of the reason that Citizens has a reputation as a doctors' hospital and a money mill rather than a true community institution. Further, Ms. Flowers is convinced that this situation is causing younger members to look elsewhere for their medical care and hospitalizations.

\* \* \*

ASSIGNMENT

Assume you are on the administrative staff and Ms. Flowers has asked you to develop a white paper on preference-sensitive patient decision making. She would also like to know how she could sell the medical staff on more patient involvement in decision making.

---

## CASE 5-11 | The Health Fair

Phil Maxwell, director of human resources for the W&T manufacturing company, recently talked to the CEO of the company about W&T sponsoring a health fair for the two shifts of employees. Maxwell has contacted the local community hospital for help in designing and implementing the health fair.

\* \* \*

ASSIGNMENT

Assume you are director of the benefits section within the human resources department of W&T. Maxwell has asked you to be the point person on the health fair. He wishes to understand the costs and benefits of the fair and is now having second thoughts about partnering with the hospital on the project. He is waiting for a memo from you on the scope of the fair, the costs and benefits, and a recommendation about going forth with the project.

---

## CASE 5-12 | ER: What's Next?

| MEMO | |
|---|---|
| From: | CEO |
| To: | Associate Director, Clinical Services |
| Subject: | ER Services |

As you are no doubt aware, this 4th of July holiday weekend was a royal disaster in our ER. The overcrowding, the wait times, and the diversions are unacceptable. The statistics I looked at indicate that as of July 6, our ER has been on diversion 411 hours. At that rate, we will be on diversion about twice the national average by the end of the year.

Our ER wait times are simply out of hand. I have already received complaints from four board members about waits in excess of 3 hours. More importantly, I think there are people who are in need of care who are simply either leaving the ER or waiting too long for urgent care.

Finally, there is a serious problem with the slowness of admitting people and the wait for beds—even on a holiday weekend. In fact, this morning I heard from Mr. Hugh E. Luigi, the vice president of our board, who told me about his mother-in-law's experience coming in with a possible stroke. She waited more than 90 minutes to see a doctor, another 2 hours for an MRI, followed by hours waiting for blood work, and then when the decision was made to admit her, she wound up lying on a stretcher in a hallway for 8 hours before being moved up to a floor.

*All of this is bad medicine, opens us up for potential litigation, and is bad PR. This has to change!*

Please put together a task force to immediately examine this problem and report back to me with your analysis, conclusions, and recommendations.

\* \* \*

## QUESTIONS

1. Are there any problems with the CEO's memo?
2. Who would you want on your task force?
3. Do research on the problems mentioned in the memo.
4. What are your recommendations?
5. How can these recommendations be implemented?

| CASE 5-13 | The Consultation |

The international consulting firm of AB&C has recently finished an engagement for Rolatel, a publicly owned (NASDAQ) chain of 130 nursing homes headquartered in California, with facilities in California, Arizona, Oregon, and Washington. For the past 5 years, the chain has been plagued with problems of high labor turnover, particularly with administrators, nursing directors, and nurse's aides. In some years this turnover has reached in excess of 50%. These problems generally have been more pronounced in central and southern California and Arizona, where 80% of the homes are located. Turnover is minimal in Washington and Oregon, and in northern California turnover is in the 30% range.

The study by AB&C has confirmed what Rolatel's senior management has long suspected: high turnover is affecting the bottom line through increased labor costs as well as increased regulatory problems. The study concluded that the staff at all levels were "alienated" from "corporate" and that they did not feel invested in the individual facilities or in the organization. The major suggestion from the consultants was that Rolatel move toward a more Japanese-style organization including having the local nursing home staff participate more in local decision making, giving local administrators and the director of nursing more control over their budgets, providing senior staff with significant stock ownership in the company, and finally, providing guaranteed employment after 5 years of satisfactory service with the company.

\* \* \*

QUESTIONS

1. What would be the advantages and disadvantages of such changes?
2. Is there a better alternative to reach the goals of reduced turnover, more employee buy-in, and better quality of care?
3. Can Rolatel implement a Japanese-style change in just the regions where there are problems, leaving alone those areas with fewer problems (such as Washington and Oregon)?

## CASE 5-14 | **A Prescription for Change**

After reading an article in a medical journal on medication problems in nursing homes, Myra Quinn, MD, the newly appointed medical director of the Wayside Home, a 200-bed skilled nursing facility, decided to undertake an evaluation of the drug usage situation at Wayside. Her study involved a review of drug and medical records of all the residents, most of whom are not her patients.

The results of her research were only slightly better than those reported in the literature: Close to 40% of the residents received at least one inappropriate medication. With these findings in hand, Quinn decided to embark on an educational program and sent the following letter to each physician on the home's medical staff.

*Wayside Skilled Nursing Facility*
*Snowville, State*

*Dear Colleague:*

*As you can see from the enclosed article, there is a serious problem with inappropriate drug-prescribing behavior in nursing homes. In response to this article, I reviewed the drug and medical records of each of our 200 residents, and I am sorry to report that we are doing about the same as the 12 homes reported in the study. What this means in practice is that we all need to be more careful about our prescribing habits. My research indicates that about 40% of our residents are getting drugs that they simply should not be receiving. It would be appreciated if you would review the enclosed article and also review your prescriptions for your patients in the home and make any adjustments as appropriate.*

*Thank you for your attention to this matter.*

\* \* \*

QUESTIONS

1. Are there likely issues with Quinn's research methodology?
2. Is the gross 40% inappropriate drug rate enough information?
3. In what other ways could Quinn have handled this issue?

4. What might be the implications of Quinn's memo for:
   a. Her relationship with the medical staff?
   b. Potential litigation?
   c. Resident/patient relations?

---

## CASE 5-15 | Off-Label Dilemma

> UNIVERSITY HOSPITALS MEMO
>
> From:     CEO
> To:       Deputy Director, Professional Service
> Subject:  Off-label drug use

As you know, as part of my orientation to my new position, I have been having meetings for the past few weeks with the various hospital department heads as well as clinical chairpersons.

Today I spent close to 4 hours with Dr. Vanessa Rubingrave, head of our pharmaceutical services and associate professor of pharmacology at the state university. In addition to the briefing on her department, operating budget, and likely future capital expenditures, she provided me with an extensive briefing on our use of off-label drugs. Their use appears to be most prevalent in the Washington Children's Hospital, the Adams Family Psychiatric Facility, the intensive care unit, and the Jefferson Cancer Institute.

There does not appear to be any institution-wide policy on off-label use. I am definitely concerned about this and would like you and your staff to look into this immediately.

\* \* \*

ASSIGNMENT

1. Prepare an institutional policy on off-label drug use. This policy must look into all aspects of the issue and provide a defensible rationale. Ultimately, the medical staff must approve the policy.

2. What objections to this policy do you anticipate? How can these objections be handled?
3. How can the administration be certain that the policy is being followed?
4. What remedies exist if the doctor chooses to operate outside the policy parameters?

---

| **CASE 5-16** | **Kratzkup** |

For the past 10 years, the Kratzkup Medical Center (KMC) has employed approximately 35 full-time physicians including hospitalists, radiologists, emergency department specialists, and primary care physicians in two hospital-based ambulatory care practices. Since the first MD was hired, there has been a debate about the proper compensation and system for compensation for these physicians. At this point, each individual physician, on an annual basis, negotiates his or her contract with the Senior Vice President of Medical Affairs. Traditionally this negotiation is rubber stamped by the CEO and the board. In every instance, the initial salary that a physician was hired at was based on supply and demand, and subsequent salaries tend to be merely cost-of-living increases unless someone threatens to leave and the senior vice president wants to retain this person. When that occurs, there is usually a bump up in the base pay.

Last year the CEO announced his retirement, and it now appears that the senior vice president will also retire when the new CEO takes over. During the interview process for CEO, one important question that was asked of all candidates was what they would do about physician pay in the future. Aileen Benmoshe, a successful candidate said the following, "Your present system is antiquated. Pay should be based on quality, productivity, and patient satisfaction. If I am selected, I will work with the new Senior Vice President of Medical Affairs to develop a better and more equitable system for paying our medical staff."

The board liked that response, and now that she has had time to settle in, they want to hear from her about the plan to change the physician payment system.

* * *

ASSIGNMENT

1. Prepare a presentation for Ms. Benmoshe on a proposed system for paying the medical staff that meets the objectives of being equitable and based on productivity, quality, and patient satisfaction. Consider the role of bonuses.
2. Once you have decided on a new plan, what steps will be necessary to implement the plan?
3. What objections should be expected with implementing the plan?
4. How will these objections be handled?

---

## CASE 5-17 | Caleb Roberts Medical Center

> MEMO
>
> From:    I. M. Angri, CEO
> To:        Associate Director, Professional Services
> Subject: Patient Safety

As you know, last week we had a case in which one of our medical staff mistakenly removed the breasts of a patient subsequent to a pathology report that turned out to be incorrect because the report was for a different patient. This matter is being handled in a variety of ways, but I think we need to implement a system to minimize all of these problems!

Based on some quick research, it seems that Dr. Gawande's (Brigham and Women's Hospital) concept of checklists needs to be implemented immediately in our surgical area. Many of his ideas have found their way onto the World Health Organization's Surgical Safety Checklist.

The essence of the Surgical Safety Checklist is that prior to the induction of anesthesia we verify the patient's identity, double-check the site that will be operated on, confirm that all machinery is operating properly (e.g., anesthesia machines and pulse oximeter), and check to see that the patient has no known allergies or conditions that will interfere with surgery or anesthesia. The second part of their checklist occurs before the first incision and ascertains that the team is present and that the procedure is clear, as are any potential problems. Afterward, there are postsurgical procedures to be checked.

Please review this immediately (on the WHO website) and let me know your thoughts on the following questions:

1. Do we need to develop our own customized checklists, or can we use the WHO checklist and modify as we go along?
2. How do we get buy-in from the physicians and nurses?
3. What costs might be associated with these checklists?
4. Who should lead the effort on this project?
5. How do we sustain a patient safety program?

\* \* \*

ASSIGNMENT

Respond to the CEO's questions.

---

## CASE 5-18  Child Pornography

Natalie Bamberg, CEO of Millville Hospital (a 176-bed facility), recently read a press release from U.S. Immigration and Customs Enforcement with the headline "Former hospital director sentenced to 10 years in child pornography case." As she read further, she learned that a 39-year-old man who was the Director of Case Management in a south Texas hospital was found to have more than 100 videos and 1,800 image files depicting child pornography on his home computers and related equipment. Nothing in the press release or other media suggested that pornography was found on his hospital equipment. This led Bamberg to send the following memo:

---

MEMO

From:     CEO
To:       Director, Information Technology; Associate
            Director, Professional Services; Chief, Security
            Department; and Director, Human Resources
Subject:  Integrity of our computer systems

---

As you are aware, our computer systems here at Millville are for transacting professional business only. Effective immediately, I want the following policies implemented:

1. Only hospital-owned devices are to be used on our network. NO PERSONAL DEVICES MAY BE CONNECTED TO OUR NETWORK AT ANY TIME!
2. Effective immediately, access to YouTube is blocked. I am not convinced that viewing it during business hours serves any useful purpose.
3. I am directing the IT department to arrange for the installation of key word and key site filters on our system as well as to upgrade all our firewalls.

All of the above are in the service of our patients and to ensure that our computer systems are used in an appropriate manner. If you have any questions about this, contact me.

\* \* \*

QUESTIONS

1. Is Ms. Bamberg overreacting?
2. Is this a good memo?
3. What types of questions is she likely to get?
4. Is her plan a good one?

## CASE 5-19 | MODHOME

The Victoria Life Center (VLC) is an umbrella nonprofit organization located on a beautiful 32-acre campus in a suburban community. Since its inception 40 years ago, it has been recognized as the premier provider of services to the elderly through its network of five off-campus day-care centers, two nursing homes (one off-campus), an assisted living center, a medical clinic, and most recently a 200-unit apartment house for independent living. This apartment house is not subsidized, offers one meal daily, and is limited to people who are at least 55 years old and older.

The CEO of the center, Bart Pearson, has been approached by Lila Samuels, the owner of a company named MODHOME. This company, which was started by Ms. Samuels, is in the business of modifying homes and apartments so that senior citizens can most easily continue to live in their own space. According to Ms. Samuels, the typical job has three phases: First, she or a member of her staff visits the elderly or disabled people in their homes and examines each space, including the kitchen, bathroom, bedroom, and living room, in order to determine how safe the space is and what modifications will make the home more conducive to healthy living. Second, modifications are made as determined by the inspection. Samuels went on to show the CEO a dozen photos of modifications that had been made, including lowering cabinets in a kitchen and cutting out some cabinetry so a woman in a wheelchair could easily use the sink and cutting area. Other examples involved grab-bars in a shower, a raised toilet, raised washing machine and dryer, and the entire redoing of a bathroom with a roll-in tub. Third, Samuels told the CEO that she also helps clients find devices that would make their lives easier, such as furniture risers, reacher devices, and knob turners.

As the conversation was coming to an end, Pearson told Ms. Samuels that he was intrigued by what MODHOME did and he was certain that such services were desperately needed in the community. Next, he asked her the obvious question: "Why are you sharing all of this with me?" Samuels replied, "I am looking for one of two things. I would like either to obtain your endorsement, which would certainly help with our marketing, or to enter into a joint venture with VLC to further develop our product line." Pearson said, "Let me think this over and I will get back to you next week."

* * *

QUESTIONS

1. Is MODHOME a legitimate business (in terms of what it offers)?
2. Does this seem to be an appropriate activity for VLC? How might it help or hinder VLC?
3. What issues might come up in a joint venture?
4. What would be your recommendation to Mr. Pearson? Why?

---

## CASE 5-20 | Lost Patient Data

> MEMO
>
> From:     CEO and Director, Information Technology
> To:       All department heads
> Subject:  Unauthorized computer usage

As you may have heard, in the past few years there have been numerous instances of patient information being made public, compromised, or otherwise not being maintained in the strictest confidence that is required.

For example, in 2010 the Children's Hospital in Stanford, California, learned that the medical records of more than 500 patients were missing when an employee stole a desktop computer. That incident resulted in a significant fine for the hospital.

Closer to home, Massachusetts General Hospital was fined a million dollars when a staff member lost records of almost 200 patients being treated for HIV. These papers were accidently left on the T (the Boston subway).

In our judgment, every day at this hospital someone takes home a computer or records that have patient information that could put us in a compromising position. Further, we are convinced that too many of our computers are left on and unattended, sometimes in easy view of probing eyes.

The security of all patient information must be a top priority at our hospital. Toward that end, we are implementing the following policy immediately:

## POLICY

1. No hospital-owned computer can be removed from the premises of the hospital without the express written approval of a department head.
   a. Security is hereby empowered to check the briefcases, backpacks, or other carry-in baggage/luggage of any employee or staff member entering or leaving the hospital premises. This includes every member of administration, the medical staff, and the nursing staff.
      i. In the event a hospital-owned computer is found (without authorization), it will be held by security until the next morning and turned over to the IT department for examination. In the event that patient information is found on the computer, disciplinary action will be taken.
   b. Staff members are personally responsible for securing their own computers when they are not at their workstations.
   c. No patient information may be transferred to any personal computer or device such as a flash drive.
2. Failure to follow these policies will result in disciplinary action, up to and including dismissal.

* * *

## QUESTIONS

1. Does this seem like a serious enough problem to warrant such a policy?
2. Is this a good policy? Why or why not?
3. What other ways exist to both deal with this issue and develop a new policy?

| CASE 5-21 | **The Luxtown Medical Center** |

The Luxtown Medical Center (LMC) is a 73-physician multi-specialty group practice with two locations in southern New England. Because of changing federal laws, the U.S. Supreme Court decision on pharmaceutical marketing in Vermont (*Sorrell v. IMS Health*), and the evolving strategies of drug companies, the executive committee of the group has held several discussions about relationships between physicians in the group and detailers. These discussions led to the following memo from the group's CEO:

---

MEMO

From:     Bob Rudyard, CEO, Luxtown Medical Center
To:       All physicians
Subject:  Pharmaceutical reps

---

As many of you know, for the past several months the executive committee has been discussing the issue of how we deal with drug detailers. On the one hand, they sometimes provide useful information, and on the other hand, they more often waste the time of the staff and sometimes the physicians. During my most active practice years, I always tried to maintain an arm's-length relationship with them and learn what was useful. Frankly, I did appreciate many of the samples that I dispensed to patients on a trial basis or in some cases to patients who could not afford prescribed medication.

On occasion, some companies have tried to be a strong influence, not through the lunches, donuts, pens, etc., but by hiring me to give dinner seminars. These sparsely attended events are designed to change your prescribing habits because of the preparation you need to do before the seminar and, of course, the honorarium attached to said seminar.

Today our concern should be the best interests of our patients. The committee is deeply concerned about the privacy of our patients as well as the confidentiality of our own decision making.

We do have an option of opting into the AMA Physician Data Restriction Program. If we choose to do this, all of our prescribing data will be withheld from the pharmaceutical sales people. Our next general meeting is in 2 weeks. I want to take a vote on this issue. In accordance with our bylaws, any vote will bind the entire medical group. In other words, we either all opt in or all opt out. I look forward to an interesting and lively discussion!

\* \* \*

QUESTIONS

1. What objections are likely to be raised about joining the data restriction program?
2. How is the current system of drug detailing of value?
3. What is in the best interest of the patient?
4. How can a group practice make effective use of what drug reps have to offer?

**CHAPTER 6**

# PLANNING

 **INTRODUCTION**

When thinking about planning, two famous quotes come to mind. The first is from the poem written in 1785 by Scotsman Robert Burns titled "To a Mouse on Turning Up Her Nest With a Plough"; Burns wrote, "The best laid schemes of mice and men gang at agley (go often askew)." The second quote is from the Bible, Psalm 33:10: "The Lord bringeth the counsels of nations to nought: He maketh the thoughts of the people to no effect." The second quote is often translated as "Man plans and God laughs."

Despite the pessimism—or perhaps cynicism—inherent in the previous quotes, it is still both imperative and often a legal requirement to plan and prepare. At an organizational level, planning is primarily concerned with the organization's need to survive and flourish in a competitive, often quagmire-like environment. All planning begins with a clear statement of organizational mission. Without a clear mission statement, the organization is going 75 miles per hour but does not know where it is headed. A mission statement clarifies the objectives necessary to accomplish the goal. For example, if one has a plan to be a physician, one's objectives could be as broad as graduating from college and getting into medical school. More immediately, one's objectives could be passing biology and organic chemistry. Finally, smart planning requires recognizing roadblocks, opportunities, and threats along the way and developing strategies to overcome those problems. Using the educational analogy one last time, a strategy might be to skip the party and study or perhaps hire a tutor to get through a critical course.

It should be emphasized that planning is an integral function of all management at all levels, not simply a function delegated to a special group of people labeled planners. Theoretically, the higher a person is on the organizational chart, the more time he or she should spend in that aspect of planning identified as strategic planning. While this is likely accurate, the unfortunate reality is that even the most senior executives still spend a good chunk of their time involved in day-to-day organizational management. Hopefully, though, they are thinking more about preventing fires than merely putting them out.

Planning is an activity that requires a synthesis of virtually all the skills within an organization, and strategic planning involves a probing analysis of organizational objectives, strengths, and weaknesses. It also must address organizational opportunities and organizational threats.

There are inherent difficulties in all aspects of planning. Problem number one is, who does it? Theoretically, planning ought to be an organizational effort. Because strategy and tactics are involved, however, the senior management staff (sometimes just the chief executive officer) often takes the responsibility for strategic planning, delegating subsets such as project planning, to subordinates. As noted earlier, it is easy to get caught up in the dynamics of the day-to-day running of the organization and not set aside the ideal planning time. In fact, a common criticism of strategic planning is that the senior executives do not give it sufficient thought, which leads to the second problem: continuity. To be successful, a strategy must have a certain element of continuity. Otherwise, the organization that is to implement the strategy is likely to provide more of a hindrance than help in the implementation.

All planning activities require an enormous amount of information and data. The subordinate problems here, of course, are the availability, timeliness, and quality of information. For example, how does an ambulatory care program determine the potential demand for its services? Census data are usually out of date, and it is difficult to get straight answers from physicians about their practices. Without actually undertaking an expensive and time-consuming survey, management is effectively forced to rely on informed guesses.

When it comes to a strategic planning process through which it is necessary to look at the strengths and weaknesses of the organization as well as the opportunities and threats (SWOT analysis), another set of problems arises. Specifically, who will evaluate the strengths and weaknesses of the organization? Analyzing strengths is always a pleasant and usually self-serving job, but what about the weaknesses? How does management say that the institution is losing its patient base because of a move to the suburbs that had been vehemently opposed by the board chairman? In less dramatic terms, how many organizations ever sit back to analyze their success? Or, for that matter, to what extent do they understand what success is for their organizations? In business organizations, success usually refers to the bottom line, or profit. An organization that cannot produce a profit is an organization that simply must leave the marketplace. In healthcare organizations, other than the few proprietary ones, the measure of success has never been profit. But what has it been? Prestige is one of the intangibles that healthcare organizations have striven toward, as is technical excellence. To some extent, survival has been a major goal in the last few years; although society is not asking many of its charitable organizations to make a profit, it certainly is saying, "Stop losing so much money." And, as noted at the beginning of this chapter, even publicly traded healthcare companies are not immune to organizational failure.

On the one hand, healthcare organizations must deal with a mystique about what they do; on the other hand, they must consider some realities, such as a payroll that must be met.

To complicate these basic considerations, healthcare organizations must also consider their role as socially responsible organizations. These responsibilities have many dimensions; for example, they have a responsibility toward the overall financial well-being of the nation; toward patients, medical staff, and personnel employed by the organization; and toward the community.

At one time, a hospital in a small upstate New York town took upon itself an interesting social responsibility. For many years, it operated the only food service facility in the area that was open to the public 24 hours a day. In the early hours of the morning, not only were the late-night workers at the hospital, but also a range of others, including local police and late-night partygoers.

According to the hospital's administrator at the time, the hospital felt a special responsibility toward the community, and opening the cafeteria to the community 24/7 was one way to meet that responsibility.

A more dramatic example comes from a New Jersey hospital that was in the process of closing down patient rooms because of a decline in census. In the interest of good management, such cutbacks would normally result in staff layoffs. In this case, however, there were no layoffs because the hospital was concerned about the economic implications to its community if 100 people were unemployed. Here again can be seen the reality facing the healthcare organization; it is both a social organization with special responsibilities because of what it does as its daily work and an economic organization with a vast influence on the total economic system because of the resources it commands. The point is emphasized by the fact that, in many parts of the United States, health services may be the largest industry in town.

An organization interested in strategic planning would have considered a range of basic issues in this case, such as its definition of success, its view of its social responsibility, and, most importantly, its objectives. In the business sense, this would answer the fundamental question: What business are we in and why?

The cases in this chapter provide a range of opportunities to consider a variety of planning issues as well as the impact the regulatory schemes have on that planning.

The final case in this chapter is titled Obituary. It is perhaps rather unusual as far as casebooks go in that it asks the reader to review several obituaries and then write one's own obituary. The three obituaries presented are the slightly altered versions of the lives of real healthcare administrators. Perhaps in seeing how people lived their lives, each of us can make plans about how we would like to live our own!

---

## CASE 6-1 | Tsunami

On March 11, 2011, a devastating tsunami inundated the coastal town of Rikuzentakata, Japan, destroying most of the houses, businesses, and the Takata hospital. Of the 23,000 residents of the town, one-third of whom were over age 65, it appears that as many as 10,000 people might have died.

The loss of the hospital and many staff has presented ongoing problems with the care of the remaining citizens, most of whom are not interested in relocating.

* * *

ASSIGNMENT

Assume you have been called by an international agency and asked to provide the town of Rikunzentakata with consulting assistance on rebuilding its local health system.

1. What data do you need before making your recommendations?
2. What information do you need about the Japanese health system and the role of hospitals before issuing your report?
3. What changes in the health system have occurred that will likely influence your recommendations?
4. What is your initial impression about what should be on the table for consideration?

---

## CASE 6-2 | Hospital Disaster Plan

Assume the following:

1. You are a consultant to the new CEO of a 180-bed community hospital that has a catchment area of 110,000 people. The CEO has asked you to look into the issue of disaster planning.
2. To the west the nearest hospital, a tertiary care facility, is 47 miles away and can be reached only by a two-lane road that oftentimes is snow covered in the winter and can also be dangerous in other inclement weather.
3. To the south there is an 84-bed community hospital, 9 miles away, and a tertiary medical center 23 miles away. There is an interstate highway running north and south.
4. To the north the closet hospital is 18 miles away, and it is a 91-bed community hospital.
5. To the east the closest hospital, which can be reached only by a two-lane road that is often snow covered in winter, is 31 miles away.

Although the hospital and community have not experienced any disasters that have caused the hospital to activate the disaster plan, you are convinced, based on your experiences during Hurricane Katrina (when you worked at a hospital in New Orleans), that it is essential that disaster plans are current and functional.

The CEO is particularly concerned about the following issues:

1. Freeing up beds in case of massive disaster
2. Transferring patients
3. Staffing all shifts
4. Housing and feeding staff
5. Triage
6. Record keeping
7. Chain of command
8. Communications—internal and external
9. Legal issues

You have just reviewed the hospital disaster plan standard operating guidelines from the state of Wisconsin and now wish to present a proposal to the new CEO about his hospital's disaster preparedness. Based on your review of the Wisconsin document and other relevant material, what will be the focus of your presentation?

---

## CASE 6-3   Certificate of Need

A majority of U.S. states have some type of certificate of need (CON) legislation that requires various healthcare providers to obtain governmental approval prior to embarking on a range of projects. This case focuses on the state of Connecticut. A copy of the Connecticut policies and procedures on certificate of need[1] is presented here, as well as several determination of need (DON) scenarios.

\* \* \*

1. http://www.ct.gov/dph/lib/dph/ohca/lawsandregspdf/policiesproceduresforpublicact10-179final10-25-10.pdf

ASSIGNMENT

1. Read the Connecticut CON policies (following DON scenarios).
2. Review the DON scenarios and determine whether a CON is required in the following four situations.

## Determination 1

A surgeon who has been doing outpatient surgery in his office, which is not licensed as an outpatient surgical center, wishes to open a new office with an operating room.

## Determination 2

A for-profit substance abuse center has a contract with the state department of motor vehicles for the provision of substance abuse services. The center now wishes to expand its business to provide substance abuse services to the state adult probation department.

## Determination 3

A nonprofit community-based cancer center that is a consortium of nonprofit hospitals wishes to acquire a CT simulator. Presently it has a conventional (non-CT simulator).

## Determination 4

A urologist wishes to acquire extracorporeal shock wave lithotripsy equipment for his office.

## CERTIFICATE OF NEED, STATE OF CONNECTICUT POLICIES AND PROCEDURES FOR IMPLEMENTATION OF PUBLIC ACT 10-179 §§87, 89-93

These policies and procedures shall govern the implementation of Public Act 10-179 §§ 87, 89-93. In accordance with Public Act 10-179, the Department of Public Health is adopting these interim policies and procedures to administer the certificate of need process under Public Act 10-179, until official regulations are adopted by the General Assembly. Accordingly, the policies and procedures set forth below supersede the current Office of Health Care Access (OHCA) Administrative Regulations. Additionally, in light of the merger of OHCA with DPH in September 2009, the Rules of Practice for DPH at 19a-9-1 et. seq. applies to OHCA.

## I. DEFINITIONS

(1) "Acquisition" as used in subdivisions (8), (9), and (11) of subsection (a) of section 19a-638 of the general statutes means the acquisition through purchase, lease, donation, or other comparable arrangement of a computed tomography scanner, magnetic resonance imaging scanner, positron emission tomography scanner, positron emission tomography-computed tomography scanner, linear accelerator, or equipment that utilizes technology that has not previously been utilized in the state.

(2) "Central Service Facility" means a healthcare facility or institution, person, or entity engaged primarily in providing services for the prevention, diagnosis, or treatment of human health conditions, serving one or more healthcare facilities, practitioners, or institutions and satisfying the criteria for a central service facility as discussed in section II, Criteria for Determining if an Entity is a Central Service Facility.

(3) "Freestanding Emergency Department" means an emergency department that is not located on the main campus of a hospital and is held out to the public (by name, posted signs, advertising, or other means) as a place that provides care for emergency medical conditions on an urgent basis without requiring a previously scheduled appointment.

(4) "Interventional cardiology" means non-surgical procedures used in the treatment of coronary artery and peripheral vascular disease and performed in the cardiac catheterization laboratory. Procedures include, but are not limited to, angioplasty, valvuloplasty, cardiac ablation, coronary thrombectomy, and congenital heart defect correction. Only those procedures that are authorized pursuant to a Certificate of Need may be performed by a healthcare facility or provider, and several procedures may be authorized under one Certificate of Need.

A facility that is authorized to provide open heart surgery is authorized to provide all of the above procedures.

(5) "Provider" means any person or entity that provides health-care services.

(6) "Psychiatric residential treatment facility" means a psychiatric residential treatment facility as defined in 42 CFR 483.352.

## II. CRITERIA FOR DETERMINING IF AN ENTITY IS A CENTRAL SERVICE FACILITY

(a) An entity shall be a central service facility if it meets one or more of the following criteria: (1) The entity is institutional in nature and practice; (2) Patient care is or will be the responsibility of the facility rather than of the individual physician, physicians, practitioner, or practitioners; (3) Nonmedical personnel, owners, or managers can or will be able to influence the operation of the entity to a significant degree; (4) There are physicians from one or more physician practices, partnerships, or corporations who practice or will practice there or who will control a business involving health services; (5) The physician or practitioner is not practicing medicine in the area of his expertise and training or does not hold a Connecticut license to practice medicine; and (6) A partnership with general and managing partners exists.

(b) Additional considerations: In determining whether a particular entity meets any of the criteria in subsection (a) (1) through (6), the commissioner, commissioner's designee, or deputy commissioner may consider the following: (1) The entity is or will be licensed or designated as any type of healthcare facility or institution by the department; (2) the patients have no prior familiarity with the physician or practitioner or any ongoing relationship with the physician or practitioner; (3) services such as laboratory, pharmacy, x-ray, linear accelerator, and imaging are or will be available with no free choice of the provider of such services by the patient; (4) the entity can continue to function even if the license of its physician or physicians has, have been, or might be suspended or revoked, since the entity can simply retain another physician or practitioner; (5) bills and charges are or will be determined by the entity rather than the individual physician, physicians, practitioner, or practitioners who provided the care or the service; (6) income distribution is or will be determined by the entity rather than entirely by the physician, physicians, practitioner, or practitioners who provided the care of service; (7) there are present interlocking relationships, corporate relationships, or entities with other health-related corporate relationships, entities, or properties; (8) the location and services provided are a small part of a larger entity; and (9) any other information the officer deems relevant or pertinent.

## III. INCREASE IN OPERATING ROOMS

Any outpatient surgical facility that increases its operating rooms on and after October 1, 2010, shall file a notification with the office indicating the date on which the operating room was added, the number of operating rooms added, and the total number of operating rooms including the new operating room(s).

## IV. REPLACEMENT OF IMAGING EQUIPMENT

Any healthcare facility, person, or provider that replaces equipment shall notify the office of the date on which the equipment was replaced and the disposition of the replaced equipment pursuant to subdivision (18) of subsection (b) of section 19a-638 of the general statutes. The notification shall also include the docket number of the certificate of need or certificate of need determination, and the office shall place the notification in the original file for that docket number.

## V. DETERMINATIONS

All requests for determinations shall be submitted to the office on a determination form, which is available on the office's website. The office will not review a request for determination until a complete form has been submitted and all required information has been provided to the office. Requests for determination may be submitted electronically in PDF format or via facsimile.

## VI. PUBLIC NOTIFICATION OF A CERTIFICATE OF NEED APPLICATION

Pursuant to section subdivision (b) of section 19a-639a of the general statutes, not later than 20 days prior to the submission of a certificate of need, the applicant shall publish notice that an application is to be submitted in a newspaper having substantial circulation in the area where the project is to be located.

The notification must contain at least the following information: (1) The applicant is applying for a certificate of need pursuant to section 19a-638 of the general statutes; (2) a description of the scope and nature of the project; (3) the street address where the project is to be located; and (4) the total capital expenditure for the project.

## VII. NEWSPAPERS WITH SUBSTANTIAL CIRCULATION IN TOWN WHERE PROJECT IS TO BE LOCATED

A list of towns in Connecticut and the corresponding newspapers of substantial circulation in each town are available on the office's website. The office will update the list as necessary.

## VIII. CERTIFICATE OF NEED APPLICATION

(a) The application shall consist of the following:

(1) Copies of the notices of the certificate of need application demonstrating that such notice was published for at least 3 days in a newspaper having substantial circulation in the town in which the project is going to be located pursuant to subsection (b) of section 19a-639a of the general statutes.

(2) A description of the project setting forth the proposal in as much detail as possible. The description should reference the applicable subdivision under subsection (a) of section 19a-638 of general statutes.

(3) The specific location of the facility, service, or equipment.

(4) A detailed description of how the proposal satisfies each of the guidelines and principles enumerated in section 19a-639 of the general statutes and any supporting documentation.

(5) All other information as required by the specific application form, which is available on the office's website. The application form should be filled out in its entirety and all supporting documents should be attached to the application and referenced as either an attachment or exhibit in the order in which they appear in the application.

(6) Application forms for specific types of proposals are available and may be downloaded from the office's website.

(a) Establishment of a new healthcare facility as defined in section 19a-630.

(b) Establishment of an outpatient surgical facility.

(c) Establishment of a freestanding emergency department.

(d) Transfer of ownership of a healthcare facility.

(e) Termination of inpatient or outpatient mental health or substance service by a short-term acute care general hospital or children's hospital.

(f) Termination of an emergency department by a short-term acute care general hospital.

(g) Establishment of cardiac services.

(h) Acquisition of any of the equipment enumerated in subdivisions.

(i) Increase in licensed bed capacity; and

(j) Increase in operating rooms by an outpatient surgical facility pursuant to subdivision (12) of subsection (a) of the section 19a-638 of the general statutes.

(b) One original and four copies of the application shall be submitted to the office at 410 Capitol Avenue, MS#13HCA, Hartford, CT 06134. The application shall be accompanied by the $500 filing fee pursuant to subsection (a) of section 19a-639a of the general statutes. If the application including attachments or exhibits does not exceed 50 pages, it may be filed electronically in accordance with subsection (c) of this section.

(c) Applications of less than 50 pages may be filed electronically in PDF format. All applications exceeding 50 pages must be filed in accordance with subsection (b) of this section.

(d) Applications shall be deemed received on the date and time at which the office receives the document or the complete electronic version of the document. Any documents received after normal business hours shall be deemed received on the following business day.

## IX. CERTIFICATE OF NEED, COMPLETENESS REVIEW

(a) Pursuant to subsection (c) of section 19a-639a, the office shall have 30 days to review the application and request additional information as necessary to complete the application. The applicant shall have 60 days from the date of the request to provide responses to the completeness questions. Said responses may be filed electronically in PDF format or via facsimile. If the applicant fails to respond within the 60-day time frame, the application shall be deemed withdrawn in accordance with subsection (c) of section 19a-639a.

(b) Upon receipt of the responses, the office shall have 30 days to review the responses and make a determination with respect to whether the application is complete or if further information is needed. If additional information is sought, the applicant will have another 60 days to respond. If the applicant fails to respond within the 60-day time frame, the application shall be deemed withdrawn in accordance with subsection (c) of section 19a-639a.

(c) The review cycle described above shall continue until the office deems an application complete.

## X. CERTIFICATE OF NEED, REVIEW PERIOD

(a) The review period will begin on the date on which the office publishes notice on its website that the application is complete with subsection (d) of section 19a-639a of the general statutes. The office shall publish notice on its website as expeditiously as possible and in no instance more than 7 days beyond the expiration of the 30-day review period. Additionally, the office shall provide notice that the application is complete to the applicant via first class mail, facsimile, or electronic mail. The notice to the applicant shall also notify the applicant of the date on which the review period expires. The notice on the website shall serve as notice to any interested members of the public.

(b) Extensions of the Review Period:

    (1) The office may extend the review period for good cause as defined in section 19a-630-1 of the Regulations of Connecticut State Agencies for a total of 60 days in

accordance with subsection (d) of section 19a-639a of the general statutes.

(2) Where a public hearing is held pursuant to subsections (e) or (f) of section 19a-639a of the general statutes, the review period will be extended for another 60 days beyond the date of the hearing.

## XI. NOTICE OF PUBLIC HEARING

The office shall provide notice of the date, time, and place of the public hearing in a newspaper having substantial circulation in the town in which the project is to be located 2 weeks prior to the date of the hearing pursuant to subsection (f) of section 19a-639a of the general statutes. The office shall also provide a copy of the notice via first class mail, facsimile, or electronic mail to the applicant and any individuals or entities that have requested a hearing pursuant to subsection (g) of section 19a-639a of the general statutes.

Additionally, the office shall post the notice of public hearing on its website.

## XII. VOIDANCE AND EXTENSION OF CERTIFICATE OF NEED

(a) A certificate of need shall be void 2 years from the date of issuance by the office unless the applicant has requested an extension of the certificate of need at least 30 days in advance of the expiration of the certificate of need pursuant to subsection (b) of section 19a-639b of the general statutes.

(b) At a minimum, a request for an extension of a certificate of need shall contain the following:

(1) A detailed description of any change in the cost, configuration, services, or scope of the project.

(2) A detailed description and documentation of any progress on the project including preparation of construction drawings, securing of necessary funds and building permits, and commencement of any construction.

(3) An estimated timetable for commencement and completion of all remaining components of the project.

(4) Documentation of an extenuating circumstance, including, but not limited to, delays occasioned by negotiations

with vendors or contractors, beyond the control of the applicant that prevented the applicant from completing the project by the expiration date.

(c) The following criteria shall be used to determine whether an extension will be granted to the applicant.

(1) Site procurement: The applicant must have made progress toward permanent acquisition of the intended site for the project.

(2) Financial status: The applicant must be able to provide documentation regarding finalizing any necessary loans or lease purchase arrangements.

(3) The applicant must provide reasonable assurance that the project will be under construction or implemented within the requested extension time frame.

## XIII. NON-TRANSFERABILITY OF THE CERTIFICATE OF NEED

A certificate of need is non-transferable. A certificate of need or rights thereunder may not be sold, assigned, leased, transferred, mortgaged, or pledged. Any attempt to transfer a certificate of need shall result in the immediate voidance of the certificate of need.

## XIV. RELOCATION OF A HEALTHCARE FACILITY

Pursuant to section 19a-639c of the general statutes, any healthcare facility that proposes to relocate its facility shall submit a request for determination. A form for the relocation of a healthcare facility is available on the office's website.

Based upon the information submitted by the applicant, the office shall determine whether there has been substantial change in the payer mix or the population served by the healthcare facility that proposes to relocate. The applicant shall provide the percentages of total patient volume by payer source prior to the relocation and following the relocation.

## XV. RELOCATION WITHIN THE SAME TOWN

For a relocation of a healthcare facility within the same town, the office shall not require the submission of information concerning the payer mix or population served as it will be presumed that the proposed relocation will not result in a substantial change in the payer mix or population served. Accordingly, no determination is required for relocation of a healthcare facility within the same town.

## XVI. CERTIFICATE NEED FOR RELOCATION

Any healthcare facility that proposes to relocate its facility and is unable to demonstrate to the satisfaction of the office that the relocation will not result in a substantial change in the payer mix or population served shall file a certificate of need for the establishment of a new healthcare facility pursuant to subdivision (1) of subsection (a) of section 19a-638 of the general statutes.

## XVII. TERMINATION OF A HEALTHCARE FACILITY

(a) Any healthcare facility that was authorized through a certificate of need shall provide notice that it is terminating services not later than 60 days prior to the termination. The notification shall contain the following: (1) the name and location of the healthcare facility; (2) reasons for closing the facility; (3) other facilities where patients will be able to obtain the services that are currently provided by the facility; and (4) date on which the facility will be closed.

(b) Any healthcare facility that was not authorized through a certificate of need and intends to close the facility shall notify the office not later than 60 days prior to the termination of the facility. The notification shall contain the following: (1) The name and location of the healthcare facility; (2) reason for closing the facility; (3) other facilities where patients may obtain the services that are currently provided by the facility; and (4) date on which the services will no longer be provided or on which the facility will be closed.

## XVIII. TERMINATION OF SERVICES PROVIDED BY A HEALTH-CARE FACILITY

(a) Any healthcare facility that intends to terminate services which were authorized pursuant to a certificate of need shall file a modification of the original certificate of need on the forms available on the office's website. The applicant shall provide the following information to the office: (1) The service(s) that the facility will no longer provide; (2) reasons that the facility will no longer provide the service(s); (3) other facilities where the patients can obtain the service(s) which the facility will no longer provide; and (4) date on which the service(s) will be terminated.

(b) Any healthcare facility that intends to terminate a service which was not authorized pursuant to a certificate of need shall notify the office not later than 60 days prior to the termination of the service. The notification shall contain the following: (1) The service(s) that the facility will no longer provide; (2) reasons that the facility will no longer provide the service(s); (3) other facilities where the patient may obtain the service(s) which the facility will no longer provide; and (4) date on which the service(s) will be terminated.

## XIX. RULES OF PRACTICE

The Office of Health Care Access Division of the Department of Public Health shall follow the Rules of Practice under section 19a-9-1, et seq.

## XX. NOTIFICATION OF A CIVIL PENALTY

The commissioner or the commissioner's designee, prior to the imposition of any civil penalty under this section, shall notify any facility, institution, or person subject to such civil penalty in accordance with subsection (b) of section 19a-653 of the general statutes.

## XXI. CIVIL PENALTY–REQUEST FOR HEARING

Pursuant to subsection (c) of section 19a-653, any healthcare facility or person to whom the notice of civil penalty was addressed may request a hearing to contest the imposition of the civil penalty. Upon receipt of the request, the office shall have 10 days to notify the facility, institution, or person of the date, time, and place of the hearing.

## XXII. CIVIL PENALTY–REQUEST FOR EXTENSION OF TIME

(a) A request for an extension of time within which to file required data or information shall contain the following: (1) the reasons why the healthcare facility or person was unable to comply with the original due date; and (2) the date on which the information or data will be filed.

(b) In reviewing the request for an extension of time, the office shall consider the following: (1) any extenuating circumstances that prevented compliance with the original due date; (2) demonstration of a good-faith effort to comply with the appropriate statute, act, order, or regulations; (3) past history of compliance with the submission of data or information requirements; (4) length of the delay in filing; (5) degree of incompleteness or inaccuracy; and (6) any other relevant criteria.

(c) If the request for a time extension is granted, it shall be granted to a date certain. Failure to submit the required data or information by that extended date may result in the imposition of a civil penalty from the day after the extended due date onward. The civil penalty shall become effective at the expiration of the time extension, and OHCA shall provide notice of the same to the person or healthcare facility.

## XXIII. RESCISSION OF CIVIL PENALTY

Upon receipt of the data or information or the filing of a certificate of need, the office may rescind the civil penalty in whole or in part.

## XXIV. PUBLIC INFORMATION

The public may inspect the regulations, decisions, and all public records of the Office of Health Care Access at its office. Written requests for public information shall be filed on the FOI request forms available on the office's website.

## Certificate of Need Requirements and Exemptions for Physicians

### CON Required

- Related information
- Acquisition of imaging equipment
- General statutes § 19a-638 (a) (8) & (9):
  - Includes CT scanners, MRI scanners, PET scanners, PET/CT scanners, and non-hospital based linear accelerators
  - Acquisition of equipment utilizing technology that has not previously been utilized in the state
- General statutes § 19a-638 (a) (11):
  - Generally does not apply to x-ray, mammography, ultrasound, or cineangiography equipment as those types of equipment do not require CON authorization

### No CON Required

- Related information
- Replacement of existing imaging equipment
- General statutes § 19a-638 (b) (18):
  - Provider shall notify OHCA of the date on which the equipment was replaced, the disposition of the replaced equipment, and the docket number for the original CON or CON determination
  - Acquisition of cone beam CT scanner
- General statutes § 19a-638 (b) (19):
  - Must be used exclusively by a dentist licensed by DPH
  - Establishment of offices by a licensed private practitioner whether for individual or group practice
- General statutes § 19a-638 (b) (2):
  - CON required if establishing a healthcare facility such as an outpatient surgical facility or freestanding emergency department or if acquiring imaging equipment

## CASE 6-4 | Greenbridge Medical Complex

### BACKGROUND

Alfred Newman, Chairman of the Greenbridge Corporation, a major builder of commercial property including shopping centers and office buildings, is a longtime trustee of the Lakeview Medical Center (LMC) in North Metropolis, an affiliate of the University Medical School. LMC is the parent corporation of four hospitals totaling 1,125 beds in four suburban locations and a 500-physician multispecialty group practice that operates out of more than 40 locations. Shortly after a board meeting where Kent Clarkson, CEO of LMC, presented a less than optimistic picture of the medical center's ability to increase market share or improve its finances, Newman asked to schedule a private meeting with Clarkson.

During the meeting, which took place at the members-only Metropolis Union Club, Newman broached the idea of a joint venture between Greenbridge and LMC. The proposed plan called for Greenbridge to finance and build approximately 10 physician centers (medical office buildings) that would carry the LMC name and would be located in communities where LMC had minimal presence. Newman's idea was that these centers would be leased to a combination of LMC physicians operating satellite offices as physician groups presently operating in the communities where the offices were being built. Additionally, each building would have a host of ancillary services such as labs, radiology, ultrasound, and rehabilitation services associated with or owned by LMC. In order to get local physician groups into the new buildings, Newman proposed that an arrangement be worked out where LMC would subsidize the rent of local physician groups for 30 months. Clarkson liked the proposal and detailed one of his subordinates to work with the Greenbridge Corporation to develop a comprehensive package for the approval of the trustees. Three months later the package was ready, distributed to the trustees, and at the next board meeting approved.

## THE FIRST BUILDING

The plan that was approved by the LMC board was to begin by building the first physician center as a prototype and to open it in Oak Bluffs, 21 miles north of LMC's flagship hospital, an area where LMC has traditionally had poor market penetration due to competition from the 193-bed Oak Bluffs Community Hospital (OBCH). Anticipating potential objections from OBCH, particularly after they had rejected overtures to merge with LMC 5 years earlier, Greenbridge set up a new corporation to purchase an available tract of land for the medical office building. The land is less than a mile from Oak Bluffs Community Hospital. Within a few days of the land purchase, Wayne Debruse, CEO of OBCH, learned that Greenbridge and LMC were behind the purchase and that they intended to build a physician center. Additionally, Debruse learned that three physician groups in Oak Bluffs were engaged in negotiations with Greenbridge to lease two floors of the proposed building.

## THE OAK BLUFFS COMMUNITY HOSPITAL BOARD MEETING

Upon learning of the Greenbridge–LMC plan, Debruse called an emergency meeting of his board. At that meeting, he presented his board with the background information about the medical office building project and stated the following:

"I think we have a serious problem on the horizon. Greenbridge seems to be expanding into our area with a joint operation involving Lakeview Medical Center. There is no question in my mind that this is a huge threat to our hospital and that we need to launch a campaign that will prevent this building from being built in our community. This campaign needs to involve the commissioners of our town and the community in general. Although it's going to cost us a lot of money in terms of PR as well as legal expenses to fight the Greenbridge–LMC alliance, it is imperative that we do this. If we don't, I believe that we will be forced to either downsize our hospital or merge with LMC. I do not believe this building is in the interest of our community, our medical staff, or our patients. Today I am asking for your approval to both launch a campaign against this project and fund that campaign."

After 2 hours of discussion, Debruse's request was approved and the fight against the building began.

* * *

QUESTIONS

1. Assume you are Kent Clarkson, CEO of LMC. What objections to this plan do you anticipate from the Oak Bluffs Hospital? Oak Bluffs general community? Your medical staff?

2. Assume you are the Oak Bluffs medical staff. How do you plan to deal with these objections?

3. Assume you are Wayne Debruse. Why would you object to the building of a new medical office building in your community? Is the project really a threat to the hospital? Is it possible that the project may be good for the health of the community? What can you possibly do to stop the project?

4. Should either party be concerned about their actions being perceived as antitrust violations?

---

## CASE 6-5   Koffee Klub

No one seems to know how it all got started, but what is affectionately known as the Koffee Klub has been in existence at the 150-bed Gremlin Hospital for more than 30 years. There is nothing formal about the Klub except that it occurs between 10:00 AM and 10:45 AM in the main hospital cafeteria (a time when the cafeteria is ostensibly closed for cleanup and luncheon preparation). The Klub meeting occurs at the same set of tables, and the people who drift in and out are all members of senior and middle management, senior nursing staff, and physicians (around 30 people per day). Everyone helps himself or herself to coffee provided by the food service staff, and on sporadic occasions there are Danish or donuts.

Over the years, the Klub has served as an informal vehicle for communications, ironing out problems and developing a sense of community among people who commonly work together but don't socialize.

The retirement of Harry Bird, a longtime administrator, has caused the board of trustees to look for a new administrator who would tighten up the organization and trim costs. The person they selected, Molly McGee, is the former Vice President of Finance from a successful midsized lawnmower manufacturing company. Although McGee has no experience in health care, she is confident about her managerial skills and feels that Gremlin is ripe for an overhaul. One of her first orders is the elimination of the Koffee Klub, which she estimates will save $750 per year in direct costs and $150,000 per year in lost productivity.

* * *

QUESTIONS

1. What assumptions are being made to come up with these numbers?
2. Are these real or imagined savings?
3. Is the Klub of any value? If so, how can that be quantified?
4. Is McGee making a mistake? If so, how could she rectify her mistake?

---

## CASE 6-6 | Electronic Medical Record

Myron "Mick" Mowse is the founder, CEO, and majority stockholder of Mowse Health, a 27-facility, for-profit regional chain of nursing homes based in Fort Lauderdale, Florida. Mowse Health operates in the largest cities of five neighboring states. The homes total 3,400 beds and are generally well staffed and well regarded. Although they use some electronic systems for recording their nursing activities for reimbursement purposes, they have not yet developed an electronic medical record that integrates financial and clinical information.

Because of the various developments in the federal government with regard to health care, Mowse is convinced that within the near future some form of accountable care organizations will come into being and that the hospital will play an even more central role from a financial perspective. At a recent senior staff meeting, Mowse stated he wants to move ahead at warp speed developing an integrated medical and financial record that provides the individual facility with every conceivable bit of information about each resident, such as the cost of every treatment and the effectiveness of the treatment. Mowse's Chief Financial Officer and a significant shareholder of the company, his sister Mina, disagrees with him. She thinks that the idea of the Mowse chain developing from scratch an integrated electronic medical record is daffy. Her opinion is that Mowse Health should either adapt the electronic medical record marketed by Company A, which presently has the largest share of the nursing home market (about 15%), or work with two separate vendors—Company B, which has the hospital electronic market cornered in three of the five cities where Mowse operates, or Company C, which controls the hospital electronic record market in the other two cities where Mowse is operating. However, there is a problem with Companies B and C. Although they both have well-developed electronic medical records for hospitals, they are still in the development stages of their electronic medical records for nursing homes. However, they are both interested in working with Mowse on the development of a record.

\* \* \*

QUESTIONS

1. Are there any significant questions that the Mowse organization needs to consider before going ahead with any developments?
2. What are the costs and benefits of each of the Mowse alternatives?
3. What is your recommendation and why?

## CASE 6-7 | House Calls

At a recent meeting of the strategic planning committee of the board of trustees of County Wide Memorial Medical System (CWM), it was suggested that the management of the system investigate the possibility of developing a house calls department.

This idea has the enthusiastic support of the board's president, who was influenced by an article in the *New York Times* (December 5, 2011) that argued that house calls are a good way to offer less expensive and more personal care to the chronically ill. The chairman, who is 80-years-old, also seemed to have fond memories of the days when doctors made house calls throughout the county. Additionally, the board treasurer lived for 5 years in Cowbridge, Wales, a short distance from Cardiff, and he recalled that physicians in Wales routinely made house calls.

Emily Jacobs, CWM's chief executive officer, is generally supportive of this idea, but she does have some serious reservations. Her own background as a clinical nurse practitioner in the inner city has clearly sensitized her to the importance of the home environment in determining the quality of care. Additionally, years prior to joining the CWM staff she worked near Chinatown in San Francisco, where she was exposed to the On Lok program that later gave rise to the government's Program of All-Inclusive Care for the Elderly (PACE). Finally, Ms. Jacobs is knowledgeable about the U.S. Centers for Medicare and Medicaid Services's Independence at Home Demonstration Program, for which CWM did not apply.

\* \* \*

QUESTIONS

1. Ms. Jacobs has commissioned you to develop a position paper on the costs and benefits of their 500-bed acute care general hospital developing a home care service. Specifically, she wants to know what the staffing would be, assuming all the patients were on Medicare (part A and B).
2. What are the implications for hospital admissions?
3. What other issues would likely arise?

## CASE 6-8 | Clanghorn's Future

Last year the 96-bed Clanghorn Memorial Hospital (CMH) celebrated its 100th anniversary with 3 months of festivities including a black tie dinner at the American Legion Post and a parade at which more than 1,500 people who had been born at the hospital marched down Main Street. All of these activities, though, including the nostalgia about the centrality of the hospital in the community, mask a few realities. There is a continuing decline in hospital census to a point now where the average daily census is approximately 51 patients. The hospital barely squeaked through the last accreditation survey because of problems with the hospital's physical plant. The hospital has been losing money for the past 5 years, and fund raising is down 43%. Although the hospital has a monopoly in the community, its in-patient business has been steadily eroded by the State University Medical Center, which is 25 miles away. This erosion is a product of both technology and the physical plant. The technological issue is a critical one for CMH because it continually has trouble raising the funds for new technology as well as the staff to run the technology. Further, its catchment area is generally too small to support cutting-edge technology but too large and sophisticated to do without.

Within the past week, confidential preliminary discussions have begun between CMH and the State University Medical Center regarding a takeover. If this occurred the plan would be for the CMH to be torn down and the land sold to developers, with the money placed into a foundation to benefit the new CMH division of the State University Medical Center. The new CMH would be a 35-bed primary care hospital with an extensive ambulatory care center. CMH would be located approximately 2 miles from the present CMH site on the Clanghorn Campus of the State University.

\* \* \*

QUESTION

Assume word has leaked about these preliminary discussions, and the CEO of CMH has asked you to prepare a press release about this situation. What arguments for and against this preliminary plan can be anticipated?

## CASE 6-9 | The Playground

A donor has approached Peter Piper of the Peck Geriatric Center (PGC) with the following proposal.

He would like to donate $35,000 to the PGC for the purpose of building a children's playground on the grounds of the center. He would like the playground to be a place for grandchildren and great grandchildren of residents to gather and sit outside during a visit to the center.

\* \* \*

ASSIGNMENT

Piper is inclined to accept the offer, but before going ahead he would like your analysis of the costs and benefits of this proposal.

## CASE 6-10 | Rural Telemedicine Grant

Marcus Welby, CEO of Green Valley Hospital, recently had a meeting with some of his younger medical staff (all family physicians), and they urged him to try to find funding for a telemedicine project that would be used for several services now covered by physicians who visit the hospital twice a month. The particular services of concern to the physicians were cardiology, neurology, psychiatry and dermatology. Through his contacts, Welby learned that the Star Valley Medical Center in Afton, Wyoming, had received a $191,925 telemedicine development grant from the U.S. Department of Agriculture's Distance Learning and Telemedicine Program. The Star Valley Medical Center is located in a rural community about half the size of Green Valley. It is a facility with 20 beds and 25 nursing-home beds compared with Green Valley's 47 beds and no nursing-home beds. Green Valley is located in a town of 3,700 people and is 87 miles from the nearest large town with 39,000 people and a 150-bed hospital. Like Star Valley, Green Valley is located in rural Wyoming.

\* \* \*

ASSIGNMENT

You have been hired as a consultant to Green Valley to look into the feasibility of developing the telemedicine services that interest the medical staff. Prepare a short report about the following:

1. The theoretical cost/benefit of telemedicine.
2. Possible sources of funding and the application process—with particular attention to the Helmsley Trust and the U.S. Department of Agriculture.

---

| CASE 6-11 | **Graham-Kracker Hospital** |

The CEO sent the following memo to the associate director of Clinical Services.

---

MEMO

From:     CEO
To:          Associate Director, Clinical Services
Subject:  Blood transfusion policies

---

In the 9 years I have been here, we have never had a patient challenge our blood transfusion policies or request that they not be transfused. I suspect this could change and we need to be prepared. My reasoning is simple: I recently noticed that a Kingdom Hall is being planned for the old and abandoned RKO movie theater downtown. This suggests that our community could soon see an increase in the number of people whose faith is that of Jehovah's Witnesses. This group traditionally refuses blood transfusion.

As you know, our present policy would require people in this situation to be counseled about the dangers of refusing the transfusion. When a minor is at risk, we will need to get our lawyer involved in the situation. Frankly, our surgeons are a very conservative group, and I believe they would all refuse to operate if they couldn't have the option of blood transfusions.

I do know that in Topeka, Kansas, the Kansas appeal court ruled that when the University of Kansas Hospital refused to do a liver transplant on a patient because she refused to allow a blood transfusion (she was a Jehovah's Witness), the woman went to the University of Nebraska hospital where they respected her no-transfusion request, and the court ruled that the Kansas Medicaid program would have to pay.

I would like to have you examine the current state of blood management programs and make recommendations that we can take to the medical staff executive committee. Thanks.

* * *

ASSIGNMENT

1. Assume you are the Associate Director, Clinical Services. Prepare a response to the CEO's request.
2. Your research should begin by reviewing:
   a. C. Tokin et al. Blood Management Programs: A Clinical and Administrative Model with Program Implementation Strategies. *The Permanente Journal*, Winter 2009, 31:1, pp. 18–28, http://www.thepermanentejournal.org/component/content/article/48-review-articles/427-blood-management-programs.html
   b. *Stinemetz v. Kansas Health Policy Authority*, 45 Kan. App. 2d 818; 252 P. 3d 141 (2011).

---

## CASE 6-12   Florida Center for Geriatric Assessment

The Florida Center for Geriatric Assessment (FCGA) was developed by three entrepreneurial health professionals who were interested in "doing good and doing well." Their focus was on starting a new type of organization that would offer high-quality diagnostic services to the elderly of South Florida in a freestanding office setting. In discussing their project, they described it simply as "Mayo Clinic-quality medical services in a Ritz Carlton environment." If successful, they planned to move from the original prototype center to several others in

Florida, and they hoped to eventually build other centers in large retirement communities.

The model for their clinical operation was the Mayo Clinic's executive assessment program. As explained by Dave Hodges, a former senior executive in the nursing home industry and a partner in FCGA, the executive assessment at Mayo provided not merely a comprehensive physical examination but an exam that was preceded by an extensive written history submitted by the patient prior to the 2-day visit to Rochester, Minnesota. Hodges himself had gone through the executive assessment at Mayo and described it as ". . . totally amazing. In less than 48 hours I met with a primary care physician who spent over an hour reviewing my questionnaire and then examining me. Next I had blood tests, an EKG, a stress test, a special nuclear cardiac test, and consultations with everyone from nutritionists to a physiatrist because of a knee injury. At the end of the 2 days, I met again with the primary care physician and he discussed everything that was needed for me to be in optimal health. For example, he suggested a change in my cholesterol medication and explained the change. Additionally, he told me that he would provide my regular primary care practitioner and me the results of my testing. He also made sure that I was up to date on my immunizations. It was the most satisfying clinical experience I have ever had."

Hodges's experience and the logic of the proposed FCGA quickly found two partners, Mort Reese and Dan Robinson. Reese had been a medical school dean in a neighboring state, and Robinson came from a finance background and had extensive experience in the health field. Together the three put together a business plan for the FCGA to service the needs of the population of Palm Beach, Broward, and Miami-Dade Counties in South Florida.

The following is a summary of the plan.

## A PROPOSAL TO ESTABLISH A MODEL FREESTANDING GERIATRIC ASSESSMENT PROGRAM

The proposed center would offer senior citizens a 2-day comprehensive health and social evaluation that would be available to the patient and the family for the purpose of a family and patient making short-term and long-term decisions with regard to the patient's health and welfare.

Proposed elements of this GAP are as follows:

1. First-class facility, easily accessible, with high-quality public areas
2. Model apartment as part of facility to test for ability to conduct various activities of daily living
3. High-quality exam and conference rooms
4. Health education DVDs available and/or playing in a theater-style room
5. Healthy snacks while waiting
6. Concierge to arrange for non-health–related issues
7. Full range of clinical examination as per Mayo Clinic and U.S. Age-Specific Guidelines for Preventive Medicine
8. All patients will have the following:
    a. An extensive history taken
    b. A thorough physical administered
    c. A psychiatric evaluation with particular attention to dementia
    d. A nutritional review
    e. A social work review to examine living conditions
    f. An OT evaluation, performed in the model apartment
    g. If appropriate, a site visit at the patient's home to evaluate it for safety and utility

## THE NEED FOR A GERIATRIC ASSESSMENT CENTER IN THE TRI-COUNTY REGION

Most seniors in the Tri-County area, regardless of economic status, receive the bulk of their medical care from local practitioners. The typical encounter, perhaps with the exception of a select group of people, who have signed up for VIP/concierge medicine, lasts only a few minutes. Practitioners simply do not have the time or maybe the inclination to do extensive fact-finding with the elderly.

## FINANCES

The key to the finances of this project is that the client or their family will be responsible for paying the estimated $3,250 fee privately. The FCGA will not participate in the Medicare or Medicaid programs or accept any private insurance payments.

The program will be staffed to accommodate 15 clients per week. It is estimated that at 80% capacity the FCGA will generate $1.7 million per year with fixed operating expenses of $490,000 and variable expenses of $687,000 (of which approximately $400,000 is in program marketing).

## MARKETING

From a demographic perspective, there are (based on the 20__census estimates) 831,000 persons over the age of 65 in the Tri-County region. The largest group is in Broward County, with 306,400 people, but Palm Beach County, with 272,620 people, represents the area with the highest percentage of senior citizens (21.5% vs. 14%+/−).

The initial market plan contemplates the first center's location in the Delray Beach area of Palm Beach County. This area was selected because it is easily accessible to a significant percentage of the target population and a startup facility was readily available.

Marketing efforts will initially be concentrated in the New York Metropolitan area because 80% of the elderly in Palm Beach County have no relatives in South Florida but rather family in the NY area. Marketing would utilize a website as well as targeted print ads.

## A CRUCIAL AFFILIATION

The partners realized that in order for the FCGA to have credibility it would be advisable to either develop a medical advisory board or, alternatively, an academic affiliation. Because it was more expedient, they immediately began assembling an advisory group. Fortunately, before commitments were made, Dr. Reese was able to interest in the project Dr. Alvin Campanella, a former colleague who had been a medical school dean and now was the president of a nearby university with a medical school. This led to a series of discussions between the partners and the university and a "loose affiliation" for marketing purposes with the expectation that the affiliation would be formalized if the project showed signs of success.

* * *

QUESTIONS

1. Does the concept of freestanding geriatric assessment centers make sense? Why isn't the service widely available already?
2. Why would the founders choose to not accept Medicare, Medicaid, or insurance funding?
3. Are there likely licensure issues associated with their plan?
4. Do you think the idea will be successful?

---

## CASE 6-13 | Webster Home for the Aged

The Webster Home for the Aged (WHA) is a nonprofit community nursing home now in its 50th year. During its existence, the WHA has had three sites, the latest of which is a 160-bed facility located on a 32-acre site in Timber Creek. The home, which is entirely certified by Medicare, maintains close to a full occupancy.

Presently, the WHA operates with a staff of 176 full-time-equivalent persons, of whom 67% are in nursing, 10% in food services, 9% in housekeeping, and 5% in laundry.

Over the past few years, the resident population has changed from a younger and less physically debilitated group to one that now has an average age of 86 and an average length of stay of just fewer than 3 years. Approximately 79% of the residents are paid for by Medicaid, 6% are paid for by the State Commission for the Blind or the Veterans Administration, and the remaining 15% pay privately for their care. Data from a recent resident survey indicate that 83% of the residents are from the Webster-Timber Creek area.

The home is under the general direction of a 45-member self-perpetuating board of trustees that meets semiannually. Each year this board elects a seven-person executive committee that meets twice monthly, provides direction to the home's management, authorizes the expenditures of funds, and approves critical personnel decisions. This executive committee group is composed of people who have a long history of active involvement in the affairs of the home, including a number of former presidents as well as presidents of related groups such as the women's auxiliary.

## FINANCES

As noted earlier, the primary source of revenue for the WHA is Medicaid payments. These payments are further subdivided into current revenues that are provided on a regular basis and an adjustment payment that is paid as many as 2 years after costs have been incurred. This latter payment, amounting to several hundred thousand dollars, reduces a deficit that may have been incurred in a given year.

A second source of revenue is the private payments from residents. The rate is presently set at $197 per day. Additional income comes from nonresident sources, primarily donations through ongoing fund-raising activities and the income from the home's $14,000,000 endowment.

As with all service institutions in the health field, the largest single expense category is salaries (and related payroll expenses). Data from the most recent budget indicate that at the WHA this expense category accounts for 73% of all expenses. Almost 50% of these expenses are for nursing services, 13% for dietary salaries, and 9.3% for the salaries and related payroll expenses of the housekeeping staff. Other areas of major expenditures were 10% for food and dietary supplies, 6.5% for building insurance and mortgage interest, and 6% for plant supplies and utilities.

## LOCAL TRENDS LIKELY TO AFFECT THE HOME

There are approximately 38,000 nursing home beds in the state and an occupancy rate of between 97% and 98% for those beds. Recent reports from the state government indicate that approximately 4,000 more beds will be authorized in the near future. It is unclear how these beds will be distributed throughout the state, but, based on population figures, between 500 and 1,000 new beds can be anticipated for the Webster-Timber Creek area.

A second trend likely to have an impact on the home is the general perception that nursing homes in the Webster-Timber Creek area are becoming more competitive. A recent example is the level of advertising and promotion associated with the opening of the Home2000 in East Webster. As the number of beds increases, it can be anticipated that more competition (clinical or financial) will be experienced for the most desirable residents.

Finally, the Webster-Timber Creek area has seen a significant population increase of newcomers who generally have no long-term connection to the region. For example, a decade ago the younger members of the community were most frequently children of longtime residents of the area; that is no longer the case. Typically, the newcomer has no familial connections to the Webster-Timber Creek Metroplex but rather is a refugee from one of the large neighboring cities and is looking for a particular lifestyle that the Webster-Timber Creek area offers. As many longtime friends of the home have said, the newcomers do not know of the home's existence, reputation, or needs.

## ORGANIZATIONAL STRENGTHS AND WEAKNESSES

### Strengths

A particular strength of the WHA is that its accommodations are among the best in the region. Despite its age, the home's physical plant appears to be in excellent condition and the grounds continue to be beautifully maintained. The space available for activities is, in general, adequate.

Second, the location of the home is excellent and has long-run viability. The home is located in an affluent suburb and proximate to other community-sponsored facilities and agencies.

The home enjoys an excellent reputation in the area. It is considered a "five-star" institution in terms of facilities and quality of services offered by staff.

The home also continues to enjoy the strong support of the community as manifested by the success of fund-raising activities and the active volunteer program.

Another strength is that there is a stable and high-quality clinical staff. The medical director and the consultant physician are respected members of the medical community. The home's commitment to medical care as manifested by its half-time medical director distinguishes it from almost every other nursing home in the region and is a particular strength.

The endowment funds represent an important strength of the home. These funds allow the home to provide those additional services and programs that distinguish it from other facilities in the region.

In terms of policy direction, the executive committee members provide an impressive number of hours of volunteer activity to the home. Particularly noteworthy is the commitment of the board president, who provides both the time and perspective that is required by this organization.

A final strength is that the management team at the home is both professionally trained and experienced and dedicated to the provision of quality services to the elderly. The team has the skills and commitment to provide the management and leadership necessary to implement the board's present and future programs.

## Weaknesses

One weakness of the WHA is that it lacks a clear mission. Although the bylaws provide the basic framework of a mission statement, goals and objectives are not provided in this statement. Such goals and objectives could provide the standards against which the organization would chart and evaluate its progress.

Related to this is the observation that the current functioning of the home is not in accord with the roles and responsibilities of the various organizational components as delineated in the home's bylaws. This suggests the need to either rewrite the bylaws or require the board and the committee to act within the scope of their authority and responsibility.

A second weakness is the local orientation of the home. The organization still behaves as if its mission is to serve only the Webster-Timber Creek area. There is a clear lack of knowledge and understanding of the broader community in the region. The home has, until recently, not marketed itself in an effective manner outside of a very narrow community.

A third problem is that of loss of support. Although the home continues to raise funds in impressive amounts, such funds appear to represent, when corrected for inflation, a steady decline; that is, fund-raising has not kept pace with inflation. Equally important is that funds continue to be raised from the same sources. The ability of the home's activities to engage new area residents is limited. Even in the Webster-Timber Creek community, energy that might once have been directed toward home activities has now shifted to other organizations, including the new YMCA and several new and revitalized social service agencies.

The home may also be a victim of some community myths. While the home enjoys an excellent reputation in terms of quality, there is an undercurrent of animosity toward it in the community. This hostility is related to unclear admission standards that are thought to relate to the willingness and ability of a family to provide donations to the home.

Another weakness is that there has been no organized or effective program of board education. There is now an attempt by the administration to remedy this lack of knowledge, but much work still needs to be done.

Finally, there appears to be some ambiguity about the roles and responsibilities of the board and administration. As part of the planning process, these roles should be clarified. Specifically, there needs to be a clear delineation of responsibility and authority for policy and organizational administration.

* * *

## ASSIGNMENT

1. Develop a presentation to the board that summarizes the case study.
2. Develop a management action plan to address the issues raised by the case study.

## CASE 6-14 | Planning a Child-Care Center

The Good Folks Nursing Center of Northampton, Massachusetts, is a 150-bed, skilled nursing facility. The administration is interested in renovating the facility's empty 1,500-square-foot general storeroom into a day-care center for children of employees (and other children, if necessary). A marketing study indicates that there is a need for these child-care services and that if the home opens an attractive and well-staffed facility, there should be enough demand to make the project self-supporting. However, the administrator has been advised that a special permit might pose regulatory impediments to such a project, so she is interested in receiving a memo that details what steps will be required to make the project work. Relevant excerpts from the regulations appear in the following Exhibits.

* * *

ASSIGNMENT

Prepare a memo to the administrator detailing the feasibility of the home developing a day-care center in light of the attached regulations.

## Exhibit | Code of Massachusetts Regulations

105 CMR 151.500 Storage Areas
General Storage. A general storage room or rooms shall be provided in each facility with a total of at least 10 square feet per bed for 100% of the total beds authorized.

## Exhibit | City of Northampton Use Regulations

Section 5.1—Applicability of Use Regulations. Except as provided in this Ordinance, no building, structure, or land shall be used except for the purposes permitted in the district as described in this article. Any use not listed shall be construed to be prohibited. Uses permitted by right, by special permit, or by a variance granted under the provisions of Section 10.9, shall be subject, in addition to the use regulations contained in the Article, to all of the other provisions of the Ordinance.

Any use that is accessory to a principal use shall be allowed only in connection with the bona fide operation of a principal use allowed under the Table of Use Regulations, and subject to the provisions of Section 5.3 where applicable.

Note. See also:

Article VI for dimension and density regulations
Article VII for sign requirements
Article VIII for parking and loading regulations
Article XII for site plan review/approval requirements

**Section 5.3—Accessory Uses.** Any use that is accessory to a principal use allowed by right shall be allowed only in connection with such allowed principal use. Any use that is accessory to a principal use allowed by special permit, and that is not specifically included in the original special permit, shall be allowed only after issuance of a new special permit. Cessation of a principal use shall require cessation of any accessory use that is not otherwise allowed as a principal use. The Building Inspector shall be responsible for determining what uses are principal, and what uses are accessory.

**Section 10.1—Special Permits.** Certain uses, structures, or conditions are designated within the Table of Use Regulations as requiring a special permit. Such permit shall be granted only after application to a hearing by the special permit granting authority and subject to the provisions of Chapter 40A of the Massachusetts General Laws and this Ordinance. The special permit granting authority responsible for hearing a particular proposal shall be that board or other entity designated by the coding in the Table of Use Regulations. In situations where there is no specific board indicated as having the authority to issue a special permit, the special permit granting authority shall be the Board of Appeals.

1. Application for a special permit shall be made to the Building Inspector on forms provided for that purpose, accompanied by the required fee. Specific rules governing the application and fee shall be adopted by each special permit granting authority along with its rules of procedure

and shall be applicable to those special permits that are under its jurisdiction. When the application has been received in a completed form as defined by said rules, a copy shall be forwarded to the City Clerk. The stamp of the City Clerk shall designate the date of filing. Copies shall also be delivered to the special permit granting authority, to the Planning Department, and to such other departments and boards as may be determined in the rules of the special permit granting authority.

2. Special permits shall only be issued following public hearings held within sixty-five (65) days after filing of an application. Advertising and notice of hearing shall be conducted by the Planning Department subject to the rules of procedure adopted by the special permit granting authority having responsibility for the particular proposal in question. Costs of advertising and notification shall be paid by the special permit granting authority.

3. Before granting an application for a special permit, the special permit granting authority, with regard to the nature and condition of all adjacent structures and uses, and the district within which the same is located, shall find all of the following general conditions to be fulfilled:

    (a) The use requested is listed in the Table of Use Regulations as a special permit in the district for which application is made or is so designated elsewhere in this Ordinance.

    (b) The requested use bears a positive relationship to the public convenience or welfare.

    (c) The requested use will not create undue traffic congestion or unduly impair pedestrian safety.

    (d) The requested use will not overload any public water, drainage, or sewer system or any other municipal system to such an extent that the requested use or any developed use in the immediate area or in any other area of the City will be unduly subjected to hazards affecting health, safety, or the general welfare.

    (e) Any special regulations for the use as set forth in Article XI are fulfilled.

    (f) The requested use will not unduly impair the integrity or character of the district or adjoining zones, nor be detrimental to the health, morals, or general welfare. The use shall be in harmony with the general purpose and intent of the Ordinance.

4. The special permit granting authority shall also impose, in addition to any applicable conditions specified in this Ordinance, such additional conditions as it finds reasonably appropriate to safeguard the neighborhood or otherwise serve the purposes of this Ordinance, including, but not limited to, the following: front, side, or rear yards greater than the minimum required by this Ordinance; screening buffers or planting strips, fences, or walls, as specified by the special permit granting authority; modification of the exterior appearance of the structures; limitation upon the size, number of occupants, method and time of operation, time duration of permit, or extent of facilities; traffic features in accordance with the regulations of loading; or other special features beyond the minimum required by this Ordinance. Such conditions shall be imposed in writing, and the applicant may be required to post bond or other security for compliance with said conditions in an amount satisfactory to the special permit granting authority.

## CASE 6-15 | Outpatient Imaging: The Perfect Storm

By *Alex Szafran*

### BACKGROUND

#### Business Environment

State Medical Center (SMC) is a large tertiary medical center that provides a full range of services at its main hospital campus. Because space at the hospital campus is in high demand, the hospital chose to relocate many of its outpatient services to three dedicated outpatient sites located within a few miles of the hospital. The largest of these sites includes office space leased by community physicians and is also adjacent to a medical office building owned by the hospital.

The hospital's department of radiology has established imaging services at all three of the outpatient facilities, and at the largest of the three, provides a full suite of imaging technologies including mammography, radiography, ultrasound, CT, MRI, and PET/CT services.

One of the largest specialty medical practices in the community, Specialty Medical Associates (SMA), runs its main practice in office space at this location. The patients from this practice require frequent CT scans as part of their care, and referrals from the practice account for about 30% of the CT work performed at this location.

CT scan technology has gone through rapid technical improvement during the last 8 years. Hospitals, wanting and needing to provide the most up-to-date technology, have been replacing their equipment on shorter time frames than ever before. As a result, equipment vendors have taken in on trade CT scanners that are still serviceable and usable in some settings. The vendors see medical offices as a potential secondary market for used equipment and have been heavily promoting "value-priced reconditioned equipment" in this marketplace.

Coincidentally, as this secondary marketplace is coming under heavy promotion from the vendors, continued reimbursement pressure from health insurance companies is causing medical practice incomes to shrink or at best remain stagnant. In response to this pressure, many medical practices are looking for new ways to generate revenue to replace the lost income, and some are seeing opportunity in medical imaging.

## Regulatory Environment

The state in which SMC is located has a long history of heavily regulating healthcare activities. The state's certificate of need regulations include not only specific dollar thresholds for acquisition of new technology, building new facilities, and the like, but also limit the aggregate dollar value of all CON projects approved each year. Competition for CON approvals is, as a result, fierce. The dollar value threshold for new technology acquisition is $1.5 million. The price of the refurbished CT scanners that the vendors are promoting to medical offices falls well below this threshold; the price of the new technology that the hospitals are purchasing typically falls above the threshold.

In addition to CON regulations, the state has recently implemented legislation that tightly controls hospital operating expenses and profit margins. This legislation limits growth in cost per discharge from year to year and also places a cap on hospital margins. The combination of strong reimbursement rates for outpatient imaging and the way the financial formulas embedded in the regulations calculate cost provides a way for hospitals to reduce the negative impact of the cost and profit regulations by encouraging growth in outpatient services, particularly in imaging.

The payor mix in the community in which SMC and SMA exist is about 50% Medicare and 15% Medicaid, with the rest a mix of commercial indemnity, managed care, and self-pay. For many years, hospitals have been paid for outpatient services under a fee system that is different than the system used to pay medical offices for their services. Hospitals have typically been paid less than medical offices for identical services. The Centers for Medicare and Medicaid (CMS), the federal agency responsible for establishing Medicare fee structures, is considering fee schedule changes in response to new legislation called the Deficit Reduction Act, which will primarily impact fees paid to nonhospital providers. The exact impact is unknown, but it is clear that the regulatory intent is to level the playing field by eliminating the differential pricing structure in a way that will be unfavorable to medical offices.

Growth in office-based medical imaging has also captured the attention of congress, and concern is growing about the impact self-referral is having not only on the growth in Medicare spending for imaging services, but also on a perceived growth in unnecessary utilization of expensive medical tests. Congress is debating legislation intended to address this; however, it is early in the process and there is no consensus on what the legislation will contain. It is also unclear that this legislation will survive the legislative process.

## The Business Dilemma

SMA has been approached by an equipment vendor who is promoting a low-cost CT scanner with a price that falls below the CON threshold. Recognizing that so many of its patients require CT scanning on a regular basis, SMA believes that opening its own CT service inside its office would provide a much-needed contribution to its bottom line. In order to maintain its relationship with SMC, SMA discloses to SMC its intent. SMC management considers a variety of options and decides to respond to SMA with a proposal to lease a portion of its CT scan capacity to SMA for its own use. Since SMC's CT scanner is located in the same building as SMA's practice, SMC believes that this will meet SMA's need to provide its own CT service while allowing SMC to maintain the productivity of its equipment and staff. Both SMA and SMC see this as a "win-win" opportunity, and both begin their due diligence reviews. Legal counsel approves of the approach.

\* \* \*

QUESTIONS

1. What does each party give up if this deal is consummated?
2. What does each party gain?
3. What are the long-term risks for each party?
4. If you were negotiating the contract that would govern the business aspects of this new relationship, what protective language would you consider necessary if you were representing SMC? What if you were representing SMA?
5. If you were the key decision maker at SMA, would you accept SMC's proposal or continue with your original plan?
6. What other options might you consider?

| CASE 6-16 | **The Tower** |

Five years ago, the Central Medical Center (CMC) committed itself to building a new 36-story clinical tower that would have state-of-the-art ancillary facilities, 34 operating suites (about 20 replacing those in older buildings), administrative and conference space, 6 floors for condominium medical offices, and 22 floors devoted to patient rooms. The steel skeleton of the building would be covered with an aluminum skin. Additionally, to provide a bit of drama as well as a protected space for passenger cars and ambulances using the various entrances, the entire building would sit on four-story-high stilts.

The board, medical staff, and CMC administration, led by Shane Ferguson, MD, decided that even though it might cost more money, the new tower should be a landmark building in the city. Toward that end, they hired the region's most distinguished architect who in turn hired the country's most distinguished structural engineer. While the project was simple, in many senses there were some complications because the building site was located about two blocks north of the convergence of the city's main river and the ocean in the city's downtown business section. Another complication was that the building would be tall, thin, and asymmetrical.

As the building progressed, the board, medical staff, and Ferguson watched in awe. Donations poured in and Ferguson, now 62 years of age and looking forward to retirement, viewed this as the crowning achievement of his years at CMC. Accolades came in to the organization, the medical staff were finally happy, and, for Ferguson, life could not have been better. Clearly the building was a masterpiece of design and engineering. In fact, 2 months after it opened, the architect was given a prestigious international award for its design.

A day ago Dr. Ferguson got a phone call from the architect and structural engineer. He was told that there was an emergency and they needed to meet with him immediately.

An hour after they left he sat in his office alone trying to decide what to do next. The news he had received from the architect and structural engineer was the following.

The building had been built in total accord with all applicable codes and it would withstand wind, rains, and storms coming from one direction (the one required under the code). However, they had, as an intellectual exercise, run the data to see how the building would handle strong winds and rain from other directions or perhaps floods. And, based on these calculations, which theoretically might happen once every 100 years, the building could collapse. The architect and engineer told Ferguson that they accept full responsibility and are prepared to remediate the problems immediately. They suggested several options. The fastest and easiest would be to evacuate the building and do the necessary retrofitting to strengthen the core and make it less vulnerable. The second option would be to retrofit on a floor-by-floor basis.

Ferguson wasn't certain of his next move. Should he evacuate? Retrofit? Whom should he inform?

\* \* \*

QUESTION

You are Dr. Ferguson's consultant. What should he do?

---

## CASE 6-17 | Tyler Memorial Hospital

Marti Quinn knew she was in for perhaps the most difficult board meeting of her 19-year career as a hospital administrator. Five years earlier she had been hired as CEO of Tyler Hospital, a 140-bed, financially troubled facility that was now on the verge of bankruptcy despite all her efforts at cutting costs and increasing revenue. Five months earlier, at her own suggestion, Tyler had entered into discussions with St. Catherine's Medical Center, a 300-bed financially healthy facility located 7 miles from the Tyler building. St. Catherine's was supportive of a merger; however, there were several conditions that Quinn was going to present to the board at this meeting.

She began her presentation.

"Good afternoon. I will try to be brief. I now have the final merger proposal from St. Catherine's. In a few minutes I will distribute a copy, but first I wish to highlight a few aspects of the proposal. The positive aspects are simply that if we accept this merger agreement all of Tyler's debt will be absorbed by the St. Catherine's system and their foundation. Next, for the immediate and perhaps foreseeable future, the physical facility of our hospital will remain right here in town and its name will not be changed, although it will be identified as part of the St. Catherine's Health System. The present board of Tyler will be dissolved, although some members may be asked to serve on the St. Catherine's board or its foundation board.

"As you know there is an 85% overlap of medical staff between the two hospitals, and I have been assured that every member of our medical staff will be part of the St. Catherine's staff. With regard to employees, I anticipate several problems since we are a unionized facility and St. Catherine's is not. There could be a transition period where questions of fringe benefits, pensions, seniority, and so forth are worked out, but I don't see this as a major stumbling block. Additionally, there could be some overlapping and duplication of services where one service might be closed or merged with another. None of this has been decided as of this moment, and I do not anticipate any major cutbacks in staffing.

"A major issue I want to call to your attention is the one service that Tyler offers that will have to be curtailed. It certainly comes as no shock to anyone in this room that a non-negotiable component of the merger proposal is that Tyler must shut down the portion of our women's health program that offers abortion and birth control services. As you know, this is a major issue for all Catholic hospitals and has not been an issue here at Tyler. Obviously this will affect the practices of some of our most loyal physicians and will place a burden on the women of Tyler who will have to travel the 19 miles to Jamesville Memorial for those services. Also, nothing in the merger will have any impact on what physicians do in their own private offices that are not on our campus or in hospital-owned medical office buildings.

"Finally, some of you have asked about my professional future subsequent to a merger. At this stage it is somewhat unclear, although Sister Elizabeth, CEO at St. Catherine's, has said she would like me to stay on at Tyler to help with the transition, and after that 6- to 12-month period we would discuss future employment.

"I will now distribute the proposal and we can open the discussion."

* * *

QUESTIONS

1. Should Ms. Quinn have distributed the proposal before her presentation?
2. Is the closure of the abortion and birth control services truly non-negotiable?
3. What opposition can be anticipated about this merger?
4. Is there any way the merger can go through and allow the women needing the services to be better accommodated?
5. Assuming the merger happens, what is your prediction about the future of Ms. Quinn?

---

**CASE 6-18** | **Lunch at Applebee's**

The ABC Health System, a nonprofit organization, is the fifth-largest healthcare provider in the state with 4 hospitals, a total of 814 beds, and several ambulatory-care facilities. Recently, its CEO, Robby Jackson; its medical director, Page Bagg, MD; and the chairman of the board, Hodge Gilson, were having lunch to get a briefing from Jackson about his recent trip to Washington DC, where he was attending a seminar on accountable care organizations (ACOs) held by the American Hospital Association. The conversation went as follows.

*Hodge:*

So Robby, what is the latest on these ACOs?

*Robby:*

From a legislative standpoint there is some lack of clarity. But I can tell you that I do expect the government, and probably the private insurers, to start bundling payments to us in one way or another, so that we are going to be on the hook financially for an entire episode of care.

*Page:*

And Hodge, I think that means we have to be quite careful about how long we keep people in the hospital and where we send them after hospitalization, such as what nursing home.

*Hodge:*

Am I reading you folks right? Are you suggesting we buy or build a nursing home in order to control what happens after patients get discharged?

*Robby:*

Absolutely not! The last thing in the world we want to do is own nursing homes! But what we have to do is find good-quality, skilled nursing facilities that provide rehabilitation care at competitive prices and most importantly don't generate readmissions for our hospitals. Any readmission costs us a fortune!

*Hodge:*

How do you do this?

*Page:*

Well, for quality we will examine their Medicare surveys. Basically, if they are certified and don't have any glaring inspection problems, we will go with that. It is also crucial that they have electronic medical records that integrate with our system. Generally, there shouldn't be a big issue as long as they have some EMRs.

*Robby:*

Next we need to do some digging about their readmission history. We need to see it across the board, perhaps a few MDs, or maybe even some diagnostic groups. We need to also be certain that our work at the hospital is not complicit in readmissions. For example, if patients get discharged too soon, that may be a setup for a readmit. Finally, we are going to have to do some serious staff education about all of this. Everyone needs to be on board if this is going to work for us!

*Hodge:*
> Sounds like a plan. Let's eat!

Sitting at the adjacent booth having lunch is Kelly O'Reilly, CEO of Old Towne Nursing Center, a 200-bed for-profit facility that has been examining its own position and strategy for becoming the primary referral facility for the ABC Health System. After overhearing the conversation (and finishing lunch), she goes back to the Old Towne Nursing Center to work on the ACO issue.

* * *

QUESTIONS

1. Ms. O'Reilly wants to have a meeting about ACOs. Who should attend the meeting and why?
2. What items should be on the agenda for the meeting? Why?

---

## CASE 6-19 | Obituary

Please read the following three obituaries.

### EDWARD HEWLETT, METRO UNIVERSITY CEO

Edward E. Hewlett died on March 9, 20___ at Metro University Hospital of complications from a stroke. Born in 19___ in Patterson, New Jersey, Mr. Hewlett had a long and distinguished career as a healthcare manager. After graduating from Whitman College in Walla Walla, Washington, he attended Columbia University where he received his Masters Degree in Hospital Administration. His career included positions at New York University Hospital, the Hospital of the University of Pennsylvania, and the Metro University Hospital, where he served as Chief Executive Officer for 21 years before retiring 9 years ago. During his tenure at Metro, he oversaw $217 million in new construction, the development of an affiliation with the State University Medical School, and the inauguration of the 2-year fellowship program in healthcare management that the trustees named in his honor at his retirement. Subsequent to retirement, Mr. Hewlett began a new career as professor of health management at State University.

Mr. Hewlett was active in numerous community activities, including the United Way, Friends of Metro Museum, and the Alzheimer's Association. Mr. Hewlett's first three marriages ended in divorce. He is survived by his fourth wife, Brittany. He is also survived by two sons from his first marriage, Edward Jr. and Mario, both of Milford Sound, New Zealand, and a daughter from his second marriage, Edwina, of Cape Town, South Africa. Donations in Mr. Hewlett's name can be made to the Metro University Hospital.

## ELLIE BOUDREAUX, PUBLIC HEALTH EXECUTIVE

Ellie Boudreaux, MD, MPH, former Chief Health Officer of the state, died yesterday at her home at the age of 66. The family said her death was the result of complications from multiple sclerosis.

Former Governor P. M. Clark, who appointed Dr. Boudreaux to Chief Health Officer, issued the following statement, "Our state is diminished by the loss of Ellie Boudreaux. She was a great human being, public health leader, and national figure. Her activities on behalf of the underserved and underprivileged were monumental. She spotlighted the problems of AIDS, malnutrition, and auto safety. Her diligent work led to reforms in our state as well as the nation. She will be missed by all."

Dr. Boudreaux served as the state's Chief Health Officer during the 8 years of Clark's administration and then became dean of the State University's School of Public Health until her retirement last year.

A graduate of Bryn Mawr College and Yale University School of Medicine, Boudreaux had an MPH from the Johns Hopkins University. After her residency in dermatology at the University of Rochester, Dr. Boudreaux worked in the State Health Department's Division of Infectious Diseases where after 5 years she became director of the division.

She is the author of 123 professional articles and 14 chapters in various textbooks.

In 19___ she spent a year in Washington DC as a White House Fellow and then returned to the Health Department in a newly created position as Deputy Commissioner for Governmental Relations.

Dr. Boudreaux is survived by her husband of 42 years, Oscar D'Piot, MD; a daughter, Sally Boudreaux D'Piot of Brookline, Massachusetts; and three sons, Dr. Oscar D'Piot, Dr. Peter D'Piot, of Metro University Hospital, and Rabbi Eli D'Piot of Jerusalem, Israel; as well as 11 grandchildren. Boudreaux is also survived by a twin sister, May, of Philadelphia, Pennsylvania.

## HAROLD NEW, 41

Harold New, 41, died on Tuesday of complications following surgery for pancreatic cancer.

Mr. New was Associate Director, Nonprofessional Services, at Metro University Hospital. Mr. New began his professional career 19 years ago at Metro as an administrative resident and then became Assistant to the Associate Director, Professional Services. Four years ago he was promoted to Associate Director. Mr. New had an undergraduate degree in healthcare management from Bison University.

In addition to his work at Metro University Hospital, for the past 17 years New was an umpire in Metro Little League, the organist at St. Mary's Church, a weekly volunteer at the St. Agnes Homeless Shelter, and a member of the Metro Citizens' Crime Watch. Mr. New, a former U.S. Navy Corpsman, who was awarded two Purple Hearts and the Bronze Star with a Combat V for service in Iraq, was a chief petty officer in the Naval Reserve.

His wife of 16 years, Daisy Mae New, and his twin 11-year-old sons, Michael and Todd, survive him.

\* \* \*

QUESTIONS AND ASSIGNMENT

1. Based on these obituaries, how would you evaluate the careers of these people?
2. Does it appear that any of them have paid a high price for their success?
3. Whose career would you most like to emulate?
4. Write your own obituary!

**CHAPTER 7**

# MARKETING

 **INTRODUCTION**

In the last few decades, healthcare marketing has shifted from being a dirty term to becoming an organizational necessity and academic discipline. Organizations have multiple constituencies that require both understanding and nurturing.

The art and science of marketing require a broad array of talents, including those ranging from quality research to productive promotion, whether that be in the traditional media or in the various components of cyberspace. Healthcare marketing also has a host of constraints typically not found in other sectors of the economy.

Consider the following scenario. A person checks into a hotel, arrives in his or her room, and finds the bathroom messed up with soap scum in the tub and encrusted soap in the soap holder. What happens? The manager calls, apologizes, sends the customer to an upgraded room, sends up a basket of cheese, fruit, and wine, and perhaps cancels the bill—great marketing! In a different scenario, a state inspector walks into the room of a resident in a nursing home and the soap scum problem results in a Medicaid or Medicare violation. A fine may be levied. A plan of correction will definitely happen, and if the nursing home wants to fight the violation (called an F-tag), it will cost thousands of dollars. Here marketing's role is limited, at best.

| CASE 7-1 | **Sleep Apnea**

The following letter came into the office of a congressman who is on the House Finance Committee.

*Dear Congressman:*

*As one of your constituency, a concerned citizen, and a beneficiary of both Medicare and the VA, I am very upset about the dollars wasted by the government on sleep apnea studies.*

*Specifically, it seems that all the sleep doctors want a potential person with sleep apnea to have at least one and sometimes two overnight sleep studies in their centers. For example, I went to a sleep MD and had to see him for 2 minutes before he would prescribe a sleep study. He then read the study and I had to see him a second time for another 3 minutes to have him tell me I had sleep apnea. Then he prescribed a second study to titrate the machinery for me and find the right mask. Another overnight study and another meeting with him! So, Medicare was billed for two overnight studies and three doctor visits. And who knows how much money the hospital made!*

*Then my buddy, who gets his care in the VA, went to his VA hospital. Like me, he snores like a train, is obese, and hardly sleeps. At the VA they gave him a little gadget called a WatchPAT-200 that he wore on his fingers overnight, he slept with it (without all the wires I had), and that was that. The VA checked the data from his home machine and gave him a CPAP.*

*Mr. Congressman, no wonder the government is going broke! What are you going to do about this?*

*With Concern,*

*J. P. Jones, Retired*

\* \* \*

QUESTIONS

Assume you work for the Congressman.

1. How do you respond to this constituent?
2. What additional facts do you need from CMS and the VA?
3. What are you going to do about this situation?

---

**CASE 7-2** | **Credential Dilemma**

For 11 years Charles Michael Madison, PhD, has been Director of Human Resources at Joshua Valley Health System (JVH), which includes 3 acute care hospitals totaling 843 beds and 3,700 employees; 7 hospital-affiliated medical clinics employing more than 150 staff; and 4 nursing homes with a total of 400 beds and 500 employees. JVH is a nonprofit organization whose foundation raises close to $15 million per year.

Madison has been a core player in the success of JVH through his careful but innovative recruiting activities, his nationally recognized orientation and training programs, and his careful management of potential problem areas such as Workers' Compensation and sexual harassment. And most importantly from the administration and board's perspective, he has been able to have cordial relations with the union.

The board and administration well recognize the importance of Madison to the accomplishment of the system's mission, and they have rewarded Madison handsomely. He is now the third highest paid person in management (directly below the CEO and COO). Additionally, he has a range of perks similar to those of the CEO and COO such as a luxury automobile, expense account, unlimited business travel, and a million-dollar life insurance policy. The only thing that the CEO and COO have that Madison doesn't is a contract. That is, he is an employee at will, like everyone else at the health system, with no severance package.

On Monday evening when the CEO returned home from work, she received in the mail a letter with no return address or signature. The letter read as follows:

*Dear Ms. CEO:*

*Charles Michael Madison is a fraud. He is no doctor. His so-called PhD is phony. He went to a matchbook school. He doesn't even have a college degree. He is a big fat liar. Don't trust him.*

*Yours truly,*

*A friend*

\* \* \*

QUESTIONS

1. What is (or should be) the system's policy about false credentials?
2. What are the CEO's next moves and why?

---

## CASE 7-3 | Chutzpah

The following editorial appeared in the *Metropolis Gazette*, an alternative newspaper in the community.

OUTRAGEOUS SALARIES FOR TOP NONPROFIT EXECS

No wonder the quality of care at The Metropolis Geriatric Center (MGC) has slipped from five stars to four stars since the money that is raised through their extensive fund-raising activities (auctions, dinner dances, casino nights, annual dinners, etc.), which is supposed to go for the care of the residents, is going to the pockets of the two senior executives. This year's Form 990s tell the story. The CEO is making $1.1 million, and his chief deputy is making $425,000. Not bad for running a $75 million dollar nonprofit company that is consistently losing money. The board allows this to go on! Here is our community where the real unemployment rate is in excess of 12%. Our hospital systems that are much bigger don't make that money, and the heads of private geriatric systems that are 20 times the size of MGC (in terms of revenue and employees) make only slightly more than MGC's CEO. And they want to raise money from the community? Get serious! Clean up your house first!!!!!

\* \* \*

QUESTIONS

1. What is a Form 990?
2. Assume you are the executive vice president of Metropolis Bank and a member of MGC's executive committee and you have seen this editorial. What should you do?
3. How should salaries be set for senior executives of non-profit healthcare corporations? Should there be performance bonuses?

---

## CASE 7-4 | Celebrity

At the February 2012 meeting of the Board of Trustees of the Metroplex Memorial Medical Center, an extremely animated discussion took place about the handling of celebrity patients and their family members. The trigger for this agenda item was what several board members perceived as the negative publicity that Lenox Hill Hospital received for its actions surrounding the birth of a daughter to the singer Beyoncé and her husband, the rapper and entrepreneur, Jay-Z, on January 7, 2012.

According to one board member who is an aficionado of pop culture, Beyoncé and Jay-Z, in anticipation of the birth of their child, built two five-star private suites at Lenox Hill at a cost of close to $1.5 million. But according to this board member, the reason for the bad publicity was that once Beyoncé was admitted to the maternity floor the entire area essentially went into lockdown mode to control activity on the floor.

Another board member, definitely not a fan of pop culture, pointed out that the lockdown prevented other parents from visiting their newborns on the newborn intensive care unit (NICU). A third board member chimed in, "It sounds fair to me. The hospital gets $1.5 million, and a few folks get inconvenienced. Further, in this competitive environment, it is good to have ultra-luxury suites to attract the high rollers."

Finally the chairman of the board asked the CEO her opinion and she replied, "I don't think we have all the facts yet. It does appear that the complaints made to the Health Department resulted in no negative sanctions at Lenox Hill. But there definitely was a steady drumbeat of negative publicity over the barring of patients from the floor during Beyoncé's hospitalization. On the lighter side, Lenox Hill certainly did get a lot of free PR for its VIP facilities. But, I suspect some lawsuits will be coming as a result of this."

The board chairman thanked the CEO for her remarks and then instructed her to develop a hospital policy for handling VIP patients.

* * *

ASSIGNMENT

As the associate CEO, you have been asked to develop a policy for handling VIP patients.

1. Identify the elements of the policy.
2. Draft the policy.
3. Prepare a defense of the policy.

---

## CASE 7-5 | Marketing Admissions

Frank Fleet, Associate Director of the Grant Geriatrics Center, has just received the following confidential memo from the Center's director.

| GRANT GERIATRIC CENTER MEMO |
| --- |
| From:     Ms. Wendy Field |
| To:       Mr. Frank Fleet |
| Subject:  OBRA regulations and our admissions agreement |

As you are aware, our one-page admissions agreement is hopelessly out of date and fails to include a number of important points brought out in the OBRA regulations. Would you please review the section of the regulations on patients' rights and let me know how we could incorporate these rights into our admissions agreement and use them to our marketing advantage?

\* \* \*

ASSIGNMENT

Assume you are Mr. Fleet. What is your response to Ms. Field's request?

*Note: The student can review the OBRA regulations on Resident Rights and Quality of Life on the Internet. Also, the Internet has a range of commentary on these rights and requirements.*

## CASE 7-6 | Chamber of Commerce Presentation

Jillian Reilly, the CEO of the Plaidsville Hospital, has sent you a memo asking that you prepare a 5- to 7-minute speech for him to deliver to the local chamber of commerce. The title of his speech is "Health Care: National Trends and What It Means to Plaidsville." In his memo he has asked you to include some national data but to also focus on the local scene (Plaidsville is the ultimate average hospital in the average community). Finally, Mr. Reilly has urged you to not prepare a sterile presentation but rather find a way to humanize the presentation.

\* \* \*

ASSIGNMENT

Write the speech using current and accurate data available from the Internet. As noted, the Plaidsville Hospital is "totally average"; thus it will be necessary to explore a range of data in order to define "totally average."

---

**CASE 7-7** | **Patient Satisfaction at Pineview**

---

The following is an executive summary of a consulting report.

---
THE ABC CONSULTING GROUP
---

### EXECUTIVE SUMMARY, Pineview Group Practice

The following executive summary reviews the three areas that your group asked our firm to examine.

1. Patient Utilization
2. Patient Satisfaction
3. Net Practice Income

1. Patient Utilizations

    a. Over the past 3 years, there has been an 11% net decline in patient census. During the same time, the group had a net increase of two physicians.

        i. There are likely several reasons for this decline, including issues in patient satisfaction, a patient population that is generally older (to put it succinctly, dying off), and increased competition from new practitioners in the community as well as alternative competition such as the walk-in clinics at Target, Walmart, and Walgreens.

2. Patient Satisfaction

    a. There is no baseline study to compare the present results with previous surveys.

        i. You clearly have mixed results when it comes to issues such as hours of operation, access, parking, and communication with patients. These issues need to be addressed!

3. Net Practice Income

    a. Despite the decline in census, the group has managed to keep its net income from similarly declining. However, it also has not grown and will not likely remain stable in light of declining reimbursement.

## RECOMMENDATIONS

1. Use the present patient satisfaction survey as a baseline for future surveys.
2. Consider a change of hours to include appointments in the early evening and weekends.
3. Consider adding specialists who will focus on younger age groups (e.g., sports medicine-oriented MDs).
4. Consider adding alternative and complementary services such as acupuncture.
5. Parking is a problem at your facility; consider a valet system.
6. Bring in an interior design firm to update your nonclinical and waiting areas.

\* \* \*

QUESTIONS

1. Based on the limited comparative data, are these recommendations premature?
2. Assuming you accept these recommendations, how would you as an administrator sell them to the medical group?
3. What problems would you anticipate in convincing the group about the needed changes?

---

## CASE 7-8 | International Marketing Case

After learning that a number of America's major medical centers have been actively expanding their presence in the overseas market, Larry Liverless, the CEO of the South Florida Jewish Geriatric Center (SFJGC), has decided that his institution should also consider getting into this activity. From his background research, he learned that the University of Pittsburgh Medical Center already has a presence in four foreign countries and is planning to open 25 oncology centers outside the United States. He also learned that other medical centers are actively building branches in the wealthy Middle Eastern and Asian countries. Liverless also learned that in order to develop a successful program it is necessary to have a reliable foreign partner.

Based on this information, Liverless is about to prepare a presentation to his board of directors that will outline his goals and strategy to developing an off-shore program. The SFJGC is one of the two largest nonprofit providers of long-term and rehabilitative care in the state. Presently it operates five nursing homes with a total of 944 beds, as well as seven rehabilitation clinics and a total of 140 rehabilitation beds. Although the organization is profitable, its "bottom line" has been shrinking because of a decline in the private census and a decline in the number of Medicare patients.

Liverless thinks that because South Florida is the gateway to Latin America and many affluent Jewish people from Latin and South America own condominiums in South Florida, it makes sense to recruit rehabilitation patients and nursing home residents from these countries. The CEO's thinking is that any of these international clients would be private-pay because of their ineligibility for Medicare and Medicaid.

* * *

ASSIGNMENT

Prior to the board meeting, you have been asked to think through the CEO's idea and develop a comprehensive list of likely issues that need to be resolved before a program can be implemented to import new patients and residents. Additionally, the CEO wants your thoughts on strategies to market any new program.

---

## CASE 7-9  Kayland Community Hospital

Each Labor Day weekend, the 3-day Kayland Community Fair is held at the county fairgrounds. Typically, the fair has a midway with various games, a 4-H barn where children compete in various agricultural-related activities, a host of vendors selling everything from tractors to kitchen supplies, and some events such as a tractor-pull contest and performances by daredevil drivers with their monster trucks.

Until a decade ago, the Kayland Community Hospital was a sponsor of the fair and participated with a gift of $25,000 to the fair. In return the hospital had the use of approximately 2,000 square feet in which to set up a health screening clinic and to hand out various health education brochures. A year after Alfred E. Newman arrived to take over as CEO of the hospital, he decided that the fair was a waste of money. Since Newman's arrival, the hospital has neither been a sponsor nor offered any services at the fair. Newman was adamantly opposed to involvement with the fair. Indeed, in response to a question about pulling out of the fair he was quoted as saying, "What do you think? I'm mad? It's a waste of money." Six months ago Newman retired, and the new CEO, Kendra Clark, wants to revisit participation in the fair.

\* \* \*

ASSIGNMENT

Prepare the Analysis:

Assume you are the Director of Community Relations of Kayland Community Hospital and Ms. Clark has asked for an analysis of the costs and benefits of the hospital's and staff's involvement in the Kayland Community Fair.

---

## CASE 7-10 | Amenities

COMMUNITY HOSPITAL, CONFIDENTIAL MEMO

From:     CEO
To:       Director, Marketing
Subject:  Amenities

Charlie:

I'm concerned! In the past few years we have recruited a number of new splendid MDs, added a range of community-oriented services such as our breast cancer clinic and our men's health center, and bought millions of dollars worth of high-technology equipment. And, despite all this, we have not gained 1% in market share!

The one area where we are still at a significant disadvantage is in amenities. At a recent conference, I heard that the new UCLA Medical Center is filled with patient amenities, and as a result the number of patients who would recommend the facility to friends and family has increased by 20%. I would like you and your staff to look into ways in which we could enhance our amenities and be perceived more as a five-star place. Obviously cost is an issue. Please try to cost out your ideas.

Thanks

\* \* \*

QUESTIONS

1. Are amenities really important in attracting patients?
2. Assuming that amenities are important, what suggestions can be made to the CEO? What are the cost benefits of these suggestions?

---

| CASE 7-11 | Not #1 |

---

MEMO

From:    Chairman of the Board
To:      CEO
Subject: Can't we do better?

---

As you know, every year the weekly magazine *U.S. News & World Report* has an issue that ranks the best hospitals in a variety of specialty areas. And, as you know, our hospital, despite its size and the quality of our programs, never gets acknowledged.

Three years ago we finished our cancer center. As you recall, we spent a fortune on the facility and more on recruiting national stars, who seem to have done nothing for our image.

We continue to spend way above our budget for this program, and I don't believe we have had appropriate recognition for the money spent.

Finally, last week we opened a new state-of-the art children's hospital, and other than local TV coverage and newspaper PR, it doesn't seem as if anyone is interested.

So I have the following questions:

1. What can we do to change things and get national recognition?
2. Is it important to have national recognition?
3. Should we relinquish our slogan of World Class Care in Your Own Backyard?

\* \* \*

ASSIGNMENT

Answer the board chairman's questions.

---

## CASE 7-12 | Top Performer?

On September 14, 2011, The Joint Commission issued the following press release:

### JOINT COMMISSION ANNUAL REPORT NAMES TOP PERFORMING HOSPITALS

*405 Hospitals Achieve Recognition as Top Performers on Key Quality Measures*

(OAKBROOK TERRACE, Ill. – September 14, 2011) For the first time, The Joint Commission's 2011 annual report on quality and safety, Improving America's Hospitals, lists hospitals and critical access hospitals that are top performers in using evidence-based care processes closely linked to positive patient outcomes. The 405 organizations identified as attaining and sustaining excellence in accountability measure performance for the full previous year

(2010) represent approximately 14% of Joint Commission-accredited hospitals and critical access hospitals that report core measure performance data.

Based on performance related to 22 accountability measures for heart attack, heart failure, pneumonia, surgical care, and children's asthma care, the Joint Commission report singles out hospitals in 45 states. The list of top-performing hospitals and the measure set or sets for which the hospital was recognized are available online.

"Today, the public expects transparency in the reporting of performance at the hospitals where they receive care, and The Joint Commission is shining a light on the top-performing hospitals that have achieved excellence on a number of vital measures of quality of care," Mark R. Chassin, MD, FACP, MPP, MPH, President, Joint Commission said. "Hospitals that commit themselves to accreditation-related quality improvement efforts such as the use of evidence-based treatments create better outcomes for patients and, ultimately, a healthier nation."

The Joint Commission's sixth annual report, which presents scientific evidence of hospital performance and how it relates to common medical conditions and procedures, demonstrates continual improvement on accountability measures over a 9-year period. The newest data, drawn from more than 3,000 accredited hospitals, show:

1. Significant progress in consistently using evidence-based treatments. In 2002, hospitals achieved 81.8% composite performance on 957,000 opportunities to perform care processes related to accountability measures. In 2010, hospitals achieved 96.6% composite performance on 12.3 million opportunities—a 9-year improvement

of 14.8% points. A composite result sums up the results of all individual account-ability measures into a single percent-age result and can be calculated at the measure set level or overall reported accountability measures.

2. The heart attack care result is up 11.5%, from 86.9% in 2002 to 98.4% in 2010.

3. The 2010 pneumonia care result is 95.2%, up from 72.3% in 2002—an improvement of 22.9 percentage points.

4. The surgical care result has improved to 96.4% in 2010 from 82.1% in 2005 (14.3 percentage points).

5. The 2010 children's asthma care result is 92.3%, up from 79.8% in 2008—an improve-ment of 12.5 percentage points.

6. The percentage of hospitals achieving composite accountability measures greater than 90% has also dramatically improved. In 2010, 91.7% of hospitals achieved 90% compliance, compared to 20.4% in 2002.

Although hospitals·achieved 90% or better performance on most individual process-of-care measures, the report contends that more improvement is needed. For example, hospitals finished 2010 with relatively low perfor-mance on the following two measures intro-duced in 2005:

1. Providing fibrinolytic therapy within 30 minutes of arrival to heart attack patients—only 60.5% of hospitals achieved 90% compliance or better.

2. Providing antibiotics to immunocompetent intensive care unit pneumonia patients—only 77.2% of hospitals achieved 90% com-pliance or better.

"While the data across the annual report show impressive gains in hospital quality performance on many specific measures, further improvements can still be made," Dr. Chassin said. "By following evidence-based care processes, hospitals can improve the quality of the care they provide and meet national mandates regarding performance. The Joint Commission will continue to seek new methods to inspire and assist hospitals to excel in providing safe and effective care of the highest quality and value."

One such effort is the integration of performance expectations for accountability measures into accreditation standards. Beginning January 1, 2012, Joint Commission-accredited hospitals will be required to meet a new performance improvement requirement that establishes an 85% composite compliance target rate for performance on accountability measures. The new requirement is intended to help improve performance on selected core measures of patient care. This standard will not apply to the critical access hospital program.

Quality, safety, and patient satisfaction results for specific hospitals can be found at www.qualitycheck.org.

* * *

## ASSIGNMENT

Your medical center is not on the list of the top 405 medical centers and, like the Mayo Clinic, The Johns Hopkins Medical Center, Duke Medical Center, and several others, your facility is traditionally listed in national polls as one of the top places in the country.

1. Prepare a press release to the local media to deal with this situation.
2. Prepare a memo to your board of directors responding to The Joint Commission's press release.

3. Prepare a memo to the staff about this press release.
4. Prepare "talking points" for the CEO to use for interviews about this press release.

---

## The Complaint Department

Herbert Bushel, MD, and chief executive officer of the Tri-County Regional Medical Center received the following letter.

*Dear Dr. Bushel:*

*I am writing to tell you about a series of unpleasant experiences I recently had with one of your medical staff, Dr. Hortense Steele, who practices orthopedic surgery in your medical center. My 16-year-old son Derek had a basketball injury that required an office visit and splinting. The first visit went well. Dr. Steele x-rayed the fingers, told us there were no breaks but that the fingers would need to be splinted for 6 weeks. He made temporary splints and set us up for an appointment 3 days later, with Kate Cameron, Dr. Steele's occupational therapist, who made new splints.*

*The two fingers were splinted and 2 days later we returned to have the splints adjusted. Within a week my son's fingers were swollen and the skin was raw. So we went to a dermatologist who gave us a prescription for a topical steroid. During my son's follow-up visit 3 weeks later, Dr. Steele removed the splint and was surprised to see the inflamed skin and swollen fingers. He told us that new splints would be required and that they would have to stay on for another 5 weeks. He also told us to make an appointment for the next day with Kate to get the new splints.*

*After thinking it over I decided (and my son agreed) that we should go to a different OT for the splint. The first thing I did was cancel my son's appointment with Kate and then, assuming that my son would need to see a different orthopedist in order to get the splints made, I asked for a copy of the x-rays and medical records. The following day I went for a physical with my primary care physician and I told him about Derek's problem. He suggested that we contact Tri-County Hand Clinic and an OT named Lucas Adams. I called Mr. Adams and told him the story and he said that he often worked with Dr. Steele's patients and that he would be pleased to make new splints for Derek. He needed a referral from Dr. Steele and said he would call Steele's office and take care of the paperwork. An hour later he called me back and told me that he got a very hostile response from the Steele office and a refusal to forward a referral. I then called the office and was told rather rudely that the records were ready and that they would not make a referral because they had their own OT. I dealt with the problem by asking Derek's pediatrician to write a referral, which he did.*

*Frankly, all I was trying to do was get care for my son and I am not interested in suing anyone. I was unhappy about Dr. Steele's OT and that was all! In light of the fact that my insurance company is paying good money for these visits, Dr. Steele is on your staff and practicing in your building, I think something needs to be done to prevent these situations from hurting other patients.*

*Sincerely,*

*Rachel Morgan*

* * *

QUESTIONS

1. What leverage does Dr. Bushel have over Dr. Steele?
2. What actions could Dr. Bushel possibly take? What are the implications of any of these actions?
3. Assuming that Dr. Bushel decides to respond in writing, what should he say?
4. How would you suggest Dr. Bushel handle this letter if Rachel Morgan is:
    a. A member of the board or a big donor?
    b. A local politician?
    c. A staff RN at one of the Tri-County hospitals?

## CASE 7-14 | **Back Problems**

On February 9, 2012, an article titled "In Small California Hospitals, The Marketing of Back Surgery" was published on the front page of the *Wall Street Journal*. The primary focus of the article was the activities of Paul Richard Randall, who was hired by the 107-bed Tri-City Regional Medical Center in Hawaiian Gardens, California, to market its back surgery program.

For Randall, this marketing arrangement resulted in millions of dollars in fees as well as additional income from his hardware distribution sales to the hospital. Randall's marketing activities allegedly also resulted in kickbacks to MDs who signed on to do their workers' compensation back surgery and primary spinal fusions at Tri-City.

Prior to the publication of this article, which painted both Tri-City and Mr. Randall in a poor light, the hospital stated that it had terminated its relationship with Mr. Randall as well as the executive who had first engaged him.

\* \* \*

QUESTIONS

1. What is the range of responses that the present executive staff can make about the negative light cast on Tri-City Regional Medical by this article? What are the costs and benefits associated with these responses?
2. Assume you have decided to issue a press release. What do you say and why?
3. It turns out that there is another hospital in the region with a name similar to Tri-City Regional. How should it respond to this article?

| CASE 7-15 | The Colonoscopy Center |
|-----------|------------------------|

> MEMO     February 23, 2012
>
> From:    CEO
> To:      Director and Associate Director of Marketing
> Subject: Colonoscopy Screening Program

As you have probably heard, a recent study in Oregon has demonstrated that colorectal cancer was cut by more than 50% as a result of colonoscopies. Both of you have not likely had a colonoscopy because of your age, but I have already had my first one! Presently the preparation is worse than the procedure because during the procedure you are anesthetized. I think these reports (which have been in the national media as well as our local paper) present a unique opportunity for our hospital to educate the public and provide a useful service. I would like the two of you to look into how we can market a colonoscopy program. Get back to me as soon as possible.

\* \* \*

QUESTIONS

1. What would be the elements of a top-notch program?
2. What could this hospital do that might distinguish itself from other providers?
3. What political problems would you anticipate with a hospital-based colonoscopy-screening program?
4. Is this a good idea?

**CHAPTER 8**

# FINANCIAL ISSUES

 **INTRODUCTION**

Money is the life force of all healthcare organizations. How well an organization bills for its services, collects for those services, utilizes its cash and assets, and raises outside funds will in large measure determine the organization's future. The cases in this chapter examine a broad range of financial issues and challenges that all organization's face.

Decision making regarding these financial issues is handled in a variety of ways in any healthcare organization. Although ultimate authority for financial decisions is in the hands of ownership or its representative—that is, the board—this top level of financial management might or might not actually be involved in the financial management of the organization, depending on the board's power. If the board is powerful, its power most likely will be exercised through the purse strings. If the board is not powerful, it might simply act as a rubber stamp and might not be involved in the financial decisions at all. Quite often, boards take a middle-of-the-road position and act on annual budgets, any capital expenditure over a certain amount of money, or any major change in program that affects or risks the financial health of the organization. The daily management of finances is then delegated to the top managerial echelon, which may delegate some of its responsibility and authority to others in the organization.

Within larger organizations and/or larger boards, the functions related to finance might be delegated to a finance committee. This committee might have limited direct authority, or it might simply be a fact-finding group for the entire board. There is, of course, no simple formula for how all of this should work. The key point is that, in many organizations, the board is ultimately responsible and does indeed exercise that responsibility.

For publicly traded corporations, the early 21st century is surely the era of post-Sarbanes–Oxley. This federal law evolved as a response to eroding confidence in public corporations and developed a host of new financial reporting requirements, as well as emphasized the role and responsibility (including the composition and qualifications) of audit committees. Sarbanes–Oxley is not directly applicable to most healthcare organizational managers, but it could well be a harbinger of the future.

It should be noted that although most boards are under no obligation to select only financial experts to serve on the finance committee or to be their guiding light on financial matters, it is certainly advisable to have people with enough expertise to communicate the board's needs to management as well as management's needs to the board. I have seen more than one board's finance committee composed of lawyers or businessmen who had no particular expertise in finance, much less healthcare finance, and had learned what they needed to know by experience. For example, in one hospital, the longtime board treasurer was the owner of a restaurant and catering business who had no knowledge of the intricacies of healthcare finance. On one hand, such a situation is helpful in that the staff must make its case understandable to those who have only a general understanding of finance. On the other hand, the board is almost entirely dependent on staff for its information in such a situation and is, in a sense, a captive of its own employees.

The focus of financial activities within the healthcare organization or program is the chief financial officer, sometimes called vice president for finance or perhaps treasurer. Invariably these people are trained in accounting. Sometimes they are certified public accountants, and occasionally they have special training in healthcare finance. In this day and age, it is imperative that the senior financial officer be literate in health finance and accounting, not merely general finance and accounting. At one point, I was searching for a new CFO, and one of the board members suggested I interview a friend of his who was a CPA and had audited some hospitals in his community. The CPA was a pleasant and intelligent person but knew nothing about the current aspects of Medicare reimbursement or the local Medicaid situation. Additionally, his understanding and knowledge about the healthcare industry was spotty, at best. Despite the fact that he was likely a competent accountant, I simply couldn't afford the 2 to 3 years that would be required to get this man up to speed to be an effective CFO.

No position in the organization is more important to a CEO than that of his or her CFO. The CFO is responsible for developing and policing the systems that gather, analyze, and interpret financial and related operational data. If this data is correct and presented in a useful format, the CEO will have the proper evidence to make decisions or develop plans for the future. Inaccurate or indecipherable information will lead to disasters. Assuming the CEO does have a trusted CFO, they will undoubtedly become key partners in many of the important managerial decisions in the organization.

A major problem with an accounting and finance staff (and some might say their major value) is that they often lack experience in and perspective on healthcare operations. For example, most of the training programs in accounting and finance focus on the for-profit sector of the economy; entering the nonprofit sector with its slightly different systems, new nomenclature, and different objectives presents problems to a person trained in a different value system and who possesses tools that are only useful when modified. To make up for the deficiencies, many organizations send promising individuals to special training programs and encourage them to enroll in the various health-related professional societies. Such educational and professional involvement serves two major purposes: (1) it acquaints these people with the nature of healthcare organizations and their concerns, and (2) it assists them in utilizing their professional skills to maximum effectiveness in the organization.

One major source of manpower for the accounting and finance teams is the large public accounting firms. Until two decades ago, these firms were primarily involved in the auditing side of health care. However, they have now expanded their areas of interest and expertise by becoming involved in financial feasibility studies and a range of management consultant activities. In the late 1990s, for example, I used one of these firms to provide a financial feasibility study of a new assisted living center. Their product was a comprehensive analysis of the industry, the possibilities, the competition, and the probabilities of success (and failure). It was not merely an exercise in number crunching! Unfortunately for many people (and perhaps fortunately for healthcare organizations), the tight pyramidal structure of these accounting firms causes them to regularly jettison a significant number of their junior staff, thus providing a pool of experienced and well-trained personnel for the health industry.

Despite the expertise of the CFO, the CEO is held most closely accountable for the financial management of the organization. Administrators usually are not formally trained in finance or accounting but rather are trained in general management, which no doubt includes some background in accounting and finance. Typically, though, the board has delegated to both the CEO and the CFO considerable latitude in terms of financial expenditures. For example, in my organization, both the CFO and I had the authority to spend up to $25,000 at a time without seeking board approval. That, of course, did not mean that we could spend the money without accounting for it, but rather that each time an issue came up, we did not have to chase down the board and make a formal presentation on the expense. Thus, if a van broke down and needed a $5,000 repair, it could simply be approved by the CFO. Or, as noted earlier, if a feasibility study needed to be commissioned, it could be ordered without reference back to the board. Obviously, the organization must have money in the budget for these items, but once the blanket authorization is provided, senior executives are empowered to use their judgment to make things happen.

Like most managers, however, administrators must depend on accounting and finance specialists for financial input into decision making. That is why trusting one's CFO is critical. In some ways, an administrator's lack of training in accounting and finance is an obvious limitation; however, the administrator's primary value is in having a broad perspective on the institution's problems and opportunities. For example, one administrator pushed ahead on a money-losing geriatric program because she felt it was important to the long-range interests of the relationship between her hospital and the community. From a purely financial perspective, it might have been a bad decision; from a purely political perspective, it was certainly a reasonable choice.

Many others in a healthcare organization are important to its financial management. Among these people are business office staff, who are involved in the credit and collection systems of the organization; information systems people, who are involved in the systems that set up and record transactions; purchasing staff, whose decisions affect the cash flow and hence the financial health of the organization; and the personnel department, which through its policies affects turnover, vacation substitutions, and a range of other activities that can be translated into dollars and cents. Indeed, the importance of information systems in the vitality of organizations is such that a new senior-level position of chief information officer (CIO) has emerged.

Essentially, then, any healthcare organization operates with a series of cash registers that, if properly utilized, take in (or ensure the receipt of) revenues and disburse money in a way that is organized and related to specific objectives. The nurse on the patient care floor of a hospital must ensure that the proper record is effected when the laboratory test is ordered or some product or drug is utilized; otherwise, the finance office does not bill the patient for the service. If the patient or insurer is not billed, then the organization has expended resources, such as the nurses' and laboratory technician's time, the machinery and supplies to perform the test, and all the overhead systems necessary to support the laboratory, without even the opportunity to be reimbursed. Clearly, everyone in an organization is part of the revenue-generating function. This was negatively demonstrated to me when I was on a consulting project at a healthcare facility where staff had bar-coded peel-off strips to record billable transactions. Because the nursing staff were so busy, they would frequently pull off the bar code label from the item, and instead of placing it in the proper place on the patient's billing form, they would merely place it on their uniforms. At the end of the shift, I watched as these staff tried peeling the labels off their uniforms, tossed some of the wrinkled labels in the trash, tried to remember who should be charged for what, placed some on the correct form and others on incorrect forms, and finally, in frustration, tossed the rest. Money in the dumpster!

For historical accuracy, some of these cases have dates associated with them. Although these dates are central to the issues of the specific cases, the unfortunate reality is that the issues presented in these cases are timeless.

## CASE 8-1 | Credit Crunch

The financial crisis that led to the U.S. government's $700 billion bailout on October 3, 2008, was also on a much smaller scale a crisis for the executive staff and board of the Lowell Medical Center (LMC) in Allensville, Washington. For decades LMC had operated as a successful community hospital with a balanced budget and excellent credit. In 2005, in response to a planning study that identified Allensville as one of the "hottest" retirement centers in the Pacific Northwest, the hospital decided to make some important changes in their traditionally conservative approach to delivering medical care. The plans called for acquiring two smaller community hospitals and opening three community-based health centers, and building a new emergency room and urgent care center. Because of timing and the need to raise close to $75 million, the projects were just getting off the ground during the summer of 2008. Additionally, as the fiscal year closed on June 30, 2008, the CEO learned that for the first time in a decade the hospital would run a deficit of close to $9 million. On September 30, 2008, the Allensville Regional Bank informed him that they were being acquired by a national bank and all their lines of credit were being frozen, including the $35 million line the hospital had.

\* \* \*

ASSIGNMENT

Assume it is October 15, 2008, and the chairman has called an emergency meeting of the board and executive staff to discuss the international financial crisis and any issues that could have an impact on the medical center. What questions must you be prepared to answer—and what are the likely answers?

## CASE 8-2 | Financial Clouds Over Texas

Consultants from the Washington-based accounting firm of Jefferson, Madison, and Associates were engaged by Dallas, Texas-based, nonprofit Hamilton-Burr Geriatric System's (HBGS) new CEO. HBGS is one of the oldest and most distinguished geriatric service providers in the Southwest with nursing homes, assisted living centers, adult day-care centers, ambulatory care clinics, and independent living facilities in Texas (Dallas, Ft. Worth, Arlington, and Denton). HBGS owns five nursing homes (1,000 beds), three assisted living centers (190 units), one independent living building plus one under construction (eventually, 160 apartments), three ambulatory medical care centers, and three day-care centers. Additionally, the HBGS Foundation raises money and holds a $50 million endowment for the system.

The consultants' report confirmed what the CEO had suspected; that is, the system was on shaky financial ground. This conclusion directly contradicted the position held by the board of directors and its chairman who had assured the new CEO that the system was financially sound and that any shortfalls could be covered by fund-raising.

Excerpts from the consulting report are as follows:

- A review of the past 3 years of financial statements clearly demonstrates that but for transfers from the endowment fund and fortuitous fund-raising opportunities the system would be running significant deficits.

- Based on our review of the financials, we project a deficit of from $4 million to $6.5 million in the next fiscal year.

- The likely causes of the deficit are a combination of low Medicaid reimbursement, a failure to attract a significant portion of Medicare residents, an increase in bad debts, slow collection procedures, overstaffing, excessive food service costs, and considerable long-term debt.

- The endowment income has been steadily declining and, in the past 3 years, has seen an erosion of the corpus of the endowment as money has been transferred to cover deficits.

- The current benefits package has resulted in excessive expenses in health benefits. It is anticipated that there will be in the present fiscal year close to $1 million in excess costs.

- Numerous programs are presently losing money. Most notably, the three adult day-care centers require a subsidy of close to $500,000 per year.

- The costs associated with the new independent living center are grossly out of line and represent almost 75% more in building costs than comparable facilities. Fees for housing are projected to be similar to that of other independent living units. The expectation is that this project will be another financial drain on the system.

The new CEO met with the board to discuss this report and was promptly chastised for spending $50,000 on a "useless piece of garbage." The board chairman said he wanted the system to "run the way I've been running it for 25 years and no bean counter is going to tell me who to hire or who to fire. And, I'm determined that the independent living building, which I'm naming in honor of my parents, will not be anything other than the best facility in the world." The chairman finished his tirade by looking directly at the CEO and stating, "I hired you to run this place, not to change it. I'll raise the money; you just run it."

\* \* \*

QUESTIONS

1. What should be the CEO's next move?
2. How can the CEO make the necessary changes without offending the board?
3. How do mission and values impact financial planning?
4. How might this case provide guidance to similar organizations?

---

## CASE 8-3 | The Holy Moly Nursing Center

In mid-August 2011, Jason Moly (along with every other nursing home operator in the United States) learned that his privately owned nursing home was scheduled for an 11.1% reduction in Medicare reimbursement as of October 1, 2011. The statistics for the Holy Moly Home are as follows:

| **Statistics for the Holy Moly Nursing Center;** <br> **124 Skilled Nursing Beds** | |
|---|---|
| **Average Daily Census** | |
| Medicare | 15 residents |
| Medicaid | 100 residents |
| Managed Care | 5 residents |
| **Average Daily Reimbursement** | |
| Medicare | $450.00 |
| Medicaid | $175.00 |
| Managed Care | $399.00 |

Typically the homes have an EBITA (earnings before interest, taxes and amortization) of 12% with a net profit to Mr. Moly of 47% of the EBITA.

\* \* \*

QUESTIONS

1. What impact will the Medicare cutback have on Mr. Moly's net income?
2. What strategies can Moly follow to increase his net income (assume 70% of the revenue is used for staff salaries and benefits, of which 50% are in the nursing category)?
3. What happens if interest rates go up?
4. Should Moly sell the home? Is it likely to sell?
5. What are the implications of turning it into a nonprofit corporation?

---

| CASE 8-4 | **Homeless in Metroland** |
|---|---|

The Metroland Community Hospital (MCH) is a privately owned 131-bed acute-care general hospital. The ownership group is composed of one private investor who owns 49%

of the corporation's stock and three physicians who own the other 51% of the company. One of the physicians, Virgil Teejack, a plastic surgeon, retired from practice 2 years ago and became the hospital's chief executive officer. Due to competition from the local community hospital, a general decline in census nationally, and declining reimbursement from Medicare as well as local insurers, the hospital has started to run at a deficit.

In response to this deficit, Teejack has tried several strategies to raise the hospital's profile and develop new services that would enhance its revenue stream and profitability. For example, he offered a young plastic surgeon office space in the hospital at a below-market rental fee. The physician accepted but still maintains his major practice at a competing hospital. Shortly after the hospital received a good accreditation review, Teejack placed advertisements in the local paper, touting the hospital's excellence. Most recently the hospital has sponsored a televised tennis tournament and a free health fair. And, once again, the result was hardly a blip on the balance sheet.

Shortly after the latest attempt (the health fair), Dr. Teejack was approached by Dewey Cheatum, the CEO of Metro's Free Clinic located on the skid row of town. This area is not normally MCH's catchment area, and most patients from the clinic typically go to the city-owned hospital. Cheatum suggested to Dr. Teejack that it might be in their mutual interest to meet for lunch.

At lunch Cheatum made the following proposal, "For a cash referral fee of $250 per patient, I will steer all my patients to your hospital. All you have to do is provide me with a van and driver, and I will ship these bums who are on Medicare and Medicaid to you. The others I will send to City. I bet everyone of them needs 1,000 tests and who knows what."

Dr. Teejack likes the idea and agrees to go ahead. Within a week his ancillary services are bustling and his beds are full. Because Medicare is the insurer, the bills are getting paid, and he can finally see a financially viable future.

\* \* \*

QUESTIONS

1. What's wrong with this picture?
2. Who is at fault?
3. Is Dr. Teejack being a good fiscal manager?
4. Is it likely that anyone is violating the law?

---

## CASE 8-5 | Asset Shifting at Lenoxville

Several years ago, the Lenoxville Nursing Home, a nonprofit community nursing home, revised its admission agreement to include the following paragraphs for private-pay residents:

> The resident or the resident's responsible party agrees to pay the Home a deposit equal to 1 month's charges, with said deposit being applied to any final charges due upon the discharge of the resident. No interest will accrue to this deposit.

> All monthly bills are payable within 5 days of receipt. Residents or their responsible parties will be billed for monthly bed and board charges on the first of each month. All late payments are subject to a $100 late payment fee. It is further understood that failure to pay all charges will subject residents to discharge from the Home.

Mrs. Wilma Jefferson was admitted to the home 20 months ago as a private-pay resident. Because of her frail condition, her son and sole heir William Jefferson III, MD, was designated as the responsible party—that is, the person responsible for paying her bills with her funds. Shortly after her admission to the home, her son began to transfer Mrs. Jefferson's assets to his name with the idea of transferring enough of her assets out of her accounts that she would be eligible for Medicaid.

At present, there is an outstanding balance due the home of $27,000. Dr. Jefferson now claims that his mother is financially destitute and that she must go on Medicaid. The home's administrator has also learned that as of last month Dr. Jefferson had shifted all of his mother's assets to his own accounts.

At the most recent board of trustees meeting, the administrator brought the situation to the attention of the board and asked for guidance. Several board members were horrified to learn that the home had been carrying the account for almost a year and they were only now being informed. A second group of trustees was anxious to start litigation against Dr. Jefferson and proceed to discharge Mrs. Jefferson. A third group, composed primarily of members with the longest tenure, suggested that the home attempt to negotiate a compromise with Dr. Jefferson. One member of this last group also stated, "Jefferson is an important man in this community, president of the hospital medical staff, and probably the town's wealthiest surgeon, and we don't want to antagonize him."

Finally, the following motion was made, seconded, and passed with a slight majority:

> It is moved that the administration develop a plan and strategy to get Dr. Jefferson to pay the bill and present this plan and strategy to the board at next month's regular meeting.

* * *

QUESTIONS

1. Assuming you are the administrator, what would be your plan and strategy for dealing with the Jefferson situation? What impediments would you expect?
2. How could you avoid a similar situation in the future?

---

## CASE 8-6 | Headliner

For the past 19 years the Alpha Bravo Medical Center (ABMC) has run an annual dinner that raised an average of $50,000. Typically the dinner was at a local catering hall and began with an open bar and buffet hour followed by a sit-down dinner. Most of the medical staff, board, and active community members regularly attended. The bulk of the $50,000 came from the annual journal that was produced along with the dinner. From a financial perspective, the dinner itself made only $10,000 from its ticket sales.

This year one of the members of the annual dinner committee, Albert Katraz, proposed that instead of having the usual boring guest speakers—typically the city's mayor, a local congressman, or a state senator—the ABMC invest in a headliner. By headliner Mr. Katraz meant a celebrity singer or entertainer. The names he floated for the committee's consideration were Mandy Patinkin, Jerry Seinfeld, Garrison Keillor, and Marvin Hamlisch. Katraz argued that each of these people has some, albeit tangential, connection to the ABMC, and that having them there would result in a better fund-raiser.

* * *

QUESTIONS

1. What additional arguments could be raised for or against the use of a headliner?
2. What additional expenses would be involved with using a headliner?
3. Are there ways to defray these extra expenses?
4. Is getting a headliner really a good idea?

## CASE 8-7 | Vscan Purchase

Dr. John Adams, Chairman of the Department of Family Medicine at Constitution University Medical Center (CUMC), has sent the following memo to Tom Jefferson, the CUMC President.

---

MEMO

From:    John Adams, MD, the Franklin and Theodore Jackson Professor of Family Medicine and Chairman, Department of Family Medicine

To:    Tom Jefferson

Subject:  Purchase of GE Vscan handheld ultrasound equipment

---

Tom:

This week I was at a meeting in Atlanta and saw a demonstra-tion of the GE Vscan handheld ultrasound machine. As you probably know, this very portable ultrasound machine could revolutionize the diagnostic process. I am convinced that this device will enhance the ability of our staff to make better diagnoses and therefore better treatments. Further, I believe that the use of these devices will be the accepted standard of care in the near future in the treatment of all patients.

I am proposing that the hospital purchase 12 of these devices for use by our resident staff and our hospitalists on duty. If the hospital doesn't have the money readily available, then I propose using our medical education fund for these devices.

Let me know about this ASAP because I have already talked to a GE reseller about this and I was told that they could offer us a good deal (about $7,800 per unit). Also, I think we might be able to cut a better deal if we allow GE to identify us as satisfied customers.

* * *

QUESTIONS

*Note: Although this is a hypothetical case, the GE Vscan is a real product that was introduced to the marketplace in 2011.*

1. Has Dr. Adams made any commitments to this point?
2. How should decisions about capital equipment be made?
3. What are the risks associated with responding positively to the Adams request?
4. What are the risks associated with responding negatively to the Adams request?

---

## CASE 8-8 | Auto Fringe Benefit

One of the fringe benefits enjoyed by the seven most senior executives in the Brown and Green Health System was an automobile paid for by the system. The actual way the fringe benefit was utilized varied by the particular executive. Three had cars leased directly by the system, two leased their cars personally and were reimbursed by the system for their lease, and two received a monthly auto stipend equivalent to the average costs of the five other leases. Further confounding the equation was that some leases were 3 years in length, others 4 years, and the range of cars being leased went from one executive who leased a Range Rover with an MSRP of $78,823 to the new CEO's Volvo S-80 that listed at $37,150.

* * *

## ASSIGNMENT

In light of the obvious range of lease payments and other arrangements for automobiles, the CEO has asked you to examine these arrangements and to come up with a coherent policy. Because of a pending salary freeze and some likely layoffs, she is very concerned about image and believes these cars send the wrong message within the organization.

## QUESTIONS

1. What should be the elements of a coherent auto fringe benefit policy?
2. Should different-level executives have more expensive options available to them?
3. In light of the fact that senior management is planning a salary freeze as well as layoffs, should the auto fringe benefit be eliminated? What would be the costs and benefits of eliminating the fringe benefit?
4. What should the CEO do about the following situation? There is one senior executive who presently drives a leased Lexus 400 series. This lease will expire in one month and the executive now has requested permission to lease a Porsche 911 convertible, and she has stated that she is willing to personally reimburse the health system for the difference between her Lexus lease and the new Porsche lease.

---

**CASE 8-9 | Stranded in Florida**

By *James S. Davis, MD*

Mrs. Alvarez is a 74-year-old native of Bolivia who accompanied her daughters on a 3-week trip to visit a distant relative in Florida. Mrs. Alvarez, a retired social worker, had health insurance through the Bolivian national healthcare system, but she lacked travelers' health insurance coverage. During her visit, she developed abdominal pain and was brought to the county hospital.

Her hospital course was protracted and complex. At the hospital, she mentioned a history of hypertension, hypercholesterolemia, and smoking. She was diagnosed with a ruptured abdominal aortic aneurysm and underwent an emergent repair. Postoperatively, she initially progressed but later developed left-sided abdominal pain and bloody bowel movements due to ischemic left-sided bowel, a known complication from her initial surgery. As a result, she underwent emergent removal of the compromised intestine.

Her recovery from the second operation was much more difficult. She remained intubated in the intensive care unit for days and was treated with antibiotics for multiple infections. Unable to tolerate oral feedings, she was maintained on intravenous nutrition, and her overall nutritional status deteriorated. She suffered multiple skin breakdowns over her abdomen and legs, requiring labor-intensive biweekly dressing changes, and she was so weak that she could not get out of bed.

During this hospital course, Mrs. Alvarez's daughters returned to Bolivia, leaving her without close family or friend support. She plateaued and then lingered as an inpatient, never significantly worsening but also without improving. Due to her medical needs, her lack of insurance, and her immigration status, no step-down facility would accept her. She was incapable of taking a commercial flight back to Bolivia and lacked the finances for a medical-care flight.

After 6 months, the hospital's medical officer in charge of costs and special appropriations was contacted regarding the situation. He approved a hospital-funded medical-care flight to Bolivia ($40,000) if the Bolivian National Health Service would accept Mrs. Alvarez as a patient. Her medical team contacted the Bolivian health service officials who accepted the transfer. Six months after walking into the emergency room, Mrs. Alvarez was transferred back to Bolivia.

\* \* \*

QUESTIONS

1. What elements should be considered in estimating the cost of Mrs. Alvarez's hospital stay?
2. What should the hospital policy be in similar cases?
3. Should they have offered to transport her back sooner?
4. Should they transfer similar patients to less expensive facilities such as skilled nursing facilities with a guaranteed payment rather than incur hospital expenses?
5. How can such problems be avoided in the future?

---

## CASE 8-10  Twin Mountains Showdown

For the past decade Earl Wyatt has been the CEO of Twin Mountains Medical Center (TMMC), a teaching affiliate of the State University Medical School. During the course of his tenure, TMMC has grown from one 245-bed hospital to a health system encompassing two counties and including the original 245-bed facility plus two other hospitals (a 128-bed primary care hospital and a 348-bed tertiary care hospital). Additionally TMMC owns two skilled nursing facilities, a rehabilitation institute, and 11 hospital-owned practice sites with a total of 64 physician employees who were essentially self-governing including salary levels. Seven years ago the TMMC Ladies Auxiliary purchased a thrift shop that eventually grew into three thrift shops whose profit of $3.5 million has been extremely helpful in covering the TMMC's regular deficit.

Because of changes in Medicare and Medicaid reimbursement as well as the growth of managed care in the region, Wyatt, a CPA and former healthcare consultant (and partner) in one of America's largest public accounting firms, decided to bring in a group of consultants to review the finances of

TMMC. After receiving their report and reviewing it with his CFO, Wyatt decided to present it to the executive committee board and ask for the approval of the committee before going to the full board. There were two areas of greatest concern. The first was the financial management of the thrift shop. Basically, it was run by a group of volunteers with little retail experience. An audit of the operations indicated that there was a fair amount of leakage of expensive items at drastic discounts (below market value) to volunteer leaders. Wyatt's recommendation called for professional management of the thrift shop.

The second area of concern had to do with the doctors' practices. According to the consultants, the senior specialists (about 19 of the 64 MDs) were being paid at such a rate that their practices were financially unviable. Another problem was that, during the past 2 years, nine physicians had been recruited at inflated values during the purchase of the practices. In the judgment of the consultants, there was a potential issue of Medicare fraud and abuse. Wyatt decided he simply was not interested in skating at the edge of the compliance envelope so he proposed to the executive committee that the hospital hire a group manager and take control of the practices, which would include policies regarding salaries and benefits as well as items such as purchasing practices.

The executive committee approved the recommendations and presented them to the board members, who listened respectfully and then voted his recommendations down. It should be noted that the meeting was calm and thoughtful but in Wyatt's judgment totally staged. In analyzing what happened, he conceded that several members of the executive committee had close friends or relatives who were negatively impacted by a new practice limitation. Additionally, the husband of the board's president was one of the thrift shop volunteers most responsible for the leakage problems. The day after the board meeting, Mia Nathan, the board president, asked to meet with Wyatt and said the following, "I am quite unhappy with last night's meeting. I really don't feel like you gave the executive committee the full picture and I for one was totally embarrassed. I've talked to the other members of the executive committee, and we would like you to resign immediately. Today! Right now! We will pay you full salary and benefits for the remainder of your contract (13 months) plus provide you with 1-year full pay and benefits as a severance package. Wyatt, you have lost our confidence!"

Earl Wyatt was flabbergasted! He was not certain of his next move.

\* \* \*

QUESTIONS

1. Was Wyatt being overly cautious in his approach to reigning in the group practice?
2. In light of the fact that Wyatt is to receive the remainder of his contract as well as a severance benefit, what damages has he incurred?
3. Other than losing their CEO, what other consequences might there be for the organization? How about the board of directors?

---

## CASE 8-11 | Health and Fitness Tax Conflict

The Mason Valley Health Center is a 501(c)3 nonprofit, 178-bed comprehensive medical center that has been a leader in innovation and community services since its inception. As part of its community outreach, Mason Valley has developed a Health and Wellness Center in a neighboring town (South Nome). This center, according to its website, focuses on fitness, disease prevention, and health enhancement.

Similar to other hospital-based and hospital-owned fitness centers, there is clearly a clinical component that requires a fitness assessment (and sometimes medical consent) prior to being granted membership or access. There is also a semi-annual reassessment. Additionally, the center operates a cardiac rehabilitation program, a pediatric clinic, and a physical therapy clinic, all of which bill third-party insurers.

Several years ago the town council of South Nome raised the issue of whether the center should be taxed in the same manner as the LA Fitness facility also located in town. These facilities have the same size lap pools, a similar array of cardio and weight training equipment, and similar programs such as yoga, Pilates, Zumba dancing, and spinning classes. From the perspective of the town council, the only difference was that a small percentage of the center's members were in cardiac rehabilitation and that a nonprofit company owned the facility. Further, they felt that the distance (about a 20-minute drive) meant that the center was not really part of the hospital.

Based on their deliberations, the town council decided to assess the center for taxes in the same manner as the LA Fitness Center.

* * *

QUESTIONS

1. Is this an isolated case of a community wanting to get tax dollars from a nonprofit organization?
2. Are all nonprofit organizations similar in terms of community service and financial ownership?
3. What are your arguments for and against taxing the Health and Wellness Center?
4. If the town can prevail, what are the implications for the entire Mason Valley Health Center?
5. Is there some middle ground for negotiation between the town and the Health and Wellness Center?
6. What would be your decision and why?

---

## CASE 8-12 | Embezzlement and the FBI

The following press release (partially excerpted) came from the Office of the U.S. Attorney for the District of Connecticut on September 1, 2010.

### INDICTMENT RETURNED AGAINST FORMER DANBURY HOSPITAL CFO

David B. Fein, United States Attorney for the District of Connecticut, announced that a federal grand jury sitting in Hartford returned an indictment today charging William Roe, 56, of Wilton, with one count of wire fraud and two counts of interstate transportation of stolen moneys.

According to the indictment, Roe was employed by Catholic Healthcare Partners (CHP), a nonprofit health system that operated St. Rita's Hospital in Lima, Ohio, and by Danbury Hospital in Danbury, Connecticut, as a senior vice president and chief financial officer. He also is the registered owner of a company called Cycle Software Solutions, located in Archbald, Pennsylvania. Between approximately July 2008 and July 2010, Roe is alleged to have defrauded both CHP and Danbury Hospital of more than $150,000 by submitting false invoices from Cycle Software Solutions to Danbury Hospital and CHP for software and services that were never provided and obtaining payment on those invoices.

If convicted, Roe faces a maximum term of imprisonment of 20 years and a fine of up to $1 million on the wire fraud count, a maximum term of imprisonment of 10 years, and a fine of up to $250,000 on each count of interstate transportation of stolen moneys.

On August 17, 2010, Roe was arrested on a federal criminal complaint stemming from this alleged fraud scheme. Following his arrest, he appeared before United States Magistrate Judge Holly B. Fitzsimmons in Bridgeport and was released on a $100,000 bond under conditions including that he have no contact with anyone affiliated with Danbury Hospital and that he not travel outside the state of Connecticut without the prior approval of the United States Probation Office. Upon receiving information that Roe allegedly violated conditions of his release, the government filed a motion requesting that the court revoke his bond. On August 20, 2010, ROE was arrested in Pennsylvania where he is detained pending a hearing scheduled for September 7 before Judge Fitzsimmons.

U.S. Attorney Fein stressed that an indictment is not evidence of guilt. Charges are only allegations, and each defendant is presumed innocent unless and until proven guilty beyond a reasonable doubt.

Less than a year later (July 11, 2011) the U.S. Attorney issued another press release:

### FORMER HOSPITAL CFO SENTENCED TO 33 MONTHS IN FEDERAL PRISON FOR FRAUD

David B. Fein, U.S. Attorney for the District of Connecticut, announced that William Roe, 55, formerly of Archbald, Pennsylvania, and Wilton, Connecticut, was sentenced today in Hartford by U.S. District Judge Vanessa L. Bryant to 33 months of imprisonment, followed by 3 years of supervised release, for defrauding two hospitals where he was employed of approximately $200,000.

According to court documents and statements made in court, Roe was employed as Chief Financial Officer of St. Rita's Hospital in Lima, Ohio, from 2006 through early 2009 and as CFO of Danbury Hospital in Danbury, Connecticut, from early 2009 through August 2010. Roe also created a company called Cycle Software Solutions. Beginning in July 2008 and continuing for approximately 2 years, Roe used Cycle Software Solutions to defraud both St. Rita's Hospital and Danbury Hospital by billing the hospitals for software and services that were never provided.

Specifically, Roe billed and received from St. Rita's Hospital approximately $75,000 for services that were never provided and billed and received from Danbury Hospital approximately $95,000 for software that was never provided. Roe also billed Danbury Hospital for an additional $25,000, the payment on which was stopped.

On January 4, 2011, Roe pleaded guilty to one count of wire fraud stemming from this scheme.

Today, Judge Bryant ordered Roe to pay restitution of $75,000 to St. Rita's Hospital
and $141,166 to Danbury Hospital. The Danbury
Hospital restitution figure includes an additional $46,166 that Roe improperly received
from the hospital.
On August 17, 2010, Roe was arrested on a
federal criminal complaint stemming from this
fraud scheme. He was released on bond from
September 9, 2010, until March 29, 2011, when
Roe's bond was revoked after Judge Bryant
determined that Roe had violated a condition
of his bond. Roe was prohibited from using
the Internet but sent his probation officer
an email using his wife's email account and
his wife's name.

This matter was investigated by the Federal Bureau of
Investigation and was prosecuted by Assistant U.S. Attorney
Rahul Kale and Senior Litigation Counsel Richard J. Schechter.

\* \* \*

QUESTIONS

1. How could the hospital auditors and executive staff not
   have known what was going on?
2. Should the board take any additional action?
3. What lessons does this case offer for any healthcare
   executive?

---

## CASE 8-13 | Houdini and Blackstone

The Howard Houdini Medical Center entered into a 5-year
contract with the Baseline Mobile Imaging Corporation. The
agreement called for Baseline to be the sole provider of mobile
magnetic resonance imaging (MRI) at Lockport Hospital,
a smaller facility 7 miles away owned by Houdini. The contract was an as-required agreement. Houdini was obligated to
pay a set price for whatever MRIs were ordered. No minimum
or maximum number of MRIs was specified in the contract.

The contract also had a clause that required any successor organization to assume the obligations under the contract. Finally, the contract contained the following clause in case of any contract dispute, "The prevailing party will be entitled to reimbursement of its expenses, including court expenses, and lawyers' fees." Another section of the contract stated that the defaulting party would pay attorney fees.

One year into the contract, Houdini was acquired by a former competitor, the Blackstone Hospital and Medical Center. After reviewing the contract, the Blackstone CEO decided to simply cancel the contract because her radiology department informed her that they had ample capacity to handle the entire MRI needs of the combined system at Blackstone.

\* \* \*

QUESTIONS

1. Should the CEO of Blackstone expect Baseline to walk away from the contract?
2. If Baseline sues, what are its damages?
3. If Blackstone cancels the contract, is it in default? What does that mean?
4. Is there a way for Blackstone to honor the contract without financial consequences?

---

## CASE 8-14 | For Sale: Imaging Center

By *Andrew R. Cagnetta Jr.*

Ian Orchid, MD, has been the owner of a full-service diagnostic imaging center for the past 10 years. For health reasons, he would like to sell the center and get the highest amount of cash for his operation.

Dr. Orchid owns the property (10,000 square feet) and a broad range of equipment, much of it at least 10 years old. On his balance sheet, the furniture, fixtures, and equipment were purchased for approximately $5 million, with Dr. Orchid valuing them at $1.1 million. The land and building have an assessed value of $2.5 million. In the past few years, the gross sales have declined from a high of $5.7 million to the present $4 million. In the past year, the EBITA for the practice was $400,000.

\* \* \*

QUESTIONS

1. What is the likely range of services in a full-service diagnostic imaging center?
2. Should the local hospital consider buying the center? Why or why not?
3. Would the value of the practice be different for different buyers?
4. What do you think is a fair price for the property? Why?
5. What do you think is a fair price for the practice? Why?

---

## CASE 8-15 | Western Valley Drug Testing Company

By *Andrew R. Cagnetta Jr.*

The owner of Western Valley Drug Testing Company, located in a middle class suburb of Metropolis, is interested in selling his business. The company has been operating for 7 years and focuses its efforts on drug testing of potential employees and clients of local rehab clinics. These clients frequently have court-ordered mandatory drug testing requirements.

The most common tests are those for prohibited substances such as cannabis, cocaine, and heroin. Western Valley markets its services both online through several websites and through telemarketers who are paid approximately $100,000 per year. The company operates its 1,800-square foot laboratory in leased space with the owner and a laboratory assistant as the only two permanent staff. The testing equipment and supplies are valued at $150,000.

The business has an EBITA of $450,000 on a gross income of approximately $1.6 million. Drug testing accounts for 90% of the gross income.

* * *

QUESTIONS

1. Would a hospital or medical group practice be interested in purchasing this business? Why or why not?
2. Who is likely to be interested in buying this business?
3. How would this business be valued? What risks are involved in purchasing the business?

**CHAPTER 9**

# LEGAL ISSUES

 **INTRODUCTION**

Managers of healthcare organizations are often challenged by a perplexing range of legal issues that typically make them feel as if they need a telephone hotline to a multispecialty law practice. Although the hotline is certainly one solution, it is expensive and simply not practical. An alternative, and the focus of this introduction and the cases in this chapter, is a manager who is well versed in law and the technicalities of the legal system.

Before wrestling with the cases in this chapter, consider the following questions: Where does law come from? What does law do? What is the theoretical model of law? How does law differ from ethics? And, finally, how does the legal analysis affect a given case?

When we consider where law comes from, there are generally three major answers. First, law comes from the federal and state constitutions. For example, the U.S. Constitution has been the supreme law of the United States since March of 1789. Article II,

Section 1, states that no person other than a natural-born citizen of the United States shall be eligible to be president. Poor Arnold Schwarzenegger! In 1951, the XXII Amendment was ratified, limiting the presidential term of office to two terms. These sections and amendments are relatively clear, and litigation over them is almost nonexistent. However, the cases over interpretation of the First Amendment, which deals with freedom of speech, could fill a library. Essentially, the primary source of our laws, the Constitution, is somewhat problematic in that it is frequently ambiguous and, as a result, susceptible to changing political climates. It is, however, the source of last resort and the place where judges have found the rights that have struck down the concept of separate but equal that sanctioned racial segregation in this country and provided women with the right to legal abortions through the vehicle of the case of *Roe v. Wade.*

The second major source of our laws comes from the elected and sometimes appointed legislative bodies. Whether we are talking about the U.S. Congress, a state legislature, or a local board of health, we are generally speaking of laws that have some commonalities. In most cases, the laws emanating from these bodies are responsive to a perceived problem; they are usually comprehensive in design, tend to be prospective, and are a result of an open legislative process. Realistically, though, they are also the products of special interest lobbying and frequently are replete with ambiguities designed to appease different constituents. The Medicare drug legislation is a clear national example of this type of law. It came into being as a result of perceived problems and developed into such a comprehensive and confused bill that it took more than a year after passage for the elderly to realize how limited this highly publicized and praised bill truly was.

Another dimension of these legislatively enacted laws is that they most often require implementing regulations that are promulgated by administrative agencies. These regulations are typically developed by unelected governmental bureaucrats and follow adoption procedures outlined by the Federal Administrative Procedures Act. Although lobbyists and special interest groups can respond to the proposed regulations during mandatory time periods, the government is not obligated to listen to these views. What is perhaps most significant about many of these regulations is that the government agency not only writes the regulations but then also goes on to implement the regulations and interpret them through their own cadre of administrative law judges. The concept of separation of power is effectively absent in many parts of the statutory world.

The interplay of state law, federal law, and public policy is well demonstrated in Oregon's 1994 Death With Dignity Act. This state law, the only one of its kind in the United States, makes it legal for Oregonians who are within 6 months of dying from a terminal illness to take their own lives with the assistance of physicians who prescribe a lethal medication and pharmacists who fill the prescription. The law, passed by voter initiative, has been the focus of various political and lobbying assaults. National politics have also played a part in this bill's interesting history. The U.S. Attorney General during the Clinton administration refused to become involved in attempts to overrule this law; basically saying that the issue was a matter of state law. The Bush administration's attorney general, though, operating with a conservative philosophy, actively pursued an agenda designed to nullify the Oregon law. Oregon has not taken the matter lying down, arguing—and winning—in the Federal Appeals Court that this was indeed a matter of state law. The court sided with the state in May 2004 and the decision was upheld by the U.S. Supreme Court in a 6–3 ruling on January 17, 2006. This drama illustrates how the various interested parties get involved in a process and, depending on your political point of view, either move the process forward or else throw a monkey wrench in the machinery of progress.

The third major body of law is what we call the common law—the extensive body of what we think of as judge-made law, based on cases and precedents. A confusion might set in here, because judges often get involved in the interpretation of regulations and statutes as well as common-law decision making. Unlike statutory law, the common law is developed like a giant jigsaw puzzle, one piece at a time. The essential building blocks of the common law are cases that establish precedents. Without an appropriate case, no piece is available. The common law is thus retrospective. That is, awaiting a case before a decision can be rendered to establish the law. Unlike laws that are established by legislative bodies, these laws are established by the judiciary who may not be an elected body. For example, the U.S. Supreme Court is an appointed body, and historically many members of that court have not come from the judiciary. Warren Burger, a former Chief Justice, had been governor of California, and his successor, William Rehnquist, was appointed Chief Justice in 1986 and served until his death in 2005. Before his initial appointment as an Associate Justice in 1972, he had spent most of his career as a private practicing attorney in Arizona and was active in the Republican party.

Another and perhaps more complicated question is, what does law do? In many respects, its most significant value is that it orders relationships in six important ways. First, rights are recognized through the law. On May 17, 2004, hundreds of gay and lesbian couples throughout the Commonwealth of Massachusetts applied for and received marriage licenses. Until that date, only heterosexual couples were permitted to receive licenses; but a judgment of the highest court in Massachusetts established a new right. It was the judgment of the courts that established the patient's right to informed consent in health care, meaning that a practitioner was required to obtain a patient's permission before undertaking any procedure on the patient. Conversely, in 2012, the legislature of the state of New Jersey passed a bill allowing gay marriage; that law was vetoed by Governor Christie, who stated that he wanted a voter-wide referendum on the issue.

Law also creates privileges. For example, someone can sit on a peer-review committee and make negative judgments about a colleague. Thanks to the law, such judgments can be made without fear of personal liability (although one case demonstrates some alternate ways in which disgruntled targets can counterpunch). Similarly, the law creates power, as in the case of hospitals, which, if they follow appropriate procedures, have the right to deny an unqualified person staff privileges. Liabilities are also a creature of the law. Perhaps a good example known to many of us on April 15 each year is the subject of taxes. A for-profit corporation has tax liabilities, and those liabilities come from state and federal tax laws. The law also creates immunities. In many states there is a doctrine of charitable immunity, which allows charitable organizations to avoid or lessen their financial liability exposure because they are a charitable organization. For example, a state might have a law that limits charitable liability to $25,000 per incident. Finally, the law creates disabilities, as in the case of a minor who is disabled from the operation of the law because of his status as a minor.

From a theoretical perspective, what most of us probably want is somewhat contradictory: a legal system that is fair and unbiased, but with a heart (a bit unfair and a bit biased). This suggests we desire a system that is free of political or economic considerations and one in which the decisions would not vary from judge to judge. In many senses, then, we would like a computerized system of justice but with a heart, our heart! What we have instead is a very human system that is riddled with ambiguity for the consumer. We also have a system that has its own stylized dances and acceptable rules of intellectual and personal behavior, sometimes codified in procedural or evidentiary rules. Everyone seeks justice in the end, but when conflict exists, not everyone sees justice in the same way!

Finally, before examining the cases in this chapter, it is worthwhile to recognize the functions of lawyers, judges, and juries. The basic job of the lawyer is to represent the client or, as the old gangster movies put it, to be their "mouthpiece." The lawyers must understand the facts of the case, clarify the disputed legal issues, and research these issues and facts in order to present them in the light that is most favorable for their client. The judge is responsible for deciding issues of law and the rules that apply to a case; the jury is responsible for deciding issues of fact—essentially, whose side of the truth to accept. This was well illustrated in the famous case of the celebrity Martha Stewart, who was charged with various counts related to insider stock-trading. In this case, the judge decided (as the expert on law) to dismiss the most serious charge against the defendant. In dismissing this charge of securities fraud, Judge Miriam Cedarbaum found that the prosecution had not presented enough evidence for a jury to make a finding of guilt beyond a reasonable doubt. Later in the trial, the jury (as the experts on discerning the truth concerning facts) failed to believe Stewart and found her guilty of the charges relating to obstruction of justice, conspiracy, and making false statements about her stock transactions.

One of the most famous trials of the late 1980s occurred in New Jersey and involved an infant known as Baby M. This case illustrates how a case is characterized, that is, whether it should be considered family law or a contract case. Here the adversaries were the biological mother of the child, Mary Beth Whitehead, and William Stern, the biological father of the child, whose sperm was used to artificially inseminate Whitehead. The controversy revolved around a surrogacy contract between the two parties. Stern had agreed to pay Whitehead $10,000 in return for her having the baby and then forever giving up her parental rights in order that Stern's wife could adopt the baby. The case wound up in court when Whitehead decided, after delivering the child, that she did not want to give up the baby. In analyzing this case, the New Jersey courts struggled with classification of the case—that is, was it a family law or a contracts case? The significance of the classification is that different rules of law apply, and the differing rules can impact the final decision. For example, if the Baby M case were to be classified as a custody battle, then the best interests of the child or even termination of parental rights might be the main legal issues. If the case were merely contractual in nature, then the legality of the contract or public policy considerations might be the rules of law. The Baby M case dealt with all of these issues at various times, and different rules resulted in slightly different results. In the end, the contract was invalidated because the judge said it was against the public policy of New Jersey. This left the door open to the state legislature to articulate policy on this matter through a new law. Custody of the child, however, was granted to Stern on the basis of the best interests of the child. A lower court ruling that terminated Whitehead's parental rights was voided, as was the adoption of Baby M by Stern's wife.

This chapter offers a variety of cases covering a range of legal issues that healthcare managers might encounter in a typical organization. Unfortunately, conflict of interest issues are endemic in many organizations, and the challenge is to identify such issues and then deal with them on a professional basis. Ethics represent another challenge, particularly since many ethical issues are not necessarily illegal but rather wrong, tacky, and demoralizing. Criminal issues and statutory violations are significantly different. Here the administrator should have little hesitation in doing the right thing. Nonetheless, what should be done and what is done frequently are different. There are far too many examples of organizations trying to do damage control by handling the problem themselves and essentially sweeping it under the rug. Universities are masters at this approach—consider the Penn State football scandal!

---

## CASE 9-1 | Birthday Party

Mort Morris, the longtime executive director of the 200-bed municipally owned High Mountain Hospital, decided to have the hospital host a party in honor of his 70th birthday. All the costs associated with the party were paid for by the hospital. When Jimmy Olsen, an investigative reporter from the Pulitzer Prize-winning *High Mountain Gazette*, asked Morris about the costs of this party, he was told, "It is a fund-raiser for the hospital."

Subsequent to the party, the following article appeared in the *Gazette* under Olsen's byline.

Last night 375 people attended the 70th birthday party of Mort Morris, the Executive

Director of High Mountain Hospital. The event,
which took place in the Grand Ballroom of
the High Mountain Resort, included a cocktail
hour, sit-down dinner, and musical enter-
tainment from a band flown in from New York
at the request of Mrs. Helen Morris. The
evening's events were hosted by Mayor Calvin
Lowell and were punctuated by at least five
tributes and toasts to Morris.

In attendance were the entire Morris family,
including his five children and nine grandchildren. The entire city council was in attendance, as was the hospital's medical staff.
Morris, a former executive in the state's
Republican Party, also invited more than 50
prominent politicians from state government
and regional organizations. Amongst the guests
were Lieutenant Governor Perry White, Chief
Justice Lois Lane, and President of the State
Hospitals' Association, Lex L. Green.

Although Morris stated that the party was a fund-raiser
for the hospital, which has a $3.8 million deficit this year,
there were no fund-raising activities or announcements made
during the party. All attendees were guests of Mr. Morris, and
the invitation (see Exhibit) did not mention any charge for
the party.

In a press release after the party, Clarkson Kent, President
of the State Council of the Service Employees International
Union, stated the following:

This birthday party for the 70th birthday of
Mort Morris is another example of the excesses
of the board and administration. It was sup-
posedly a fund-raiser. It was nothing but a
family-and-friends bash that cost $100,000—at
a time when the hospital is running a
multimillion-dollar deficit and there has
been a pay freeze for the past 18 months. The
community and staff deserve better. I am calling on the State Attorney General to investigate this misuse of public funds and breach
of public trust.

| Exhibit | Birthday Party Invitation |
|---------|---------------------------|

HIGH MOUNTAIN HOSPITAL

The Trustees and Administration

Cordially Invite You

To Celebrate

The 70th Birthday of Our Esteemed Executive Director

**MORT MORRIS**

January 17

The High Mountain Resort

Black Tie

RSVP to Jennifer Jones at 555-666-7890

NO SOLICITATIONS

\* \* \*

QUESTIONS

1. What legal issues are raised by the birthday bash?
2. Who should be held responsible for any negative legal consequences stemming from the party?
3. If there is legal action against a board member, should he or she be indemnified?

| CASE 9-2 | Food for Thought |
|----------|------------------|

Marcus Tyme is the president of the Good Tyme Wholesale Paper Corporation and a nephew by marriage of Hugh Howard, Chairman of the Board of the nonprofit Williams Memorial Hospital System. Tyme is also a member of the Williams Memorial Hospital System board and sells millions of dollars in paper goods to the various components of the system. A formal contract does not exist between Tyme and the organization. His prices are generally competitive, and, at the moment, neither Tyme nor any other board member has signed a conflict-of-interest statement with the organization.

* * *

QUESTIONS

1. Is this a conflict of interest situation?
2. If it is, what should be done?
3. If not, what should be done?

---

## CASE 9-3 | The Donation Letters

The chairman of the board of trustees of Port Green Medical Center (PGMC), Robert Jardin III, has asked the CEO of the organization to send the following letter to one of his friends on the stationery of the PGMC. It has come to the CEO's attention that the chairman and his family regularly send out similar letters but never follow up on the letters with gifts; she once asked about this and was told the gifts are the time the Jardin family gives to the organization.

Port Green Medical Center<br>Port Green, MA 01060<br>May 14, 20–

*Dr. John P. Jones*
*13 Ship-Shape Lane*
*South Port Green, MA 01002*

*Dear Dr. Jones:*

*I am sure you will be pleased to know that Dana and Robert Jardin III and their children Tom and Jerry have made a lovely contribution to the Port Green Medical Center in memory of your beloved mother, Tomasina Jones.*

*The Jardin's gift was most thoughtful and generous and I am sure reflects the friendship and affection they feel for you. We are honored that they have remembered our hospital in memorializing your mother. The entire family of the Port Green Medical Center wishes to express its deepest sympathy on her passing. If we may be of help to you in any way during this time of sadness, please do not hesitate to let us know. With warmest wishes to you and your family.*

*Sincerely,*

*Danielle Russo*
*Chief Executive Officer*

* * *

QUESTION

Are there any problems with this letter?

---

| CASE 9-4 | **The Ambassadors** |

The Northville Regional Health System (NRHS) is fortunate to have accumulated an endowment in excess of $35 million over the past 25 years. One way it generates money for its endowment is through a program called the Northville Ambassadors Fellowship, known as the NAF program. To be an Ambassador, an individual must donate a total of $50,000 over a 5-year period. The NAF program has been the "baby" of Henry Higgins, the board chairman. Higgins has instituted a number of benefits for the Ambassadors. Some of these are monthly luncheons at no charge. The luncheons are fairly elaborate and often take place at the local country club or one of several high-end restaurants. The typical cost to the system for each of these luncheons is between $40 and $50 per person. Other benefits include free parking at all of the system facilities, discounted meals in the Ambassador's Dining Room at the Gideon Memorial Hospital, and free tickets to the system's annual ball (tickets cost non-Ambassadors $250 per person).

IRS regulations require that a charitable organization (NRHS is such) that receives a quid pro quo contribution in excess of $75 must provide the donor with a good-faith estimate of the value of goods and services provided. Currently, the NRHS administration provides the Ambassadors with a letter documenting their donations and stating that "this contribution provides no tickets, services, or any benefits that reduce its value for tax benefits."

\* \* \*

QUESTIONS

1. What are the implications of the "less-than-forthright" letter for the administrator signing the letter?
2. What are the implications for the NRHS? What about the Ambassador using the letter for a charitable tax deduction?

---

## CASE 9-5 | The Gunshot Wound

By *Jonathan Bloomberg, MD*

Subsequent to a gunshot wound, Jim Jones, a 16-year-old young man, was taken to Remsen Community Hospital where a local surgeon performed a left nephrectomy. When Jones awakened, he was paralyzed from the waist down and he was transferred to the University Medical Center (UMC), a tertiary care hospital. At UMC, Ben Casey, the Chief Surgical Resident, thought that the local surgeon might have mistakenly ligated the aorta so exploratory surgery was undertaken. It turned out that Casey was right, and the surgeons did what they could to remediate the problem.

After recovering from surgery, the patient was placed in a room where, in short order, he became quite angry and belligerent. The nursing staff asked for a consultation from the Department of Child Psychiatry. The department assigned Tim Doi, a senior resident, to the case. Dr. Doi reviewed the records and proceeded to interview the patient and his family. Over the next several weeks, Doi met several more times with the parents (usually separately because they were in the midst of a divorce) and the patient, who frequently complained of pain and discomfort but was not very interested in communicating beyond that.

Unfortunately, there were some postoperative complications, and the young man died after several weeks at UMC. Dr. Doi called the parents to express his sympathy and agreed to meet with them. After several postponed meetings, Dr. Doi had closed the file on the family. Then, one morning 3 months later, he received a call from the mother who said she was just calling to say hello but had a question. She said, "I heard that when Remsen transferred my boy to UMC he was already brain dead from the gunshot. But what I don't get is how I was able to talk to him for a few days before he got sick again."

Dr. Doi thought long and hard before finally answering, "Mrs. Jones, I don't think Jim was brain dead when he came to UHC. You do know that there was a surgical complication that happened at Remsen and that is why he was transferred to UMC. I think you might want to talk to Dr. Casey." Mrs. Jones was stunned. She thanked Dr. Doi and hung up.

* * *

QUESTIONS

1. How should the surgical staff handle the information concerning the initial surgical error? Does the patient have a right to this information?
2. Should the hospital chaplain be involved in this situation?
3. Was the action of Dr. Doi appropriate?
4. Should there be a policy about post-hospitalization communications?

---

## CASE 9-6 | Fall From Grace

Forty years after he began his career as a hospital administrator in Queens, New York, David Rosen was fired subsequent to a federal indictment charging him with participating in various bribery schemes involving state legislators. Six months after the indictment, he was convicted in the United States Federal District Court in New York City. The opening paragraph of Judge Jed S. Rakoff's opinion is quite interesting:

This is a sad, even tragic case, as it reveals how a widely admired hospital administrator who diligently sought to better the health care of impoverished communities nevertheless chose to entangle himself in the bribing of state legislators.

And entangle himself he did! Basically, he hired state legislators as consultants or directed business to firms with which they were connected. In return, these legislators assisted the various hospitals that Rosen oversaw to obtain state monies to build, stay afloat, and basically thrive.

* * *

ASSIGNMENT

Review the 40-page opinion of Judge Rakoff in *U.S. v. David Rosen*, 11 Cr 300 (JSR).

QUESTIONS

1. Based on a review of the opinion, is it clear that Mr. Rosen violated the law?
2. Mr. Rosen's attorney claimed that Mr. Rosen was operating in the interests of his community. Is this argument supported by the facts in the case?
3. Is it clear that the only way for Mr. Rosen to go about securing funding for the hospitals and related organizations was bribery?
4. Why did Mr. Rosen keep some staff in the dark about the contracts?
5. How careful must an administrator be in certifying the truthfulness of documents?
6. Was the board correct in firing him after all his years of service?
7. Is your opinion about Mr. Rosen in any way affected by knowledge of his salary? For example, in 2011 the head of the NYC Health and Hospitals Corporation received an annual income of $351,000. What if Mr. Rosen's salary were $200,000 per year? What if it were $1.5 million per year?

## CASE 9-7 | Peter's Peers

### BACKGROUND

Peter Adams, MD, is a board-certified surgeon who has had full privileges at Boot Hill General Hospital for 7 years. During that period, he has operated on well over 1,000 adults and children without incident or complaint. He has also not endeared himself to the hospital's administration, board, or other members of the medical staff because of his oral and written complaints about various aspects of the quality of services and equipment in the operating room as well as the care his patients have received postoperatively. For example, in the 3 years before this case arose, Dr. Adams had filed 17 complaints. Each of these complaints was investigated and not one had a basis in fact.

Horace Davis, MD, is a board-certified pediatrician and an active member of the hospital's medical staff, presently serving as chair of the Quality Review Committee. He is also a member of the medical advisory board of the Department of Family Services (DFS) in the state where Boot Hill is located. One day he received a disturbing telephone call from one of the senior staff at DFS. After getting off the phone, he thought about what he had just learned and decided he needed an immediate meeting with Mr. Henry Hill, the CEO of Boot Hill.

### THE FIRST MEETING

The meeting between Horace Davis and Henry Hill took place within 2 hours of the original phone call, and the conversation went as follows:

*Henry:*

Horace, what is so urgent about this meeting?

*Horace:*

Henry, we have trouble! Trouble right here at Boot Hill, and I mean trouble with a capital T. Our trouble is Peter Adams. I just got a very disturbing call about him and Mrs. Adams.

*Henry:*

> What's up? You do know that besides being a whiner a lot of the staff admire him and his wife because they adopted those orphan kids and . . .

*Horace:*

> Sorry to interrupt you. There is a serious problem, and it has to do with those kids. It turns out that they are now 12 years old and the kids have complained to the Department of Family Services that Peter and his wife Mary have been abusing them.

*Henry:*

> That can't be right. After all, my own kids would complain about me if given half a chance.

*Horace:*

> Hank, this is no joke. The call I got today from DFS is that they are taking the kids into protective custody. They called me to see if I knew anything about Peter's behavior that might be helpful to them.

*Henry:*

> This is potentially very serious. Let's call Max Bagelman in on this since he is Chair of the Medical Executive Committee.

## THE SECOND MEETING

*Max:*

> Okay, thanks for filling me in. Now what do you suggest we do?

*Henry:*

> I think we need to take action immediately since Peter operates and sees both children and adults. Also we need to schedule a meeting of the Medical Executive Committee to formally deal with the problem.

*Max:*

> Horace, is there any documentation about what is happening? And, do we have access to that documentation?

*Horace:*

> I don't know.

*Max:*

> Gentlemen, is this at all related, in any way, shape, or form to Peter being a world-class pain in the butt?

*Henry:*

> No, I don't think so. My focus is on protecting the hospital and the public.

*Horace:*

> I agree—I don't think this is a vendetta, and I am genuinely concerned that we need to protect his pediatric patients.

*Max:*

> What if the charges aren't true? Doesn't the DFS make mistakes?

*Horace:*

> Yes, they do sometimes make mistakes, but I think they are very careful in a situation like this. But, yes, this is risky.

*Henry:*

> Okay. I think we have to make an immediate decision. As CEO of the hospital, I am proposing that we immediately suspend Dr. Peter Adams pending further investigation and analysis. Additionally, I am calling for an emergency medical staff executive committee meeting to review the suspension and a board of directors meeting to review the decision of the medical staff. Are we all in agreement?

* * *

QUESTIONS

1. Has Hill gone about dealing with this problem appropriately? Could he have done anything differently?
2. Is he justified in suspending Adams? What if the DFS is proven wrong?

## CASE 9-8 | EMTALA

A month after Olivia Alexander began her tenure as CEO of the Dallas, Texas, JLV Community Medical Center she learned from front-page articles in the local and regional newspapers of a new lawsuit that was filed against a Houston-area community hospital and its neurosurgical group. The legal basis of the suit was a violation of the federal Emergency Medical Treatment and Assisted Labor Act (EMTALA). Having been in hospital management for a decade, Ms. Alexander was quite familiar with other EMTALA cases. She knew that the law was an anti-patient-dumping act, which has as its focus the requirement that all patients seeking care in an emergency room, regardless of their financial situation, receive appropriate medical care and be stabilized before they are transferred to another facility.

The newspaper articles Ms. Alexander read told the story of a woman, Mrs. Sally Altman, who was taken by her husband to the hospital's emergency room. Mrs. Altman came in complaining of nausea, and an "unbelievable splitting headache." She was poorly oriented and her speech was slurred. The ER triage nurse's notes indicated an intake blood pressure of 199/125. In response to her situation, the emergency room physician performed an examination of her major systems, ordered lab tests, and placed her on a stretcher where her heart, blood pressure, oxygenation, and respiration were continuously monitored. Additionally, suspecting some degree of dehydration, the ER physician ordered a saline IV drip as well as an antiemetic for Mrs. Altman.

At some point within an hour of her admission to the ER, Mrs. Altman needed to use the toilet. An internal hospital incident report investigation indicated that Mrs. Altman had pressed her call bell at least once, and apparently because the response from nursing was not immediate, she decided to climb over the rails of her stretcher, tripped on the IV line, and banged her head on the side of a cabinet. The noise attracted the staff, who found Altman on the floor bleeding from a large gash on the forehead. The ER physician immediately brought her into the surgical procedure room, ordered sedation, and sutured the gash. Her husband asked what specialist had been consulted and was told, "none." He asked specifically that a neurosurgery consultant be called in and was told by the nurse that the neurosurgeons could be seen only by appointment because they refused to be on the on-call list. When asked about her blood pressure, the nurse said that it was still as it was and that there was nothing more they were going to do for her. The ER administrator then came over to Mr. Altman and suggested that he take his wife to the university hospital where she might get more specialized care.

Worried about his wife's unstable situation but fearful that nothing was going to change at the local hospital, he agreed to the discharge but requested an ambulance take them to the university hospital. The ER administrator said they could not do that, so Mr. Altman drove his wife to the ER at the university hospital. Once there, a CT scan and an MRI were done that found a massive stroke, which had likely been developing for hours. Mrs. Altman died later that night.

Mr. Altman, on behalf of the estate of his late wife, has instituted the lawsuit.

\* \* \*

QUESTIONS

1. What specific actions should Ms. Alexander take in order to minimize the probability of EMTALA lawsuits at her hospital?
2. How can the Altman case be used as part of a staff education program? Provide a "lesson plan" for using the case with nurses and medical staff.

---

## CASE 9-9   Private Duty and Public Issues

It has come to your attention that many patients of the hospital and residents of the nursing home have private duty aides. The issue for consideration is that many of these private duty aides are in fact full-time employees of either Gideon Medical

Center or King's Park Nursing Home. Although the aides perform their private duty services during their off hours, the Northville Regional Health System, as a service to the families of the patients and residents, keeps track of their private duty work hours and issues checks for the hours spent as private duty aides. In turn, the families are billed without any additional service charge.

The checks issued to the aides are separate from their regular paychecks. No taxes are withheld, and no overtime rates are paid. The NRHS issues 1099 forms for the fees paid to the aides. Copies of the 1099 are properly filed with the Internal Revenue Service.

* * *

QUESTIONS

1. What issues arise out of this practice?
2. What might the administration do to limit any legal or negative PR exposure as a result of these private aides providing care?

---

## CASE 9-10 | Mother-in-Law Dearest

It should be noted that the CEO of King's Park Nursing Home, a 400-bed nonprofit facility, has just learned of the following situation involving Mrs. Arlene Fox, who is the mother-in-law of Ira Lockman, a member of the Home's board. Lockman's wealth is reputed to be in excess of $200 million, a part of which has been funneled into his private nonprofit foundation, the Ira and Jessie Lockman Foundation. The facts of the situation that require your analysis and recommendations are as follows:

1. Three years ago, Mrs. Arlene Fox was admitted as a long-term resident of the King's Park Nursing Home. According to the admission documents, her daughter, Jessie Lockman, agreed to be financially responsible for the bill. No information on the admission form suggests that

    Mrs. Fox would be treated differently than any other full private-pay resident.

2. Since her admission to the King's Park Nursing Home, Mrs. Fox's full charges have been written off on a monthly basis. These charges are for a private room as well as private duty aides. Her annual charges exceed $125,000, and to date she has incurred in excess of $350,000 in charges that have been written off.

3. Neither King's Park nor the system has a written "write-off" or "bill-canceling" policy.

4. There is no written authorization for the write-off of Mrs. Fox's bill; however, a memo exists from the comptroller to the accounts receivable supervisor indicating that administration had authorized the write-offs.

5. Since the time of Mrs. Fox's admission, a monthly statement of the Fox account has been sent to the secretary of the Lockman Foundation. During the course of the past 3 years, the Lockman Foundation has sent checks that in the aggregate correspond to the amount of money written off. The statement of the Fox accounts includes recognition of the Lockman receipts.

6. In response to the funds received from the Lockman Foundation, letters have been sent from the nursing home's development office indicating that a gift was made to the King's Park Nursing Home without benefit.

7. Finally, it should be noted that the CEO is an accountant by training and is aware of the IRS Treasury Regulation 1.501c(3)-1(c)2, which prohibits insiders in a tax-exempt organization from taking advantage of their status to receive any type of private benefit.

* * *

QUESTIONS

1. What issues exist for the CEO? For the organization? For the Lockmans?

2. How can these various issues be best handled?

| CASE 9-11 | **Private Matters** |

Approximately 10 years ago, Kevin Winkle, president of the board of the Tree Tops Medical Center (TTMC) was asked by his good friend Maria Von Cook to be the sole trustee of her estate, which passed into the private Von Cook Foundation. Under the terms of the will and foundation documents, Winkle is to receive a trustee's fee of $25,000 per year. For that, he is responsible for investing and monitoring the funds of the foundation, for distributing the interest from the foundation corpus to any 501(c)3 charity he deems appropriate. Typically the distribution is in excess of $100,000 per year, with at least 90% of it going to TTMC.

Within the accounts of the medical center, Winkle has established the Von Cook account, to which he directs all these donations. Mr. Winkle has required that all disbursements from that account be approved personally by him.

Several weeks ago, Winkle ordered the financial office to prepare a check for $7,500 to Macy's to purchase furniture that was to be delivered to his grandson. A further check of the accounts indicated that over the past 2 years, approximately $10,000 has been disbursed from that account to pay for presents that the senator has given to his wife, sister, and several friends. Approximately $2,000 of this went for items purchased at the medical center gift shop; $3,000 was for fund-raising activities involving the system (he used this money to buy raffle tickets for himself, his wife, and his family from the TTMC Ladies Auxiliary); and the remainder of the disbursements were used to pay for membership dues in the system and other related organizations for himself and other family members. Finally, there was a $3,700 disbursement that was used to pay for Mr. and Mrs. Winkle to travel to San Francisco to attend the annual meeting of the American Hospital Association, where they attended sessions on hospital trusteeship.

\* \* \*

QUESTIONS

1. Is there any problem with Winkle's behavior?
2. Is there anything that Winkle is doing that could have an impact on the TTMC's 501c(3) status?
3. Assuming changes are required: What are they? What would be an effective strategy for getting them done?

---

## CASE 9-12 | The Orange Jumpsuit

Hy M. Yankel, CEO of the nonprofit White Water Health System (WWHS), discovered a pattern of inappropriate behavior by several longtime members of the board who are also related to one another.

For example, one member insisted that the ABC Plowing Company (ABC) be given the annual contract for snowplowing (typically it snowed about 12 times per year) despite not having the lowest bid. When the CEO objected, this board member pointed out that the vendor often sponsored a hole at WWHS's annual golf benefit and that he had been a reliable vendor in the past. When the CEO still objected, he received another call from the board president supporting the awarding of the contract to ABC. The CEO finally relented and gave the contract to ABC. After one of the early snowfalls, he happened to be talking to one of the snowplow drivers and in the course of the conversation he learned that both board members used ABC for snowplowing at their businesses and homes. He also learned that ABC was giving these board members a generous discount because these two men had brought in the WWHS account. In fact, the snowplow driver told Yankel that, if he so desired, ABC would probably plow at Yankel's home for free.

Another issue that troubled the CEO was the way some board members were being allowed to use the health system to their personal advantage. For example, there was a longstanding practice of having the board members receiving medications for themselves and their family members from the hospital pharmacy at no cost. Indeed, the 75-year-old board president also obtained medications for his married children and his grandchildren, gratis. In other cases, board members would purchase supplies and equipment through the system, thus avoiding sales taxes.

The straw that broke the camel's back occurred when Yankel learned that three board members had set up a food distribution company, and the chairman of the WWHS board, an attorney who represented the food distribution company, had met with both the food service director and purchasing director without informing him. Further, in discussions with these two department heads, it became clear that the chairman was pressuring these two people to switch WWHS's account from Sysco, who had always been fair and reliable, to the new and untried entity.

It was absolutely clear to Yankel that the board was both trying to keep him out of the loop and operating in an inappropriate manner. In response to this, he ordered the food service director and the purchasing director to make no changes in vendors until he had studied any proposed options.

Yankel also decided to bring in an outside accounting firm to do an audit of the accounts to see if any other conflicts of interest existed. He found nine instances where there were no bid contracts between WWHS and companies owned or controlled by the board. In four of these instances the amount of money was so minimal that he decided to ignore it. In two cases the cost of the goods and services was clearly in line with what it would have cost had there been a bidding process. These too, he ignored.

The remaining three contracts had significantly higher costs associated with them than if the contract had been bid out. And, in all three instances, the attorney representing the purveyor was the chairman of the board. When Yankel met with staff about these contracts, it was clear that they knew that the numbers were not in WWHS's best interests. Indeed, after examining the accounts, it was clear that WWHS was overspending at least $600,000 per year because of these three contracts. After meeting with the appropriate staff members about the contracts, it was absolutely clear that they were intimidated by the board chairman's overt involvement in the deals.

Following his investigation, Yankel had a phone consultation with his cousin, who was a Boston-based attorney
specializing in Medicare fraud. The essence of the call was
that his cousin felt that in light of the facts and circumstances, WWHS's funding coming primarily from Medicare
and Medicaid, there was a significant chance that the U.S.
government could come forward with charges of Medicare
and Medicaid fraud on the basis of the contracts. His cousin's parting words were, "Hy, you better clean up this mess
or get used to wearing an orange jumpsuit."

\* \* \*

QUESTIONS

1. What actual options does Yankel have?
2. Assume Yankel has decided to clean up the mess. What
   does he do? What do you anticipate will happen?
3. How can Yankel best protect himself?

---

## CASE 9-13 | Consent

Lorenzo Gonzales, a newly arrived immigrant from Cuba, was
brought into a New Jersey community hospital's emergency
room with severe abdominal pains. After an examination,
lab work, and a CT scan, it was determined that he required
emergency exploratory surgery. Mr. Gonzales, who spoke no
English, was presented with a series of consent papers to sign.
The hospital's translator was unavailable. Out of frustration
because of the pressure to get Mr. Gonzales into surgery, one
of the nurses who had a rudimentary command of Spanish
told Mr. Gonzales the following, "Es necesario que firme estos
documentos antes de operar," which means, it is necessary
for you to sign these papers before we operate. Mr. Gonzales
signed.

Unfortunately the surgery went poorly; Mr. Gonzales
went into coronary arrest during surgery and died. His estate
is suing the hospital, and one of their claims is that he failed
to give informed consent.

\* \* \*

QUESTIONS

1. What does the doctrine of informed consent require?
2. Was the nurse out of line by saying what she did to Mr. Gonzales?
3. Who is likely to prevail in this legal issue?
4. How can this problem be minimized in the future?

---

## CASE 9-14 | Jehovah's Witness

José Rodriquez was born in Puerto Rico and moved to New York City at the age of 19. When he was 21, he enrolled in the associate's degree program at Manhattan Community College. He eventually earned a degree that led to a job as an administrative secretary in one of New York's medical schools. After several months of satisfactory work, which included typing and opening the mail, he was transferred to another department where he took on additional responsibilities including organizational work for doctoral fellowships. Once again, this time because of a reorganization, Rodriquez shifted jobs and was placed in a position in which he became more involved with patients. In this third position, he made patient appointments and dealt with patient accounts and some basic patient education.

For more than 10 years Mr. Rodriquez worked in his positions and periodically shared with his coworkers that he was a Jehovah's Witness. Every summer Mr. Rodriquez took time off to attend the Jehovah's Witness convention, and, when invited, he never attended birthday or Christmas parties. If asked, as was often the case, he said the reason he had to decline was because he was a Jehovah's Witness and the teaching of his religion was that such gathering was pagan and offensive to Jehovah.

Shortly after his 10th anniversary as an employee, he developed a condition that required surgery. His supervisor, Janet June, came to visit him. Upon learning that Rodriquez had refused to consent to a blood transfusion if necessary, June began to mock him, according to Rodriquez, saying that he was going to die. June allegedly then passed this word around the office.

After Rodriquez returned to work from an uneventful surgery he felt he had heard all kinds of discriminatory remarks about his being a Jehovah's Witness and their position on blood transfusions. Additionally, because of cutbacks in the administrative and secretarial workforce in the department, Rodriquez was assigned a variety of tasks he had not done since he had first started working at the medical school. These tasks included coffee details and setting up and cleaning up after parties—which was particularly offensive to Rodriquez because he viewed these holiday or birthday parties as pagan in nature.

As his work life seemed to deteriorate, his performance evaluations also seemed to suffer. He went from receiving excellent evaluations from Janet June to below-par evaluations from Ms. June. After his second below-par evaluation, plus a caustic comment from June while he was setting up for a birthday party ("I hope this doesn't spoil your chances for heaven."), Mr. Rodriquez had had enough. He filed a discrimination suit with the New York State Division on Human Rights.

* * *

QUESTIONS

1. You have been notified that a complaint was filed. What is your next step?
2. What documents does the organization typically have that will clarify the situation?
3. Regardless of the outcome of the complaint is there anything to be done?

---

## CASE 9-15 | Passing Hep C

On a warm spring afternoon, Hannah Daniels, MD, a fourth-year surgical resident, was admitted to the Town Surgicenter, a complex owned and operated by William Anthony, MD. An hour after admission, Dr. Anthony, a board-certified gastroenterologist, performed a colonoscopy on her without incident.

Anthony, who used to administer the anesthesia, had decided several years earlier that, in order to meet the evolving standard of care, he would use anesthesiologists to administer the anesthetic agent. In Daniels's case the anesthesia was propofol, an agent that Anthony had actually never administered. The anesthesiologists that Anthony used were all independent contractors associated with the Nickels Group, a corporation under the control of anesthesiologist Dr. Penny Nickels. The particular MD who provided the anesthetic to Dr. Daniels that afternoon was Brandon Samuels, MD. Samuels had been practicing for more than 20 years and had applied for a position with the Nickels group several months before participating in the Daniels case. After reviewing his credentials and speaking with his references, Nickels observed Samuels satisfactorily administer anesthesia to six separate people in the operating room. Based on what she observed in the OR, as well as the written documentation and submitted references, Nickels decided to accept Dr. Samuels into her group.

The way in which the Nickels Group worked is that Dr. Nickels would market the group's services to physicians and surgicenters and then, if selected, Nickels was the person who assigned the various anesthesiologists to the various sites for procedures. All billing was handled directly by the Nickels Groups, who billed either the patient or the insurance company.

The Nickels Group paid rent to the medical offices where the procedures took place. The rent covered office space, use of telephones, faxes, and the like, as well as space for equipment and anesthesia supplies. The only person who had access to the anesthesia supply cabinets was the anesthesiologist. So, in the case at hand, the surgical suite was in the office of William Anthony and in those offices were stored the propofol that Samuels administered.

The actual colonoscopy went smoothly, and Samuels followed his standard practice of using a multidose vial of propofol. Prior to starting her surgical residency, Dr. Daniels had undergone routine testing for hepatitis C with negative results, and again, 18 months before this procedure, she was screened subsequent to being stuck with a patient's needle; the results were negative. Two weeks after her colonoscopy,

Daniels underwent a routine hepatitis C screening, and again the results were negative. Seven months after the colonoscopy, she was screened again, this time as part of prenatal testing. This test was positive, but she was not informed of the findings because she miscarried and the obstetrician never followed up on the test results.

Two years later, a patient of another gastroenterologist had a colonoscopy. Samuels administered propofol, and a month later the patient was diagnosed with hepatitis C. This particular patient had been tested for hepatitis C the week before the colonoscopy and had been negative. Suspecting a problem, the patient reported his condition to the city's Department of Health (DOH). The DOH immediately began an epidemiological investigation and found six other cases traced to the root of the problem—the clinical practice of Dr. Samuels, who routinely utilized multidose vials of propofol and occasionally reused the needle and syringe. As part of DOH's investigation, Dr. Daniels, as well as all patients whom Dr. Samuels had serviced through the Nickels Group, was contacted. She now knew the source of her hepatitis.

Further investigation determined that the state had previously suspended Samuels's license on more than one occasion, and prior to joining the Nickels Group, his license had been suspended for 3 years. Included in the suspension was information that he had given the wrong dosages of medication and failed to properly monitor his patients. Because of this behavior, his malpractice carrier had also dropped him. None of this information had been revealed to Nickels or to Daniels.

* * *

QUESTIONS

1. What legal actions are likely to occur?
2. Assume you are the executive director of an operation similar to the Nickels Group. What procedures would you institute to avoid problems identified in this case?
3. How could this entire situation have been prevented?

## CASE 9-16 | Henry County Whistle-Blower

The Henry County Hospital is a small county-owned community hospital in a rural part of the state. For years, the hospital has had trouble recruiting medical staff. After a 3-year effort, the hospital was finally able to hire Dr. Alfred E. Oldman, a licensed MD with a strong orientation toward alternative medicine.

In addition to her clinical responsibilities, Ms. Erica Barney, an RN on the staff of the hospital for more than two decades, also held the position of Patient Safety Coordinator. Over the course of the first 18 months that Dr. Oldman was on staff, Ms. Barney noticed that Oldman had made a number of serious and unexplainable errors in treating patients. After discussing this with Lucy Sonn, another nurse involved in patient safety, she decided to anonymously report this situation to the State Medical Board. Her decision to not report it to JJ Jingleheimer, hospital administrator, was based on the fact that the administrator and Dr. Oldman had become close personal friends since Oldman's arrival. She simply felt that the administrator would bury the report.

Shortly after the State Medical Board got the information, it notified Dr. Oldman that he was under investigation. Oldman immediately called his friend the hospital administrator, who in turn called their mutual friend, the county sheriff, to investigate. It did not take long to learn that Ms. Barney was the instigator of the report and that she had sent copies of patients' records (with the names and other identifying information blacked out) to the State Board.

It is unclear whether Dr. Oldman actually requested that the administrator fire Ms. Barney or whether Mr. Jingleheimer acted on his own accord. The result, though, was that the nurse was fired based on misuse of privileged information. Further, Mr. Jingleheimer, at the suggestion of the sheriff, contacted the county attorney and brought felony criminal charges against Ms. Barney for misuse of official information.

\* \* \*

QUESTIONS

1. Does this appear to be retaliation for blowing the whistle on a friend on the medical staff?
2. Does it appear that the administrator is acting in the best interests of the community?
3. What should the State Licensure Board do about this situation?
4. What do you think the likely outcomes are in the various venues?

---

## CASE 9-17 | Watson Medical Equipment

Less than a year ago, Dr. Moriarity, director of cardiology services for Watson Regional Medical Center, began negotiations with Gavin Doyle, CEO of Watson Medical Equipment Corporation, a representative for House Medical, for the purchase of an electrocardiogram management system that was manufactured by House Medical. The total cost of the equipment, including installation and a 1-year service agreement, was $198,453.

In the terms of the sale agreement, which was a document from Doyle to Moriarity (as the hospital's representative), the hospital was offered a 6-month right of return. The exact language of this right of return was as follows: "This means that during the 6 months after installation, should the hospital be dissatisfied with the system, you may return it, and all monies paid to House Medical will be returned to you." The hospital purchased the system and paid in full.

On June 1, during the third month of operation, Dr. Moriarity and his staff were totally disenchanted with the system because of continuous problems. Moriarity contacted Watson Medical Equipment Corporation and spoke to Mrs. Jones, a salesperson, telling her that the hospital wished to exercise its right to return the equipment. He then asked her how to go about effecting the return. She replied, "No problem. If necessary we will back up a truck and take it away." Dr. Moriarity then called the head of purchasing, Val Williams, and asked her to coordinate the return and the purchase of an alternate system. On June 9, Williams sent a fax to Watson Medical Equipment and asked them to arrange for pickup in 30 days (the amount of time Val estimated was necessary for a different system to be in place).

Three weeks passed before Ms. Williams received an email from Brian House, CEO of House Medical, stating that in order to return the system there would be a restocking fee, the system would have to be shipped to House Medical's warehouse at the hospital's expense (725 miles away), and the hospital would henceforth be charged $100 per day for use of the system.

The new system did not become operational until July 8 (17 days after House Medical's email).

* * *

QUESTIONS

1. Does the hospital have to pay a restocking fee?
2. Does the hospital have to return the system to House Medical's warehouse?
3. Is the hospital liable for the $100 per day charge? If yes, how does it stop the clock?
4. How could this entire situation have been avoided?

---

## CASE 9-18 | **Home From Prison**

Peter Jameson, president of Cloud Regional Medical Center, has a problem. He has just received an application from James Peters, MD, a board-certified obstetrician who has applied for privileges at Cloud.

For 17 of the preceding 23 years, Dr. Peters had been a member in good standing of the medical staff, twice had served as chairman of OB-GYN, and once had been elected deputy chief of the medical staff. During his 22 years, no complaints had been received, and one malpractice claim was filed against him. This claim went to trial and Dr. Peters's defense prevailed.

Six years ago, Dr. Peters resigned from the medical staff subsequent to accepting a plea bargain on unrelated and non-violent federal felony charges (stock fraud). The terms of his plea bargain were that Dr. Peters would serve 6 years in a federal penitentiary, be on probation for 4 years, and provide 1,000 hours of community service during his probation. The federal court also agreed that Dr. Peters would not lose his license to practice medicine.

Now that Dr. Peters is out of prison, he has rejoined his medical practice, which has been under the direction of another obstetrician-gynecologist for the past 6 years. At the moment, Dr. Peters has no hospital privileges.

\* \* \*

QUESTIONS

1. What are the arguments for and against the reappointment of Dr. Peters?
2. If Dr. Peters were to be reappointed, what conditions might reasonably be associated with that reappointment? How would those conditions be monitored?

CHAPTER 10

# PLANNING THROUGH THE OIG ADVISORY OPINION PROCESS

##  INTRODUCTION

*Note: Because of the complex nature of the cases in this chapter, I have provided an extended introduction.*

Fortunately for the healthcare industry, the government does provide a modicum of guidance designed to explain complex regulations, answer questions, and generally assist organizations and individuals in not getting into trouble. One mechanism for the U.S. Department of Health and Human Services (HHS) to provide this guidance is through its Office of Inspector General (OIG), which periodically issues an open letter on potentially problematic issues. For example, a letter of November 20, 2001, primarily dealt with corporate integrity agreements and the power of the OIG in excluding providers from participation in government-funded programs. This letter makes clear that when determining remedies for fraudulent behavior, in particular the remedy of a corporate integrity agreement as well as what might be the substance of such an agreement, the OIG would be guided by whether and how well the wrongdoer fell on his or her sword. In this letter, the OIG made it clear what it takes to get the most lenient penalty. This initial letter was further refined with subsequent missals in 2006, 2008, and 2009—each one providing further guidance and refinement of the following: (1) whether the provider self-disclosed the alleged misconduct; (2) the monetary damage to the federal health care programs; (3) whether the case involves successor liability; (4) whether the provider is still participating in the federal health-care programs or in the line of business that gave rise to the fraudulent conduct; (5) whether the alleged conduct is capable of repetition; (6) the age of the conduct; (7) whether the provider has an effective compliance program and would agree to limited compliance or integrity measures and would annually certify such compliance to the OIG.

Other guidance from the OIG comes in the form of periodic fraud alerts, bulletins, and general memo-type guidance documents. Illustrative of the guidance-type publication is a document issued on February 19, 2004, titled "Hospital Discounts Offered to Patients Who Cannot Afford to Pay Their Hospital Bills." The problem analyzed in this alert is whether hospitals violate the federal anti-kickback statute when they offer discounts to uninsured or financially impoverished individuals. The answer, the OIG concludes, is that as long as the hospital is not using the discounts as a marketing strategy to attract business, discounts are not given as a matter of routine, and that the hospitals have a good faith method of determining whether someone is eligible for the discount, there is no violation of the statute.

Perhaps the most formal and legally binding type of document is the OIG advisory opinion, established in 1997 by rules implementing a section of HIPAA. Advisory opinions are documents prepared by the OIG that answer specific questions posed by providers about business arrangements that might violate the anti-kickback legislation.

The process itself is voluntary; that is, there is no requirement for any organization to seek the OIG's review of a project. The process also costs money because the OIG charges an hourly fee for its review (fees for this service are generally in the several-thousand-dollar range). If an organization chooses to have a review, then the OIG specifies the information needed about the potential business arrangement and proceeds to do its analysis. Its conclusions are binding upon the government. That is, if the

OIG issues an opinion that an arrangement is not in violation of the statute, and the organization proceeds with the project as initially stated in the documentation and is later accused by a governmental agency for wrongdoing, the opinion is a get-out-of-jail-free card (as long as the project has not changed).

The OIG does not review Stark Law issues (physician self-referral), theoretical questions, or straight-out Medicare fraud issues. Also, the OIG stays away from any market determination issues or Internal Revenue Service (IRS) code questions. Finally, the opinions are published and available for review by anyone (the organizational and individual names are redacted), although they are only of legal authority for the organization that requested the opinion. This being the case, one might wonder, "Why bother reading the advisory opinions?" In my judgment, they do represent useful guidance about the thinking of the government on the fraud and abuse issues. If one becomes acquainted with their thinking, one is in a better position to make determinations for one's own organization without always searching for an official OIG opinion. In other words, they are models of excellent analysis and guidance for the profession.

Over the years, I have read many of these opinions and have always made them a central part of my students' classroom work in my graduate course on corporate compliance. The opinions almost invariably follow a similar structure. The first several paragraphs state what the OIG has been asked to do, and the following paragraph summarizes the OIG's findings, which are typically either that the proposed arrangement could potentially violate the statutes or would not generate a violation of the statute. The last paragraph of the section is a statement from the OIG that this opinion may not be relied upon by anyone other than the person or organization that requested the opinion. Next the advisory opinion goes on to state the factual background, followed by a legal analysis that reviews the applicable law, and applies the facts of the situation to the law. This leads to the next section, the conclusion, which is followed by a boilerplate section on limitations, such as the aforementioned applicability only to the party who solicited the opinion. Where the OIG finds that the proposed arrangement is acceptable, there is typically a final paragraph that is almost contractual in nature, stating that the OIG will not proceed with any action against those that requested the opinion as long as they follow the proposed arrangement.

## OIG Advisory Opinions: An Example

Included here is an example of the type of advisory opinion offered by the OIG. This opinion is presented in its entirety without editing so that the reader can gain a clear picture of the type of analysis that is provided by the OIG when they publish an advisory opinion. The format of the opinion is essentially followed by every OIG Advisory Opinion (although occasionally the opinions focus on other sections of the Social Security Act). While reading this opinion, attention should be directed toward the narrow focus the government presents, the limitations it presents, and the statutory and case law foundations on which the OIG relies in its opinion making. Finally, it should be noted that the redacted identifying information is redacted not by this author but by the OIG for the purpose of protecting privileged, confidential, or proprietary information about the requestor.

---

Re: OIG Advisory Opinion No. 04-08

Dear [name redacted]:

We are writing in response to your request for an advisory opinion regarding a proposal by a physician group practice to develop and own a comprehensive physical therapy center and to lease the center's space, equipment, and personnel to physicians with patients requiring physical therapy services (the "Proposed Arrangement"). Specifically, you have inquired whether the Proposed Arrangement constitutes grounds for the imposition of sanctions under the exclusion authority at section 1128(b)(7) of the Social Security Act (the "Act") or the civil monetary penalty provision at section 1128A(a)(7) of the Act, as those sections relate to the commission of acts described in section 1128B(b) of the Act.

You have certified that all of the information provided in your request, including all supplementary letters, is true and correct and constitutes a complete description of the relevant facts and agreements among the parties.

In issuing this opinion, we have relied solely on the facts and information presented to us. We have not undertaken an independent investigation of such information. This opinion is limited to the facts presented. If material facts have not been disclosed or have been misrepresented, this opinion is without force and effect.

Based on the facts certified in your request for an advisory opinion and supplemental submissions, we conclude that the Proposed Arrangement could potentially generate prohibited remuneration under the anti-kickback statute and that the

---

Office of Inspector General ("OIG") could potentially impose administrative sanctions on [name redacted] under sections 1128(b)(7) or 1128A(a)(7) of the Act (as those sections relate to the commission of acts described in section 1128B(b) of the Act) in connection with the Proposed Arrangement. Any definitive conclusion regarding the existence of an anti-kickback violation requires a determination of the parties' intent, which determination is beyond the scope of the advisory opinion process.

This opinion may not be relied on by any persons other than [name redacted], the requestor of this opinion, and is further qualified as set out in Part IV and in 42 C.F.R. Part 1008.

## I. FACTUAL BACKGROUND

[name redacted] (the "Physician Group") is a professional corporation comprised of five physicians, three of whom hold an ownership interest in the professional corporation. The physicians practice in various fields including neurology, psychiatry, and orthopedic medicine. The Physician Group proposes forming a limited liability company (the "LLC") for the purpose of establishing a comprehensive physical therapy center (the "Center"). The Center will lease space, equipment, and the services of a staff therapist to the physicians of the Physician Group and various other licensed physicians with patients requiring physical therapy services (collectively, the "Lessees").

The Center will serve physicians in multiple fields of medicine, including neurology, cardiology, orthopedics, and internal medicine. The Center will be located in the same building as the Physician Group and each of the intended lessees. The Center will be open six days a week for eight hours a day and will be available to the Lessees on an unlimited, first-come, first-served basis. The LLC will act strictly as the owner and landlord of the Center and will not bill Medicare, Medicaid, or any other third-party payor for services provided in the Center. Each Lessee will bill the appropriate health insurance provider for services rendered at the Center to their particular patients.

Each Lessee will enter into a one-year lease with the LLC and will pay a monthly rental fee for unlimited use of the Center. Lessees utilizing the staff therapist will pay a higher monthly rental fee than those Lessees who provide their own therapist. The rental fee, excluding charges for the staff therapist, will be calculated at the beginning of the lease term by totaling the monthly rental value of all space, equipment, and administrative services provided in the Center and dividing by the total number of Lessees. Thus, each Lessee would pay the same amount regardless of actual usage. The Requestor has certified that the monthly rental value of all space, equipment, and personnel services will be verified and audited by an independent appraisal firm to ensure that it is consistent with fair market value.

## II. LEGAL ANALYSIS

### A. Law

The anti-kickback statute makes it a criminal offense to knowingly and willfully offer, pay, solicit, or receive any remuneration to induce or reward referrals of items or services reimbursable by a Federal healthcare program. See section 1128B(b) of the Act. Where remuneration is paid purposefully to induce or reward referrals of items or services payable by a Federal healthcare program, the anti-kickback statute is violated. By its terms, the statute ascribes criminal liability to parties on both sides of an impermissible "kickback" transaction. For purposes of the anti-kickback statute, "remuneration" includes the transfer of anything of value, directly or indirectly, overtly or covertly, in cash or in kind.

The statute has been interpreted to cover any arrangement where one purpose of the remuneration was to obtain money for the referral of services or to induce further referrals. *United States v. Kats*, 871 F.2d 105 (9th Cir. 1989); *United States v. Greber*, 760 F.2d 68 (3rd Cir.), cert. denied, 474 U.S. 988 (1985). Violation of the statute constitutes a felony punishable by a maximum fine of $25,000, imprisonment up to five years, or both. Conviction will also lead to automatic exclusion from Federal healthcare programs, including Medicare and Medicaid. Where a party commits an act described in section 1128B(b) of the Act, the OIG may initiate administrative proceedings to impose civil monetary penalties on such party under section 1128A(a)(7) of the Act. The OIG may also initiate administrative proceedings to exclude such party from the Federal healthcare programs under section 1128(b)(7) of the Act.

The Department of Health and Human Services has promulgated safe harbor regulations that define practices that are not subject to the anti-kickback statute because such practices would be unlikely to result in fraud or abuse. See 42 C.F.R. §1001.952. The safe harbors set forth specific conditions that, if met, assure entities involved of not being prosecuted or sanctioned for the arrangement qualifying for the safe harbor. However, safe harbor protection is afforded only to those arrangements that precisely meet all of the conditions set forth in the safe harbor.

The safe harbors for space, equipment, and personal services and management contracts, 42 C.F.R §1001.952(b), 42 C.F.R §1001.952(c), and 42 C.F.R §1001.952(d), respectively, are potentially relevant to the Proposed Arrangement.

## B. Analysis

The Physician Group and the Lessees are potential sources of referrals of Federal health care program business for one another. As such, the exchange of anything of value between them potentially implicates the anti-kickback statute.

As a threshold matter, safe harbor protection is not available for the Proposed Arrangement. In relevant part for purposes of this advisory opinion, the space, equipment, and personal services and management contracts safe harbors require that the aggregate compensation paid under the arrangement be set in advance and consistent with fair market value in an arms-length transaction. In addition, leases and arrangements that are for periodic intervals of time, rather than a full-time basis, must specify the exact intervals of use, precise length of intervals of use, and exact rent or charge for intervals of use.

The Physician Group has characterized the leases under the Proposed Arrangement as full-time leases; however, the Center is available to the Lessees only on an as-needed, first-come, first-served basis. As such, the Proposed Arrangement is more appropriately characterized as involving multiple, overlapping, and part-time leases. These leases do not meet the safe harbor requirements that periodic, sporadic, or part-time leases must specify precisely the timing and duration of the rental periods and the compensation charged for each rental period. In addition, as set forth, the Proposed Arrangement raises significant concerns with respect to the issue of fair market value.

Although the absence of safe harbor protection is not fatal, several factors make the Proposed Arrangement susceptible to fraud and abuse. Accordingly, based on the facts presented we cannot conclude that the risk of fraud and abuse is acceptably low.

For purposes of the equipment rental safe harbor, "fair market value" means the value of the equipment when obtained from a manufacturer or professional distributor. 42 C.F.R. §1001.952(c). For purposes of the space rental safe harbor, "fair market value" means the value of the rental property for general commercial purposes. 42 C.F.R. §100 1.952(b). Both the equipment and rental safe harbor require that, when determining fair market value, the value not be adjusted to reflect the additional value that one party would attribute to the equipment or property as a result of its proximity or convenience to sources of referrals or business otherwise generated for which payment may be made in whole or in part under a Federal health care program.

The structure of the Proposed Arrangement, including the overlapping, as-needed aspect of the leases, will make it difficult to monitor, assess, and document fair market value. Moreover, the Proposed Arrangement's structure increases the risk that at least some physicians will pay more or less than fair market value for the space, equipment, and administrative services actually used. Depending on the direction in which referrals flow between the Physician Group and the Lessees, there is a risk that these above or below fair market value payments could be remuneration for referrals.

Further, the Proposed Arrangement would appear to permit the LLC, and ultimately the Physician Group, to guarantee a desired maximum income stream from the Center by basing the rental payments from all Lessees on the total rental value of the equipment, space, and personnel services of the Center, rather than the usage of the Center by the Lessees. There is a risk that this guaranteed income stream could be compensation in exchange for referrals.

Accordingly, based on the totality of facts and circumstances, we cannot conclude that the Proposed Arrangement poses a minimal risk of fraud and abuse.

## III. CONCLUSION

Based on the facts certified in your request for an advisory opinion and supplemental submissions, we conclude that the Proposed Arrangement could potentially generate prohibited remuneration under the anti-kickback statute and that the OIG could potentially impose administrative sanctions on [name redacted] under sections 1128(b)(7) or 1128A(a)(7) of the Act (as those sections relate to the commission of acts described in section 1128B(b) of the Act) in connection with the Proposed Arrangement. Any definitive conclusion regarding the existence of an anti-kickback violation requires a determination of the parties' intent, which determination is beyond the scope of the advisory opinion process.

## IV. LIMITATIONS

The limitations applicable to this opinion include the following:

- This advisory opinion is issued only to [name redacted], the requestor of this opinion. This advisory opinion has no application to, and cannot be relied upon by, any other individual or entity.
- This advisory opinion may not be introduced into evidence in any matter involving an entity or individual that is not a requestor of this opinion.
- This advisory opinion is applicable only to the statutory provisions specifically noted. No opinion is expressed or implied herein with respect to the application of any other Federal, state, or local statute, rule, regulation, ordinance, or other law that may be applicable to the Proposed Arrangement, including, without limitation, the physician self-referral law, section 1877 of the Act.
- This advisory opinion will not bind or obligate any agency other than the U.S. Department of Health and Human Services.
- This advisory opinion is limited in scope to the specific arrangement described in this letter and has no applicability to other arrangements, even those which appear similar in nature or scope.
- No opinion is expressed herein regarding the liability of any party under the False Claims Act or other legal authorities for any improper billing, claims, submission, cost reporting, or related conduct.

This opinion is also subject to any additional limitations set forth at 42 C.F.R. Part 1008. The OIG reserves the right to reconsider the questions and issues raised in this advisory opinion and, where the public interest requires, to rescind, modify, or terminate this Opinion.

Sincerely,
Lewis Morris
Chief Counsel to the Inspector General

## ✌️ OIG Opinions: A Few Summaries

*Note: Before presenting the case studies, it might be useful to see a few more examples of OIG thinking by reviewing synopses of previous OIG opinions.*

### 1. Opinion No. 03-01; January 13, 2003

The storyline in this opinion is of a dutifully cautious company trying to employ someone who may be a rainmaker but had better not make rain with federal dollars. The key players in this situation are a physician who gave up his medical license after complaints were filed against him and was subsequently excluded from Medicare, Medicaid, and other federal health programs and a for-profit company in the healthcare software business that wishes to employ the doctor as a senior executive for business development. The problem is that the products the company sells are, in some respects, used by government providers for reimbursement through the federal programs. The concern on the part of the company is whether their employment of this excluded physician will impact upon the physician; in other words, whether he would be in violation of his exclusion and whether that would put the company in jeopardy for administrative violation of government statutes.

The OIG analysis is that the company does not directly bill the government, although it is in the chain that does seek governmental reimbursement. The analysis also states that employment of excluded persons is allowed but under very restricted circumstances, and the circumstances outlined by the company do fit into that framework. Essentially, then, as long as the physician stays away from anything that smells like, looks like, or tastes like a federal program, the OIG thinks it is acceptable.

### 2. Opinion No. 03-14; July 3, 2003

This might be a scratch-your-head opinion in that an organization doing the right thing for the right reason may be jeopardizing its future. In this case, a rural nonprofit hospital and a for-profit ambulance company are interested in making a deal to provide emergency transport services to trauma victims in a 17-county area. The deal they propose is that the ambulance company would buy, staff, and operate a fully equipped trauma helicopter. The hospital, for its part, would provide a landing pad next to the hospital and rest quarters for the helicopter and ambulance staffs (not restricted to the ambulance/helicopter company).

The conclusion reached by the OIG is that there is a possibility of statutory violations because there might be inducements or rewards for referrals. However, under the circumstances of this case—in particular, the level of need in this rural area, the statewide support of this project by the statewide emergency medical services program, and the community benefits of this project—the OIG concludes that they will not impose sanctions.

### 3. Opinion No. 04-02; March 1, 2004

This is another ambulance service-related opinion. In this situation, the ambulance services are provided by the city's fire department. The issue of concern is that the fire department wants to bill residents directly for their services to the extent of their insurance coverage. But the department is not planning on billing for copayments and deductibles. The question the OIG considered is whether the proposed policy of the fire department to collect insurance-only billings represents an anti-kickback violation. The reason this might be the case is that the government has looked harshly on organizations that routinely waive Medicare copayments and deductibles without first examining the service recipient's ability to pay the extra costs. These routine waivers appear to be inducements to service and as such violate the statutes. Fortunately for this municipal ambulance service, there is an exception in Medicare rules for governmental services when the government itself provides the service (as opposed to the government contracting with an outside vendor). In this instance, then, the OIG finds that the fire department's planned billing practice is not a violation of anti-kickback statutes as long as the billing procedures extend only to city residents. It states rather critically, "Nothing in this advisory opinion would apply to cost-sharing waivers based on criteria other than residency."

### 4. Opinion No. 04-04; May 26, 2004

In this case, a professional optometric association is proposing to implement a portion of the vision objectives of the HHS's national policy, as found in their Healthy People 2010 document. This portion calls for free vision screening of children between the ages of 6 and 12 months in an effort to detect a preventable condition called amblyopia (lazy eye). The project involves optometrists providing totally free screenings without any billing, even if the child is insured. Further, the project has no strings attached; that is, the free screening is not part of some package for which the optometrist charges. A final element of the project is that if amblyopia or any other problem is detected, the optometrist is obliged to offer the patient's family information about the freedom to choose any practitioner for care.

In their analysis of this situation, the OIG begins with a statement that there are provisions in the Social Security Act that generally prohibit practitioners from offering the type of incentive envisioned in this program. The idea is simple: Don't give free deals and attach other services to those deals that Medicare is then obliged to pay for. This sort of activity is viewed as an illegal inducement. However, the Social Security Act does have an exception when it comes to encouraging practitioners to provide preventive care, particularly prenatal and postnatal. The key in this analysis is the safeguard built into the program by the optometric association—in particular, the lack of overreaching by the optometrists. If a problem arises, the optometrists are obliged to inform the family of their right to freedom of choice and their options. All in all, this is a win-win situation for the patients, government, and optometrists because the patients get free screenings, the optometrists are likely to generate legitimate business, and the government does not pay anything for the screening and potentially avoids more costly health problems in the future.

### 5. Opinion No. 04-09; July 15, 2004

This is a complex arrangement with an interesting twist. A physician group practice specializing in geriatrics and nursing homes is proposing an arrangement whereby they pay primary care practitioners for consulting with them about the totality of the health situation of their former patients who are now residents of the nursing home. The ostensible reason for this arrangement is that the nursing home group claims that they have difficulty obtaining the necessary information on the patients in a timely fashion and the original primary care doctor could be helpful in their providing care. The finances of the arrangement involve a monthly consultation fee of $100 if the primary care practitioner has up to five patients with the group. If a practitioner has more than 20 patients with the group, the maximum he or she can receive is $750 per month ($9,000 per year). To me, this surely looks like an arrangement that would induce primary care practitioners to transfer their patients to this group and, henceforth, become consultants.

Although this arrangement is generally a violation of the anti-kickback provision, there is a twist in that the IRS ruled that the consulting primary care physicians are bona fide employees of the geriatric group. Because of their employment status, the conclusion is that there is no violation of the anti-kickback provisions because employer–employee arrangements are excepted under the anti-kickback provisions.

## 6. Opinion No. 05-05; February 18, 2005

In this opinion the OIG is presented with a complex arrangement that, on the face of it, could present significant problems. Here, there is a proposed arrangement between a group of cardiologists (working in a cardiac catheterization laboratory) and a hospital, whereby certain cost savings generated by the cardiologists would result in savings to the hospital, and 50% of those savings would generate remuneration to the physicians. The need for this OIG opinion originated in a study of the practice patterns of the cardiology group and a set of 12 recommendations such as standardizing the products used by the cardiology group and limiting the use of other costly devices.

In its analysis the OIG recognized that while offering incentives to physicians to get them to save money might be an appropriate business arrangement, it also has the potential to undermine the very goal it is trying to achieve through such activities as steering only the less complicated cases to the hospital or payments for patient referrals. In this opinion the OIG also recognized that the proposed arrangements clearly had the potential to be in violation of various federal regulations. However, the OIG concluded that under the proposed arrangement the HHS would not seek penalties. What saved this proposal? The answer is extensive safeguards that the hospital built into the proposed cost savings arrangement. For example, in the opinion, the OIG seemed to be swayed by factors such as the transparency of the financial arrangements and their openness to public scrutiny. Additionally, the proposed arrangement presented evidence that the cost savings would not adversely affect patient care and was not being calculated in a straightforward manner as opposed to accounting magic.

In general, the OIG seemed to be willing to accept this arrangement, which appeared to be a win–win situation for the cardiologists and the hospital while offering no downside to the patient and an upside to the government in terms of reduced expenditures.

## 7. Opinion No. 05-11; August 16, 2005

The OIG is always on high alert for instances of behavior that violate the anti-kickback statute. In this opinion a private for-profit hospital that is part of a state university's medical campus is proposing to donate a building to the state university's medical school that would become a building used by various components of the family practice program including residents, fellows, and attending physicians. Although the OIG acknowledges that there is a potential for a violation of the anti-kickback statute, they go on to say that in light of the safeguards built into the agreement between the private hospital and the state university medical school, there would not be any sanctions imposed by the OIG. It is instructive to consider these safeguards: (1) There will be no requirement or encouragement by the university to have physicians refer patients to the hospital; (2) there will be no tracking of referred patients of university doctors to the hospital; (3) university physician compensation will be unrelated to volume of patients referred to hospital; and (4) physicians associated with university practice will be advised of the above on an annual basis. Simply stated, it appears that when the gift is indeed a gift (no strings attached), the OIG is less concerned about kickbacks—particularly when the essence of the gift is public and in writing.

### 8. Opinion No. 08-07; July 7, 2008

Many of us have had the experience of being disappointed by the service we have received from a healthcare provider. Sometimes that disappointment is because of waiting time, changes in appointment time, and, if we are an inpatient, numerous things. For example, I once had the experience of being hospitalized and being awakened in the middle of the night by two nurses who were discussing the relative merits of salad bars in the community. When I complained about the noise from their talking, they suggested that I take a sleeping pill.

In this opinion, a health system is seeking to address these unmet expectations by essentially apologizing to consumers through a $10 gift card. In their proposal there are certain criteria for receiving the card, such as a delay of more than 30 minutes for service, and certain limitations on the use of the card. For example, the card cannot be used for health- and medical-related items and no more than five cards would be issued to any person in a year.

For the OIG, the central issue is whether the gift cards should be considered an inducement for patients to use the health system's services or alternatively whether the gift cards are a kickback. In both instances, the OIG says that the minimal amount of money involved, plus the fact that there are limitations on the amount of the award and where it can be spent (none of it can be spent at the health system), result in a conclusion that the gift card program would not cause the imposition of any sanctions.

### 9. Opinion No. 09-01; March 6, 2009

The issue the OIG considered in this opinion was whether the provision by a nursing home of free transportation to and from the home for friends and relatives of residents was a violation of anti-kickback and inducement to beneficiaries' provisions of the Social Security Act. The pattern in this opinion is rather straightforward: A nursing home plans to offer round-trip free transportation from defined areas of a city to their nursing home for friends and family of residents.

In its analysis of this request, the OIG finds nothing that would cause the government to prosecute the arrangement for eight reasons. Each of these reasons, if presented or organized differently by the nursing home, might have led to a different result. The following is a summary of these reasons: (1) the transportation will not be used by the nursing home's residents to get services or items from federally funded sources and will not benefit the home by getting referrals; (2) the service will be open to all family and friends and not limited to federal program beneficiaries; (3) the type of transportation will be reasonable—no limos, just vans; (4) the services will be local; (5) the nursing home will be promoting the service locally; (6) local transportation appears to not be adequate in the area—implying there is a need for this type of service; (7) this helps the nursing home provide quality care by making visits by family and friends more feasible; and (8) the nursing home will not be claiming any federal reimbursement for this service.

This opinion is particularly instructive because each of these reasons is a reflection of the government's underlying concerns about inducements and kickbacks. For example, the fact that vans and not limousines are used is significant because the government views the use of luxury or specialized vehicles as more of a valuable benefit to the recipient and thus more likely to be an inducement that requires great scrutiny.

## Legal Background for OIG Case Studies

Earlier in this chapter, under the heading OIG Advisory Opinions: An Example, an unedited actual advisory opinion (04-08) is presented. Under section II of that opinion there are several paragraphs about the anti-kickback and safe harbor regulations. In this legal background section, there is a restatement of the commentaries on four aspects of the law that have implications for the following cases. This material is a compilation of statements made as background material in various OIG opinions.

## ✎ Anti-Kickback Statute

The anti-kickback statute makes it a criminal offense knowingly and willfully to offer, pay, solicit, or receive any remuneration to induce or reward referrals of items or services reimbursable by a Federal healthcare program. See section 1128B(b) of the Act. Where remuneration is paid purposefully to induce or reward referrals of items or services payable by a Federal healthcare program, the anti-kickback statute is violated. By its terms, the statute ascribes criminal liability to parties on both sides of an impermissible "kickback" transaction. For purposes of the anti-kickback statute, "remuneration" includes the transfer of anything of value, directly or indirectly, overtly or covertly, in cash or in kind.

The statute has been interpreted to cover any arrangement where one purpose of the remuneration was to obtain money for the referral of services or to induce further referrals. *United States v. Kats*, 871 F.2d 105 (9th Cir. 1989); *United States v. Greber*, 760 F.2d 68 (3rd Cir. 1985), cert. denied, 474 U.S. 988 (1985). Violation of the statute constitutes a felony punishable by a maximum fine of $25,000, imprisonment up to five years, or both. Conviction will also lead to automatic exclusion from Federal healthcare programs, including Medicare and Medicaid. Where a party commits an act described in section 1128B(b) of the Act, the OIG may initiate administrative proceedings to impose civil monetary penalties on such party under section 1128A(a)(7) of the Act. The OIG may also initiate administrative proceedings to exclude such party from the Federal healthcare programs under section 1128(b)(7) of the Act.

## ✎ Civil Monetary Penalties

Section 1128A(a)(5) of the Act provides for the imposition of civil monetary penalties against any person who gives something of value to a Medicare or state healthcare program (including Medicaid) beneficiary who the benefactor knows or should know is likely to influence the beneficiary's selection of a particular provider, practitioner, or supplier of any item or service for which payment may be made, in whole or in part, by Medicare or a state healthcare program (including Medicaid). The OIG may also initiate administrative proceedings to exclude such party from the Federal healthcare programs. Section 1128A(i)(6) of the Act defines "remuneration" for purposes of section 1128A(a)(5) as including "transfers of items or services for free or for other than fair market value." The OIG has previously taken the position that "incentives that are only nominal in value are not prohibited by the statute," and has interpreted "nominal value to be no more than $10 per item or $50 in the aggregate on an annual basis" 65 Fed. Reg. 24,400, 24,410-24,411 (April 26, 2000) (preamble to the final rule on the CMP).

## Patient Protection and Affordable Care Act

Section 6402(d)(2)(B) of the Patient Protection and Affordable Care Act (P.L. 111-148, 124 Stat. 119), as amended by the Health Care and Education Reconciliation Act of 2010 (P.L.111-152, 124 Stat. 1029), amends the Act's statutory definition of "remuneration" by adding a new exception as subsection (F) for "any other remuneration which promotes access to care and poses a low risk of harm to patients and Federal healthcare programs (as defined in section 1128B(f) and designated by the Secretary under regulations)." No regulations relating to this provision have been promulgated.

## Safe Harbors

The safe harbors for equipment leases and personal services and management contracts, 42 C.F.R. § 1001.952(c) and (d), respectively, are potentially applicable to the Proposed Arrangement. These safe harbors generally require that an equipment lease or services and management contract: (1) be set forth in a written agreement signed by the parties; (2) cover all equipment to be leased or services to be provided for the term of the lease or agreement, and specify the equipment or services covered by the agreement; (3) specify, in cases where the lease or agreement is intended to be on a periodic, sporadic, or part-time basis, the exact schedule of intervals, their precise length, and the charge for such intervals; (4) be for a term of at least one year; (5) set an aggregate rental or services fee in advance that is consistent with fair market value in arm's-length transactions and that is not determined in a manner that takes into account the expected volume or value of referrals or business otherwise generated between the parties for which payment may be made in whole or in part under Medicare or a State healthcare program; and (6) include aggregate rental items or services that do not exceed what is reasonably necessary to accomplish the commercially reasonable purpose for the rental or services agreement. In addition, the personal services and management contracts safe harbor requires that the agreement not include any services that involve the counseling or promotion of a business arrangement or other activity that violates any State or Federal law.

*Note: All the cases presented in this section are edited and modified versions of actual OIG advisory opinions.*

## CASE 10-1 | Enhanced Practice Referral Arrangements

### BACKGROUND

The organization asking for an advisory opinion, the Requestor, is a publicly traded company that provides web-based business services to physician practices. The Requestor states that its service offerings are based on proprietary software designed to work on the web, a continuously updated payor knowledge base and integrated back-office service operations. Its services support administrative aspects of billing and clinical data management for physician practices, as well as automated and live patient communication services.

The Requestor states that its focus is providing web-based services to help physicians, among other things, achieve faster reimbursement from payors, reduce error rates, improve collection rates, improve patient compliance and satisfaction, and more efficiently manage clinical and billing information. The Requestor currently offers three principal services: (i) the Billing Service, which automates and manages billing-related functions for physician practices and assists clients with non-billing related back-office operations such as appointment scheduling, insurance eligibility verification, and account reconciliation and reporting; (ii) the EHR Service, which automates and manages medical record-related functions for physician practices; and (iii) the Messaging Service, which automates practice communications with patients and includes patient messaging services, live operator services, and a patient web portal.

The Requestor states that its typical customer is a physician or physician group that uses either the Billing Service alone, or both the Billing Service and the EHR Service, with or without the Messaging Service. The Requestor generates most of its revenues by charging these clients a monthly subscription fee in the form of either a percentage of collections or a flat monthly fee. According to the Requestor, one of its core strengths is its detailed database of multiple payers' plan and coverage information and billing procedures, which allows the Requestor to automate a substantial portion of the often difficult, time-consuming, and expensive process of generating claims that conform to each plan's specific requirements.

## THE PROPOSED ARRANGEMENT

Under the Proposed Arrangement, the Requestor would offer a new service called the Coordination Service. According to the Requestor, the Coordination Service is intended both to facilitate the exchange of information between healthcare practitioners, providers, and suppliers (collectively, Health Professionals), and to help them keep track of patients receiving services from other Health Professionals.

## MAKING REFERRALS USING THE COORDINATION SERVICE

The Requestor states that, because much of the functional benefit of the Coordination Service is derived from the data maintained within the EHR Service, only Health Professionals who purchase the EHR Service could use the Coordination Service to transmit patient information to other Health Professionals in connection with a referral. According to the Requestor, offering the Coordination Service in combination with the EHR service (collectively, the Coordination Service package) would assist Health Professionals who wish to make referrals ("Ordering Health Professionals") in: (i) sending the demographic, medical record, insurance, and billing information of a patient when the patient is seen by other Health

Professionals; (ii) issuing appropriate referral reminders; (iii) tracking communications with other Health Professionals; and (iv) exchanging information about orders, order results, and healthcare recommendations. The Requestor states that the Coordination Service Package is designed to reduce the expense and opportunity for error associated with communications among Health Professionals, which currently are principally telephone-based and often require multiple contacts, entering and recopying information, and hand-indexing.

Under the Proposed Arrangement, Ordering Health Professionals would use the Coordination Service to access an electronic database (the Network) to identify Health Professionals to which they would like to make a referral. The Requestor certified that the Network would include contact information (location, fax, and phone numbers) for the following types of Health Professionals: physicians, laboratories, pharmacies, durable medical equipment suppliers, and imaging providers. To populate the Network, the Requestor would compile contact information provided by, or collected from: (i) the Requestor's existing database of Health Professionals, which is already used in connection with the Billing Service and the EHR Service; (ii) publicly available Health Professional databases; (iii) Requestor clients (for Health Professionals the clients would like to have added to the Network); and (iv) Health Professionals that were not identified via any of the three methods listed above that wish to be included in the Network. There would be no cost to Health Professionals to be included in the Network. The Requestor states that its goal in populating the Network is to make it as complete as possible, given available information and resources. According to the Requestor, the Network already includes the contact information for thousands of Health Professionals that are either existing Requestor clients or have their contact information listed in publicly available sources.

## RECEIVING REFERRALS USING THE COORDINATION SERVICE: TRADING PARTNERS

The Requestor would offer Health Professionals that are interested in receiving referrals through the Coordination Service the opportunity to enter into Trading Partner Agreements with the Requestor. Health Professionals that enter into Trading Partner Agreements with the Requestor (Trading Partners) would be able to customize their Network profiles to include, in addition to the standard contact information, information such as their subspecialty areas or particular expertise, their availability for appointments, and any clinical information they require as part of any referral. Trading Partners also would be able to receive electronically transmitted, comprehensive referrals (Formatted Orders) from Ordering Health Professionals. Formatted Orders would be sent in a standardized format and would contain: (i) the patient's demographic and contact information; (ii) the Ordering Health Professional's contact information and NPI number; (iii) the Trading Partner's contact information and NPI number; (iv) a verified insurance package that would include the insurance plan's name and number, the patient's eligibility status for the insurance package (to the extent available), and, if necessary and available, the prior authorization information and number; and (v) to the extent available, such clinical data as is requested by the Trading Partner. There would be no cost to Health Professionals to become Trading Partners; however, the Requestor would charge Trading Partners for the services it provides to them.

The Requestor states that the level of service under the Proposed Arrangement would be the highest in cases where both the Ordering Health Professional and the Trading Partner are Requestor clients, because they use the same system and, thus, could easily communicate. For example, an Ordering Health Professional's staff could access precise scheduling information at the time of referral (thus allowing the staff to schedule an appointment for the patient in real time), the Trading Partner could easily share test results and reports with the Ordering Health Professional, and the Ordering Health

Professional and the Trading Partner could communicate securely and electronically with each other about a patient's condition, without having to speak on the telephone.

In cases where the receiving Health Professional is a Trading Partner but not a Requestor client (i.e., the Health Professional has entered into a Trading Partner Agreement with the Requestor but has not purchased the Billing Service, the EHR Service, or the Messaging Service), the Ordering Health Professional could use the Coordination Service to generate a Formatted Order containing all of the information described above, including any clinical information the Trading Partner specifically requested in its customized profile. The Requestor would endeavor to transmit the Formatted Order in an optimized manner, such as encrypted email or direct electronic interface, or in whatever manner the Trading Partner might specify.

## RECEIVING REFERRALS USING THE COORDINATION SERVICE: NON-TRADING PARTNERS

Health Professionals would not be required to become Trading Partners to receive referrals using the Coordination Service; however, Health Professionals that are not Trading Partners (Non-Trading Partners) would not be able to customize their Network profiles in the same manner as Trading Partners, and would not be able to receive Formatted Orders. An Ordering Health Professional could use the Coordination Service to transmit a clean and comprehensive referral fax containing the patient's basic demographic and insurance information in a uniform format to a Non-Trading Partner. The Requestor would not perform insurance authorization services in connection with referrals to Non-Trading Partners, and such referrals would include clinical documentation only if the Ordering Health Professional manually attached it. As with referrals to Trading Partners, the Coordination Service Package would allow the Ordering Health Professional to track referrals to Non-Trading Partners so that any responsive reports or data eventually could be linked to them.

## FEES ASSOCIATED WITH THE COORDINATION SERVICE

Under the Proposed Arrangement, the Requestor would continue to charge Ordering Health Professionals a monthly subscription fee for the EHR Service component of the Coordination Service Package; however, that fee would be discounted. In addition to the monthly subscription fee, the Requestor would charge three types of transaction-based fees for referrals made and received using the Coordination Service: (i) a base fee for transmitting the referral (the Transmission Fee); (ii) for referrals made to Trading Partners, a fee for the work performed by the Requestor to record and maintain the Trading Partner's preferences, to attach the clinical documentation in accordance with those preferences, to facilitate the appointment scheduling with the Trading Partner, and to provide report builder functionality (the Functionality Fee); and (iii) for referrals made to Trading Partners, a fee for the work performed by the Requestor to verify benefit eligibility and obtain the referral authorization (the Service Fee).

The Requestor would charge the Transmission Fee each time an Ordering Health Professional makes a referral using the Coordination Service; however, the party responsible for paying this fee would vary depending on whether the receiving Health Professional is a Trading Partner or a Non-Trading Partner. In cases where the receiving Health Professional is a Trading Partner, the Trading Partner would pay the Transmission Fee. Trading Partners that are Requestor clients would pay slightly lower fees than Trading Partners that are not Requestor clients because it would cost the Requestor less to transmit the information from one client to another within its own system. In no case would the Transmission Fee exceed $1.00.

In cases where the receiving Health Professional is a Non-Trading Partner, the Ordering Health Professional would pay the Transmission Fee. The amount of the Transmission Fee charged to the Ordering Health Professional would be the same as the amount that would be charged to a Trading Partner that is not a Requestor client. The Requestor would cap the amount of Transmission Fees paid by Ordering Health

Professionals at the difference between the undiscounted monthly fee the Ordering Health Professional would have paid if he or she had purchased only the EHR Service and the discounted monthly fee for the EHR Service. In other words, the total monthly fees assessed on Ordering Health Professionals for the Coordination Service Package would not exceed the total monthly fees assessed on Ordering Health Professionals for the EHR Service alone; however, this cap would not apply to amounts charged to those same Health Professionals when they are operating in their capacity as receiving Health Professionals.

The Functionality Fee would be assessed each time an Ordering Health Professional uses the Coordination Service to make a referral to a Trading Partner. The Service Fee would be assessed each time it is applicable (each time a benefits verification or referral authorization service is required). Both the Functionality Fee and the Service Fee would always be paid by the Trading Partner. The amount of the Functionality Fee would be fixed, whereas the amount of the Service Fee would vary based on the level of effort required to provide the related services. The Requestor certified that the Transmission Fee, the Functionality Fee, and the Service Fee all would be set at fair market value, both individually and in the aggregate.

\* \* \*

QUESTIONS

1. Does this arrangement appear to be a referral in violation of the anti-kickback statute?
2. If yes, then does the arrangement appear to be protected under the safe harbor rules?
3. What are the problems with this arrangement?
4. How likely is it that the OIG would approve this arrangement? Why?

## CASE 10-2 | The RFP

### THE PARTIES

The Noah-Victoria Company (NVC) furnishes medical supplies and equipment to skilled nursing facilities. In connection with furnishing the medical supplies and equipment, NVC also provides certain related services to the skilled nursing facilities, including emergency delivery of the medical supplies and equipment, inventory control, frequent visits by customer service representatives to check on existing orders and determine whether other patients require supplies, customized resident-specific packaging, and simple returns of products for credit.

Ava Tyler Skilled Nursing Facility (SNF) is a county-operated skilled nursing facility. The SNF is located in the State of ____.

### BILLING PROCEDURES

When the medical supplies and equipment that NVC furnishes to a skilled nursing facility are covered by Medicare Part B (Covered Items), the NVC bills the Medicare program directly. When they are not covered (Non-covered Items), NVC bills the skilled nursing facility directly. Under normal circumstances, for Non-covered Items, NVC charges a skilled nursing facility a markup, which covers the cost of providing the related services as well as NVC's overhead and profit. NVC has certified that the amount paid by Medicare Part B for the Covered Items is sufficient to also cover the costs of the related services provided in connection with the Covered Items as well as related overhead and profit.

### THE REQUEST FOR PROPOSALS

The SNF has issued a request for proposals (RFP) soliciting bids to be the exclusive supplier of Covered Items and related services to the SNF. Suppliers that submit bids in response to the RFP are also required to submit pricing for the Non-covered Items and related services, which the SNF may purchase at its option.

## PROPOSED ARRANGEMENT A

Under Proposed Arrangement A, NVC would submit a bid in connection with the RFP and, if selected, enter into a contract with the SNF to: (1) serve as the SNF's exclusive supplier of Covered Items, (2) furnish Non-covered Items at the pricing listed in its bid if the SNF chose to purchase those items from NVC, and (3) furnish the related services in connection with all Covered Items and Non-covered Items it would furnish under the contract. NVC has stated that the pricing it would offer in its bid for the Non-covered Items would be such that the total package of Non-covered Items and related services would be offered below its own costs. According to NVC, if it does not offer this below-cost pricing on the Non-covered Items and related services, the SNF would be unlikely to select it as the SNF's exclusive supplier of the Covered Items. While the pricing that the NVC would offer on the Non-covered Items and related services would not be conditioned expressly on becoming the exclusive supplier of the Covered Items, NVC has noted that a losing bidder would not be bound by the pricing included in its bid and that it is unlikely that it would offer that pricing if the SNF selected another supplier for the Covered Items. NVC has stated that the Medicare Part B payments that it would receive as the supplier of the Covered Items under Proposed Arrangement A would more than offset any losses they would incur in furnishing the Non-covered Items and related services at the below-cost pricing.

## PROPOSED ARRANGEMENT B

Under Proposed Arrangement B, the NVC's owners would form a new company (Newco). NVC and Newco would submit a joint bid in response to the RFP and, if selected, enter into a contract with the SNF whereby the NVC would be the exclusive supplier of the Covered Items and related services and Newco would furnish the Non-covered Items and related services. Proposed Arrangement B would be identical to Proposed Arrangement A in all other respects.

\* \* \*

QUESTIONS

1. What is the difference between Proposed Arrangement A and Proposed Arrangement B?
2. Do either (or both) of the arrangements appear to violate the anti-kickback rules? Why?

---

| CASE 10-3 | Transport |

## BACKGROUND

The Dylan Samuels Medical Center (DSMC) is a nonprofit, tax-exempt corporation that operates an acute care hospital and provides outpatient services. Under the Proposed Arrangement, the DSMC desires to provide complimentary local transportation (DS RIDE) to patients (and their families) that present at physician offices located on, or contiguous to, its campus; require further evaluation and treatment, including admission to the DSMC acute care facility; and are unable to transport themselves.

DS RIDE would pick up patients in a hospital-owned, wheelchair-accessible van containing basic safety equipment. A trained licensed EMT employed by the DSMC would operate the vehicle.

DS RIDE would pick up patients from physician offices located on, or contiguous to, the medical center's campus and transport them to the main entrance of the DSMC hospital. The DSMC certified that the usual distance a patient would be transported would be approximately one-fourth of a mile. According to the proposal, the transportation is necessary because its 108-acre campus has limited parking in close proximity to its hospital, and campus walkways may be difficult for feeble, elderly patients to navigate. The medical center further certified that there are limited alternative public transportation options available to patients and that a van service operated by the Requestor would be able to respond more quickly to transport patients than any public transportation option.

The DSMC anticipates that not all patients would be admitted to its acute care facility. Patients may also be treated at an outpatient facility owned by the DSMC if medically appropriate, and in those cases it would transport patients only to DSMC-owned outpatient facilities on its own campus.

Currently, 37 physicians or physician group practices maintain offices on the DSMC campus, and 4 physicians or physician group practices maintain offices contiguous to the campus. All of these 41 physicians are on the medical center staff. The system would work in the following manner: If a physician determines that a patient who needs immediate treatment at one of DSMC facilities is unable to walk the distance required and has no available appropriate private transportation options, then the physician's office may contact the DS RIDE to pick up and transport the patient to one of the DSMC facilities. The EMT driver would respond and evaluate whether the patient could be transported safely in the van or whether the patient would require an ambulance.

The Proposed Arrangement would be offered uniformly to all patients of the 41 physicians regardless of a patient's income level, a patient's source of payment for DSMC services, or the level of care provided to the patient. DSMC would not charge the passengers or any third party payer for the transportation. It would not claim the costs of the transportation directly or indirectly on any federal healthcare program cost report or claim or otherwise shift the costs of the Proposed Arrangement to any federal healthcare program. The aggregate value of the transportation services for each patient could exceed $10 for one trip or $50 on an annual basis.

DSMC would not market or advertise the Proposed Arrangement; however, the medical center would inform the physicians of the availability of its complimentary local transportation program. Additionally, DSMC's proposal states that it would only provide return transportation to the patients' cars located on the medical center campus. DS RIDE will not transport people to their homes or anywhere beyond the borders of the medical center. DSMC anticipates that it would transport approximately 1,000 patients and their families per year. It estimates that approximately 68% of the transported patients would be federal healthcare program beneficiaries.

* * *

QUESTIONS

1. How could this seemingly innocuous program potentially be in violation of the anti-kickback rules?
2. How much money could be involved in this transport idea?
3. What benefit would an MD get with such an arrangement?
4. What benefit does DSMC get?
5. What argument could be made for or against this arrangement?
6. Assume that instead of 1,000 patients per year the number was 100—would it make a difference in the analysis? How about 5,000 patients per year?
7. Does it matter whether DSMC is going to claim any part of this program for federal reimbursement?

---

## CASE 10-4 | The Eye of the Beholder

### BACKGROUND

The Brandon Eye Group (BEG) is a physician group practice that specializes in ophthalmic care. The practice's four shareholders are ophthalmologists, and it also employs optometrists. One of the group's specialties is cataract surgery. A cataract is a clouding of the eye's crystalline lens, which causes progressive vision loss. Patients typically present first to their optometrist with complaints of decreased vision. If an optometrist diagnoses cataracts that may have progressed to the point of requiring surgery, the optometrist discusses treatment options and refers the patient to a cataract surgeon for evaluation.

Cataract surgery involves removing the cloudy lens and replacing it with a permanent prosthetic intraocular lens (IOL).

The typical IOL (Conventional IOL) provides patients with clear distance vision but does not correct any preexisting refractive problems that may have been causing the patient to have difficulty seeing at near or intermediate distances. Patients receiving a Conventional IOL would still require glasses or contact lenses to correct these vision problems. Newer types of IOLs can correct vision at multiple ranges or correct astigmatism (collectively, Premium IOL). Patients opting for a Premium IOL may no longer require glasses or contact lenses after surgery.

The Medicare program covers Conventional IOLs when reasonable and necessary for a patient. In addition, even though glasses and contact lenses generally are excluded from Medicare coverage, Medicare does cover one pair of glasses or contact lenses following cataract surgery. Cataract surgery is a global surgical procedure, which means that Medicare pays the physician one global fee for the preoperative care, the surgery, and the postoperative care for 90 days following the surgery. Payment for the Conventional IOL implant is bundled into the facility fee for the surgery. When a physician transfers care to another healthcare professional during the global surgical period (the surgeon transfers the patient back to his or her optometrist for postoperative care), the healthcare providers bill Medicare using different codes. That is, the Modifier 54 is a payment limited to the preoperative and intra-operative parts of the fee schedule, and Modifier 55 is limited to the postoperative management only.

Premium IOLs cost significantly more than Conventional IOLs. In addition to the implant itself being more costly, the facility and physician might require additional resources for fitting and inserting the Premium IOL. Additional visual acuity testing may also be necessary in connection with Premium IOLs. The Centers for Medicare and Medicaid Services (CMS) considered how to cover Premium IOLs and ultimately issued two rulings explaining that both the professional fee and the facility fee are partially covered by the Medicare program. Correction of refractive errors does not fall into a covered benefit category. If a Medicare beneficiary elects to receive a Premium IOL rather than a Conventional IOL, Medicare pays for the medically necessary cataract surgery when a Premium IOL is inserted as well as the covered aspect of the IOL. However, the beneficiary is responsible for the professional and facility fees associated with increased testing and other services related to the correction of refractive errors as well as the difference in cost between the Premium IOL and the Conventional IOL.

The BEG offers all cataract surgery patients the opportunity to return to their referring optometrist for postoperative care, as long as the optometrist is comfortable completing the postoperative care and the surgeon believes that such a transfer is clinically appropriate. The referring optometrists may also advise their patients of this choice when referring the patients for cataract surgery. Except as specified below, BEG currently comanages patients receiving Conventional IOLs and patients receiving Premium IOLs who choose to return to their referring optometrists for postsurgical care. The BEG has certified that it follows all applicable Medicare billing and coding requirements for those comanaged patients. Additionally, it does not have any written or unwritten agreements with optometrists regarding comanagement; however, it requires that all patients who choose to return to their optometrists sign an informed consent memorializing this decision.

The BEG has certified that it has a broad referral base of optometric and ophthalmic primary eye care professionals in the surrounding communities, many of whom have begun discussing Premium IOLs with their patients. When a patient elects to receive a Premium IOL, the BEG charges a flat fee per eye for the additional testing and related physician services. When the BEG comanages these patients with an optometrist external to its own practice, the BEG bills Medicare with the Modifier 54, as it does with the Conventional IOL, but continues to charge the $500 flat fee. The BEG does not reduce this fee if a patient elects to return to his or her referring optometrist for postoperative services because BEG does not typically perform additional noncovered services for patients who received a Premium IOL after the point at which it would be clinically appropriate to transfer the patient back to the optometrist. In other words, the BEG performs all noncovered services associated with a Premium IOL during the time frame in which the patient is under its care, whether or not that patient is comanaged. The BEG cannot certify additional services an optometrist might perform after the transfer.

According to the BEG, some optometrists have announced their intention to charge Premium IOL patients for noncovered, postoperative services that are not required in connection with Conventional IOLs and that the optometrist determines are necessary in connection with the Premium IOLs. The BEG does not yet comanage any patients receiving Premium IOLs with optometrists who have proposed to charge patients separately for services related to the Premium IOLs; comanagement of these patients constitutes the proposed arrangement.

The BEG would not have any written or unwritten agreements with optometrists for the comanagement of patients receiving Premium IOLs. Under the proposed arrangement, the BEG certified that it would: (1) notify all patients, whether they are receiving a Conventional IOL or a Premium IOL, of their option to return to their optometrists for postoperative care if such a transfer would be clinically appropriate; and (2) notify patients receiving a Premium IOL that their optometrists may charge additional fees for the postoperative services that the patients would not incur if the BEG furnished the care. This latter notification would be incorporated into the informed consent process.

* * *

QUESTIONS

1. Can this arrangement be viewed as violating the anti-kickback statute? Why or why not?
2. Does the fact that Medicare does not cover the Premium services have any importance in this situation?
3. Is it likely that referrals back to the optometrists (at the patient's behest) will result in kickbacks?

## CASE 10-5 | Hospital Discharge System

The Nathan Corporation (Nathan) is a for-profit corporation that provides software, online tools, and related discharge planning support services to hospitals across the nation. Nathan operates an online referral service that provides hospitals with access to a nationwide listing of all licensed post-acute care providers, including skilled nursing facilities, home health agencies, and assisted living facilities. Nathan typically compiles this listing by reviewing state licensure databases of post-acute care providers.

Hospitals use the Nathan system to identify and select the providers that are best suited to meet the post-acute care needs of hospital patients who are ready to be discharged, including federal healthcare program beneficiaries, and to send referral requests to the selected providers. When initiating a referral, a hospital provides to the Nathan Corporation the patient's name and identifying information, as well as any medical records a provider needs to make an informed decision regarding whether to accept the patient. Nathan then forwards this information to the providers selected by the hospital. According to the Nathan Corporation, many hospitals provide referrals to post-acute care providers on a first-come, first-served basis; consequently, the first provider that responds to the hospital's inquiry typically will receive that patient.

Hospitals pay a fee to the Nathan Corporation to utilize their referral data system. Nathan has certified that the amounts paid by the hospitals are equal to fair market value and are not tied, directly or indirectly, to the volume or value of referrals or other business generated between the parties. The Nathan Corporation further certifies that the revenues it collects under its arrangements with the hospitals exceed the associated costs of the running the system.

Currently, nursing home providers are not charged a fee to use the Nathan system to electronically receive or respond to hospital referral requests. Under the proposed arrangement, the Nathan would begin charging providers that wish to use these online capabilities a one-time implementation fee as well as a monthly fee. The Nathan Corporation has stated that the fees would not vary based on the volume or value of referrals or other business generated between the parties.

Providers that choose not to pay the fees would continue to be listed in the system but would not be able to electronically receive or respond to the hospitals' referral requests. Rather, Nathan would notify nonpaying providers of hospital referral requests via facsimile. Nonpaying providers that wished to respond to hospital referral requests would then be required to either call or fax the hospital. According to the Nathan Corporation, nonpaying providers would be significantly disadvantaged vis-à-vis paying providers under the proposed arrangement and may effectively be eliminated from any chance of receiving the patient because they would not be able to communicate with hospital discharge planners and accept referrals in a timely manner.

The Nathan Corporation set the implementation and monthly fees based on research it performed regarding the system's value to providers. According to Nathan, some providers indicated that they would be willing to pay the estimated fees to electronically receive and respond to hospital referral requests, whereas other providers indicated that their profit margins are so slim that they could not afford to pay for such online access.

\* \* \*

QUESTIONS

1. Does this deal sound ethical?
2. Is this a thinly disguised kickback arrangement?
3. Is Nathan dealing in an unfair business practice?
4. How might this be unfair to a Medicare recipient?

---

### CASE 10-6 | Exclusive Laboratory Contract

Charles Avenue Associates (CAA) is a laboratory services management company. Under the Proposed Arrangement, CAA proposes to provide allergy testing and immunotherapy laboratory services and related items to primary care physicians and physician practices (Physicians) within the Physicians' medical offices. Specifically, CAA would enter into exclusive contracts with the Physicians to operate an allergy testing laboratory on the Physicians' behalf.

The laboratory company would provide all of the necessary laboratory personnel (including laboratory technicians), equipment, supplies, training, and billing and collection services to the Physicians on an as-needed basis. Additionally, they would assist the Physicians with marketing allergy services to patients by providing patient education materials and reviewing patient files to identify candidates for allergy laboratory services. The Physicians would provide: (1) space within their offices to operate the laboratory; (2) administrative staff for patient scheduling and other administrative tasks; (3) general medical office supplies and furniture; (4) general liability and malpractice insurance; and (5) physician supervision and interpretation of laboratory results.

The Physicians would bill Federal healthcare programs and third-party payors for the laboratory items and services provided under the Proposed Arrangement under the Physicians' provider identification numbers. CAA would provide billing and collection services on behalf of the Physicians for the allergy testing services.

The Physicians would pay CAA a fee for the items and services provided by the laboratory company equal to 60% of the Physicians' gross collections from allergy testing and immunotherapy items and services. According to CAA, this percentage fee is equal to fair market value. CAA certified that it would contract with Physicians who are not operating preexisting allergy and immunotherapy laboratories. The Physicians would agree to use CAA as their exclusive provider of antigen-based immunotherapy laboratory services and as the sole allergy testing unit for the Physicians' patients.

CAA certified that it is wholly owned and managed by Jack Charles who is not affiliated with any provider or supplier of healthcare items or services payable by federal healthcare programs and who has no experience owning or operating an allergy laboratory. Requestor certified that [name redacted] would operate Requestor's proposed allergy and immunotherapy laboratory business by identifying and hiring individuals whom he believes have sufficient experience to provide, on Requestor's behalf, the services under the Proposed Arrangement.

\* \* \*

QUESTIONS

1. Does this situation appear to violate anti-kickback rules? Why? Why not?
2. Is there safe harbor protection for this arrangement? What arguments could be raised for and against safe harbor protection in this case?

---

| CASE 10-7 | **The Gavin Institute**

The Gavin Institute is an internationally known, nonprofit institution dedicated to finding cures for catastrophic diseases in children through research and treatment. It is focused primarily on infectious diseases, pediatric cancers, non-malignant hematologies (such as sickle cell disease), and certain other genetic disorders. The vast majority of its patients are on clinical research protocols.

Gavin treats children from across the United States and around the world. To receive services at the Gavin facility, a child must be referred by a physician or an independent licensed clinician. Families that contact the Gavin Institute seeking medical care are advised to consult their pediatrician or other physician. Acceptance at Gavin's facility is primarily based on protocol eligibility, and the organization states that more patients are referred to its facility than it is able to accept under its admissions policy.

The Gavin Institute offers unique and cutting-edge research and therapy options. The highly complex nature of many of the clinical and translational trials that it designs and conducts requires greater patient participation and more time at the Gavin campus than the clinical trials conducted by most cooperative groups or single institutions. According to the Gavin Institute, the success of the therapies and the pace by which new therapies can be identified rest, in part, on the willingness of patients to comply with the rigors and requirements of the protocols and the number of patients enrolling in treatment and research activities. For these reasons, many of the patients who seek to avail themselves of these options must travel or temporarily relocate to the city where the Gavin Institute maintains it major facility.

In furtherance of its commitment to cutting-edge research and therapy options, and to ease the burdens associated with participation in its programs, the Gavin Institute maintains contractual arrangements with a network of six pediatric hematology-oncology clinics, hospitals, and universities (collectively, the Affiliates), which allows children to receive some of their therapy closer to home. The physicians and staff at the Affiliates work in collaboration with the Gavin staff to deliver protocol-related care to pediatric hematology and oncology patients.

The Gavin Institute does not bill children or their families for any part of the cost of their medical care, including copayments or deductibles, a practice that has been in place since its inception and which extends to patients at the Affiliates. To support its charitable mission, the Gavin Institute relies heavily on donations raised by the Gavin Foundation, which, historically, accounts for approximately 70% of the Institute's operating revenue. The remainder of the organization's operating revenues comes from third-party payers, including federal healthcare programs and research grants. Third-party payments, however, are insufficient to cover the patient care costs incurred by the Gavin Institute even for insured children. For example, in fiscal year 2012, the Gavin Institute recovered only about 23 cents for every dollar that it incurred in patient costs for federal healthcare program beneficiaries. The Institute certified that it does not: (i) claim any unbilled amounts as bad debt on its federal program cost reports or (ii) shift any costs to other third-party payers in the form of higher rates or charges.

## THE PROPOSED PLAN

Under the plan, the Gavin Institute will continue to offer an extensive domiciliary services program that will provide transportation, lodging, and meal assistance for patients and their families depending on criteria such as anticipated length of stay and distance from Gavin Institute's city hospital (the Domiciliary Services or the Domiciliary Services Program). The Gavin Institute states that the Domiciliary Services are intended to improve access to care, enhance infection control to reduce the risk of infection for their immune-suppressed patients, help ensure clinical research protocol compliance, enhance quality of life, and reduce the stress for patients and families receiving therapies at their facility.

The Domiciliary Services Program is not advertised or marketed to prospective patients, their families, or referring physicians; however, the Gavin Institute states that many pediatricians and oncologists who refer patients to the Gavin Institute likely are aware of the Domiciliary Services Program, either from prior experience with Gavin or as a result of the foundation's fund-raising efforts. Patients generally are informed of the availability of Domiciliary Services only after they have been accepted to the Gavin facility. The Gavin Institute states that the Domiciliary Services Program is funded by philanthropic sources through the foundation and that none of the costs of items and services provided under the Domiciliary Services Program are claimed or have their costs shifted—either directly or indirectly—to the federal healthcare programs or other third-party payers.

The Domiciliary Services provided by the Gavin Institute can be grouped into four categories: transportation assistance, lodging assistance, meal assistance, and miscellaneous items. Services within each category:

1. Transportation Assistance

   The Institute states that more than 70% of its patients live more than 35 miles away from its facility. In an effort to remove barriers to access to care and participation in research, Gavin offers assistance with plans and costs associated with travel for planned treatments and checkups to its patients and one parent or guardian who expresses a need for transportation assistance. Transportation assistance is also provided to transplant donors.

   The Gavin Institute determines the mode and schedule of transportation by selecting the most economical and appropriate means of transportation at the time of the request. For patients traveling more than 35 miles, but less than 300 miles, the Gavin Institute typically arranges for bus or rail travel or will reimburse for automobile mileage driven in personal vehicles. Patients traveling more than 300 miles are eligible to receive air transportation assistance, as well as bus, rail, or automobile mileage reimbursement. For airline, train, and bus tickets, the Gavin Institute, through the foundation, covers the cost of the lowest economy fare. Although patients who live within 35 miles of the facility are not eligible for these forms of transportation assistance, they may receive shuttle van service to and from treatments and study appointments scheduled by their attending physicians if they have no other means of transport.

2. **Lodging Assistance**

   The Gavin Institute provides complimentary lodging to patients and their core caregivers who live more than 35 miles away from the city facility when: (i) the patient's treatment requires an overnight stay and (ii) the patient or his or her parent or guardian expresses a need for lodging assistance. Patients and their families requesting lodging assistance must sign a written lodging assistance agreement and must agree to be photographed for identification purposes. The Gavin Institute typically arranges for lodging for patients and their families at one of three institute-sponsored lodging facilities. The specific facility to which a patient is assigned typically depends on the patient's anticipated length of stay. All of the lodging facilities meet the Gavin Institute's standards for infection control, including HEPA filtration systems, no carpet, and pressurized buildings. To minimize infection risk, Gavin caps the occupancy of the rooms or suites at four people.

3. **Meal Assistance**

   To address the basic nutritional requirements of the patient and one family member, the institute offers assistance with the cost of meals by issuing either: (i) a meal card that may be used at the cafeteria at their hospital, at their lodging facilities, or to buy coupons for certain restaurant chains or (ii) a grocery store gift card. Meal cards are available for patients and caregivers for the period during which the patient is in the city for scheduled treatment at the Gavin facility. The Institute allots $8.00 for breakfast, $10.00 for lunch, and $12.00 for dinner. Dollar amounts do not carry over from one meal period to another. Grocery store gift cards in lieu of meal cards are provided only to patients who are expected to stay in the city for 8 or more days for treatment. The value of the grocery store gift cards is between $80 and $100 per week. For inpatients, in-room meal service is provided in lieu of meal cards. The caregiver of an inpatient may receive a meal card as long as the family has not received a grocery store gift card. The institute's policy limits the use of meal cards and grocery store gift cards to food purchases only and specifically prohibits the purchase of tobacco or alcohol products with the cards.

4. **Miscellaneous Items and Services**
   The Gavin Institute provides certain other items and services to help patients and their families maintain their well-being and quality of life, including child restraint devices for automobiles; handling of patient mail; developmental items such as bouncy seats and strollers; and special events and dinners, such as prom, graduation, and Halloween events, and No More Chemo parties.

* * *

QUESTIONS

1. How could the Domiciliary Services Program be interpreted as functioning in a manner to induce or generate business?
2. What protections exist in this plan to prevent fraud and abuse?

# INDEX